To Sheldon ....Our adventure of a lifetime.

Now the exciting story is finally told.

ABOUT FACE

The True Story of an American Couple in China
Entangled in a Web of Intrigue and Crime

CAROLE SUMNER KRECHMAN
AND
SHELDON KRECHMAN

with Cheryl Benton

Copyright © 2024 Carole Sumner Krechman.

All rights reserved. No part of this book may be reproduced, stored, or transmitted by any means—whether auditory, graphic, mechanical, or electronic—without written permission of both publisher and author, except in the case of brief excerpts used in critical articles and reviews. Unauthorized reproduction of any part of this work is illegal and is punishable by law.

ISBN: 979-8-89419-079-2 (sc)
ISBN: 979-8-89419-080-8 (hc)
ISBN: 979-8-89419-081-5 (e)

Because of the dynamic nature of the Internet, any web addresses or links contained in this book may have changed since publication and may no longer be valid. The views expressed in this work are solely those of the author and do not necessarily reflect the views of the publisher, and the publisher hereby disclaims any responsibility for them.

One Galleria Blvd., Suite 1900, Metairie, LA 70001
(504) 702-6708

CONTENTS

Preface vii

Chapter 1   The Dinner 1
Chapter 2   Welcome to the Peoples Republic of China 8
Chapter 3   Balloons, Ballons, Ballons 18
Chapter 4   The Adventure Begins 28
Chapter 5   Chinese Medical Miracles 40
Chapter 6   Guanxi 47
Chapter 7   Americans in China 57
Chapter 8   From Roller Skating Entrepreneurs
             to Real Estate Developers 70
Chapter 9   Interlude: Our Daughter Comes to China 79
Chapter 10   Due Diligence 85
Chapter 11   The Architect, Saving Face, and Games 92
Chapter 12   The Art of Going Slow 102
Chapter 13   Expulsion from China 116
Chapter 14   Back in the Game 123
Chapter 15   Interlude: The Station Wagon 128
Chapter 16   Friendship Stores, Chinese Army, Pigeons 132

Chapter 17	Interludes: The Great Wall of China and U.S. Customs	141
Chapter 18	Mr. Yu's Other Businesses	149
Chapter 19	The Plot Thickens	156
Chapter 20	The Chinese and Israeli Ambassadors	159
Chapter 21	Interlude: The Silk Road to Couture	169
Chapter 22	Mr. Wang's Nefarious Businesses	172
Chapter 23	Interlude: The Briefcase	179
Chapter 24	Mr. Yu, LA, and the FBI	182
Chapter 25	OXY becomes a Shareholder in World China Trade	187
Chapter 26	The Beijing Asia Hotel is Open	197
Chapter 27	Mr. Wang Comes to LA	204
Chapter 28	A Visit to the Ministry of Security	210
Chapter 29	Threatened in Beijing	218
Chapter 30	The Final Negotiation	226
Chapter 31	The Deportation of Mr. Yu Xue Wen	235
Epilogue		241

PREFACE

"The greatest long-term threat to our nation's information and intellectual property, and to our economic vitality, is the counterintelligence and economic espionage threat from China."

~FBI Director, Christopher Wray, in remarks delivered to the Hudson Institute, Video Event: China's Attempt to Influence U.S. Institutions, Washington, D.C., July 7, 2020

"If I could communicate one thing to the American people ... it is that the People's Republic of China poses the greatest threat to America today, and the greatest threat to democracy and freedom world-wide since World War II."

~John Ratcliffe, Director of National Intelligence, *Wall Street Journal* Opinion piece, Dec. 3, 2020,

This book has been a long time coming—over thirty-six years. It is a story that many powerful people in corporate and political circles did not want told then, and perhaps even now, despite warnings about China's threat to our country like the above from our top U.S. intelligence people.

The 1970s opened the floodgates to trade and diplomatic relations with China, and by the early 1980s everyone wanted to do business with the Chinese, the potentially largest consumer marketplace in the world, and one of the largest inexpensive labor markets. Today, the list of U.S. companies doing business in China is a who's who of our most venerable institutions.

In the early 1980s my late husband Sheldon Krechman and I were presented with the opportunity to expand our U.S. roller rinks business into China. We jumped at the opportunity, and two innocents abroad, we entered China. We eventually abandoned all hope of building a chain of roller rinks but through a convoluted series of events, we instead became involved in a large and complicated joint venture with the Chinese to build an office and hotel complex in downtown Beijing. We called our company, World China Trade.

Over the ensuing years and amidst a variety of adventures, we became ensnared in a web that included the most ruthless of China's security agencies, the FBI, the CIA and a cast of characters who seem straight out of a Hollywood spy thriller. In a national discussion of Chinese misdeeds that is sometimes abstract and impersonal, our story is concrete and full of real people. For us, the security and espionage apparatus of the People's Republic of China has a human face. In fact, the multiple meanings of the word "face" make it a useful metaphor for describing the reality of the People's Republic.

In the mid-eighties, after a few years of intrigue of doing business in China, we told our story to a top literary agent who was certain we would find a major publisher. But as it turned out, no one wanted to touch a story that exposed the truths about doing business in China.

By the late 1990s many people, like the *New York Times's* William Safire, started to sound the alarm to the American public that the People's Republic of China had brazenly stolen our technology and exploited the naivete and financial ambition of our politicians and businessmen. In June 1998 the Cox Commission was created by the U.S. House of Representatives to investigate whether technology or information was transferred to the People's Republic of China that may have contributed to the enhancement of the nuclear-armed intercontinental ballistic missiles or to the manufacture of weapons of mass destruction. The controversial report was challenged by many in politics, and people in very high places tried to quash the recommendations.

It was in this new environment, that Sheldon and I revisited the idea of a book, and Sheldon started putting our story and memories on paper. But as they say, life got in the way, and the book took a back seat. In 2020 during the world-wide COVID pandemic, Sheldon died unexpectedly—not from COVID directly, but inadvertently from being in a hospital overwhelmed with COVID cases. In the weeks and months of grief that followed, my thoughts turned to the incredible life and adventures we had shared, especially our years in China. As I went through his belongings, I came across the draft memories he had written and that's when I knew that now is the time to tell our story.

Over the years we came to realize that China would always be a place of mystery and unanswered questions. It is a land of contradictions with many faces. We experienced the best of China, its people, its children, its rich cultural history, and we also experienced the worst—treachery, subterfuge and criminal activities. The Chinese have perfected the art of manipulation. We always knew we were being manipulated, but often did not know by whom, or why. This is our story. While it has been more than thirty years since we left China, our experience is as relevant today as it was then. It's a cautionary tale to anyone doing business in China.

Who's Who and What's What

Asia Hotel Joint Venture—The compulsory agreement between World China Trade and the Chinese to build the Asia Hotel. All foreign businesses in China must operate under a joint venture agreement.

Richard Chen—Director of Occidental Petroleum's China Affairs

Dr. Armand Hammer—Chairman of the Board and Founder of Occidental Petroleum who arranged our first trip to China in 1983.

Paul Hebner—An executive of Occidental Petroleum

Saul Leonard—Advisor and trusted friend; partner in an international accounting firm

James R. Lilly—Ambassador to China after Tiananmen Square (1992); former head of the CIA in South Korea

Madam Deng Ling—Daughter of Deng Xiaoping, good friend of Mr. Yu Xue Wen, President of World China Trade (our company).

Winston & Betty Bao Lord—U.S. Ambassador to China and his Chinese wife

Zhang Xiao Lu (Ms. Zhang)—Senior interpreter for the Chinese government; "right hand man 1 1 for Yu Xue Wen; Manager of American Affairs for World China Trade.

Paul Kelly—Secret Service agent; escorted all U.S. Presidents from Nixon to Bush to China; conducted the initial investigation of Yu Xue Wen.

Ford Hart III—Head of China Desk, Department of State, Beijing, China; senior military analyst

Jim Huskey—Senior Intelligence Analyst - State Department

Denny Barnes—U.S. Commercial Attache, U.S. Embassy in Beijing; purportedly a CIA operative.

Mayor Yi Long Ki—Personal secretary to Chairman Mao; former Mayor of Beijing

Robert Messemer—Special Agent, FBI, Los Angeles.

Lawrence Liu—President, Los Angeles Guangzhou Sister City Society

Wang Fu Sheng (Mr. Wang)—Chairman of the Asia Hotel Joint Venture, former Chief of the Beijing Ministry of Public Security; referred to as "the Mafia Boss of Beijing" by the FBI.

Jim Smith—Special Agent, FBI

World China Trade—The American company formed in China by Sheldon and Carole Krechman.

Yu Xue Wen (Mr. Yu)—President of World China Trade (our company), therefore the first Chinese man to become President of an American company based in China.

Charles Wrangham—Vice Chairman, Standard Chartered Asia Bank (Hong Kong)

Ambassador Ma Yu Zen—Counsel General (with Ambassador status) to China Consul in Los Angeles

Deng Xiaoping—Head of the Chinese Communist Party.

All the Senators below wrote letters on our behalf to the Chinese Government. These letters protested the actions of the Chinese regarding our Joint Venture.

Senator Barbara Boxer—California Senator

Senator Dianne Feinstein—California Senator

Senator John McCain—Arizona Senator

Senator John Glen—Ohio Senator

CHAPTER 1

The Dinner

*Learning without thought is deceptive;
thought without learning is perilous.*

~Chinese Proverb

In the fall of 1982, my husband Sheldon and I were looking forward to celebrating the opening of our first roller skating rink in an African American enclave near downtown Los Angeles. It was a beautiful large, modern rink and based on the positive community response, we were looking forward to building these skating centers in African American communities around the country. Amid our excitement of this new entrepreneurial venture, we received a diner invitation from Dr. Armand Hammer, the Chairman of Occidental Petroleum (OXY). We had no idea that this seemingly chance dinner would be the start of a life altering journey into China.

Our dinner invitation came about from a convoluted, unlikely series of relationships spanning several decades and two generations, between my father, B. Allen Sumner, and his accountant, Sam Shapiro. Sam was married to the niece of a colorful, controversial entrepreneur—Armand Hammer. Dr. Hammer was a physician, adventurer and friend of communists. This New York born capitalist and international deal maker had moved west to set up an oil exploration company.

When he arrived in California in 1956, he bought the tiny Occidental Petroleum Company which was located in a small office on Melrose Avenue in Los Angeles. When he needed an accountant, he hired his niece's husband. Soon after that, Sam called my parents to invite them to dinner with Dr. Hammer. The dinner was an occasion for Dr. Hammer to promote his fledgling petroleum company, which needed investors. He was a master salesman, and by the time dinner was over, my dad and Sam had agreed to split one share, for $25,0000 a piece—a great deal of money at the time. There were only nine other investors in the company.

Exploratory drilling commenced a few months later. On their fifth attempt, the fledgling company with three full-time employees tapped into the largest natural gas reservoir in the history of the state, the Arbuckle Field. One of the three employees was Paul Hebner, who remained with Dr. Hammer as his closest confident and secretary of the corporation and a member of the board of directors until Dr. Hammer's death. My father continued with investments into Occidental, and as the company grew, he kept in touch with Dr. Hammer, but and most of his relationship going forward was with Paul Hebner.

My dad would see Paul at the annual meeting but had not had much of a relationship with him for a long while, when he called inviting he and my mother to a dinner that Dr. Hammer was having in the dining room at Occidental Petroleum. He also asked how I was doing, and my father told him about our roller-skating venture. Paul then suggested that we also come to the dinner and meet Dr. Hammer. I had met him just once when I was a teenager, and we were thrilled to be included.

So, by virtue of this unusual chain of relationships we arrived at the Occidental Building on a beautiful fall evening, as the guests of the world-famous, eccentric octogenarian who, as it turned out, had an interest in China. To say the least, it was an unlikely circumstance—and it would lead to an even more unlikely series of events.

The Dinner

Just getting to Armand Hammer's dining room was an event in itself. His office building was part fortress and part museum. It lacked the crenelated towers and portcullis of a medieval castle, but it certainly had the functional equivalent of a moat full of alligators—alarm systems, security cameras and poker-faced men with guns. The reason: It was a citadel for art. Dr. Hammer had a private collection that would be the envy of anyone, anywhere. The tight security protected not only his person, but his possessions. After showing identification and clearing security, we took the elevator to the top floor and walked silently to the dining room, passing walls decorated with original paintings by Rembrandt, Van Gogh, Cezanne, Monet, Picasso and others.

As we approached the entrance to the dining room the hushed quiet of the hallway gave way to the cheerful voices of people engaged in conversation. Through the double doors we could see a large, opulent room furnished with Chippendale antiques, green leather chairs, heavy velvet drapes and more paintings. Nine tables were arranged in the center of the room, set with fine China and silver flatware. The windows on the west wall looked out to the Pacific Ocean and the Santa Monica mountains.

People were gathered in small groups around the perimeter of the room, sipping champagne and drinking cocktails served by uniformed waiters. This was a collection of people who had long, historic ties to Occidental Petroleum. We looked around until we found my parents, fortified ourselves with champagne, and were taken to meet the Great Man.

Dr. Hammer was an imposing presence, but not because of his physical stature. He was a tiny, slight figure, old as Methuselah, little more than five and half feet tall, with big, coke-bottle glasses and a ready smile. He had a commanding demeanor that conveyed a sense of supreme confidence, high intelligence and personal power. This was the man who had bargained with Lenin, traded with Stalin, served as an intermediary between the US and the USSR, built a hugely successful petroleum company, hobnobbed with heads of state and inhabited news headlines for a generation.

Much to our surprise, he began to ask us about our roller rink business. It was more than polite conversation, and he asked many questions. Then, after a pause, he told us about all the children in China who would enjoy roller skating, asked us if we had ever traveled there, and suggested it would be a very good idea for us to go to China and see what business opportunities might present themselves.

We stood there, saying little, as he continued to talk for several minutes. It was obvious that Dr. Hammer had invited us to this dinner for a reason. This was not just a spontaneous conversation; he had an agenda.

We really hadn't thought about expanding our business into China until that moment, but we found the prospect very exciting. But on the way home my father told us not get our hopes up that Dr. Hammer would help us in any way. Occidental Petroleum was an energy company, and our roller-skating business would be of no interest to him.

But that didn't stop us from thinking about China. The next day (Saturday) we called my father at least five times. Was Dr. Hammer really interested in us? On each call my father repeatedly told us how much he loved us—the equivalent of a pat on the head to a naive child—but kept on reminding us that we were kidding ourselves to think that Dr. Hammer had a genuine interest in roller skating.

And he was right, there was no rational reason to think that Occidental Petroleum Company would have any reason whatsoever to promote roller skating in the People's Republic of China. Nevertheless, we spent many hours that weekend dreaming about the possibilities. On Sunday night we went to bed with our thoughts oscillating between our fantasies and the level-headed rationality of my father.

At 9:00 am on Monday morning we received a telephone call at home from Dr. Hammer's private secretary. She told us to expect a call at 10:00 am from a Mr. Richard Chen, whom she identified as Occidental's Director of China Affairs. We asked her the purpose of the call, and she told us that Mr. Chen was in charge of all China business for Dr. Hammer and that he had personally spoken to Mr. Chen about our roller skating centers. Dr. Hammer wanted us to talk to Mr. Chen in the hope that we might go to China.

Richard Chen was the interpreter for the United States Government when China's Chairman Deng Xiao Peng came to the United States for the first time and visited with Jimmy Carter. Several months later, at a dinner party, Richard met Dr. Hammer and subsequently introduced him to Chairman Deng Xiao Peng and the Chinese Government. Within a short period of time Dr. Hammer hired Richard to be Director of China Affairs for OXY.

When the call with Dr. Hammer's secretary ended, we looked at each other in stunned disbelief. An hour later the phone rang again, and Richard Chen was on the line. He asked if we could join him for lunch at the Occidental Building in two hours. Of course, we agreed, but things were happening so fast that we hardly had time to think.

What happened next seemed very strange at the time, and even more so when we reflected on it later. When we arrived at the Occidental building, we checked in with the guard in the lobby who called upstairs, and then we headed for the bank of elevators behind him. But before we could push the button to summon a car Dr. Hammer appeared, seemingly from nowhere, and motioned for us to follow him to his private elevator. On the way up to the executive floors he asked us to listen very carefully to Richard Chen and report to him, privately, as much information as we could. He spoke to us in quiet tones, as though we were trusted confidants, strange since we had only just met him three days before.

The elevator stopped on the fifteenth floor and Dr. Hammer stepped out. As the doors closed, we just stared ahead silently. What was this all about? What information? It was one of those events that happened, and after it did, you wondered if it really happened at all. The elevator rose one more floor and we emerged into the art-filled hallway and made our way to the now familiar dining room.

Richard Chen was waiting for us near the door. We introduced ourselves, sat down, and as lunch was served made small talk. Richard told us how he was hired to by Dr. Hammer to be his Director of China Affairs.

He explained that Dr. Hammer was interested in doing business in China and had his eyes on a large coal-mining concession. After briefing us on their China involvement, he got around to asking about our roller-skating business. He listened with interest as we described what we did, and then asked if he could visit our offices the next day.

On Tuesday morning Chen appeared at our offices and spent nearly the whole day with us. He left in the late afternoon, promising to get back to us shortly.

We heard nothing for three months, although we did wonder what could possibly interest Dr. Hammer in our roller-skating business—or anyone else? If we had been close over the years, and he had wanted to help us out of friendship, his interest would be understandable. But we had not been friends, did not know him personally and had met him only once; twice if you count the elevator encounter.

Why would someone who had the ambition and financial means to conduct business on a billion-dollar scale even give a moment's notice to a recreation business run by a couple he hardly knew? The unusual request he made of us in our mysterious meeting in the elevator receded in importance in our memories even though, years later, it would explain part of the puzzle. At that time, we had no context for it. Our enthusiasm for China obliterated all rational analysis of the situation. We knew that Dr. Hammer had a reputation for eccentricity and let it go at that.

Then, on a December evening, we received a call at home from Paul Hebner inviting us to attend a dinner at the University of Southern California hosted by the Guangzhou Sister City Society. Guangzhou, China is the sister city of Los Angeles. Occidental had purchased a table and we were to be guests of the company.

On the following Saturday evening we drove to the USC campus to attend the dinner. Paul was the host at our table and among the guests was a man named Lawrence Liu. Liu was the president of the Sister City Association. Paul introduced us to Liu and then said something quite unexpected. "The Krechman's will travel with you to China next March." Our reaction was a mixture of surprise and excitement. Of course, the obvious question still remained: Why? In our enthusiasm we didn't give it a moment's thought. A free trip to China? Who cares why we're going? Paul Hebner told us that Dr. Hammer would like to see us to discuss the trip.

A week later we met with Dr. Hammer who told us he had arranged a trip to China for a group of American artists and they would be accompanied by several Los Angeles officials, including city councilman David Cunningham, Bea Lavery, protocol chief for Mayor Tom Bradley and Warren Thomas, the director of the Los Angeles Zoo. The artists were supposed to meet their counterparts in several cities in China and Thomas was along for the ride, with two Lesser Pandas who would be exchanged for two Greater Pandas, in Guangzhou.

Suddenly, in a conspiratorial tone Dr. Hammer leaned forward and told us that we were not to disclose to anyone what our purpose was for going on the trip. This would be easy, because we didn't have a clue ourselves. He went on to say that we would meet several Occidental employees and they would assist us in anything we might want to do. He told us to keep our eyes open and look for opportunities to forge relationships with Chinese individuals.

We were then shuttled from his office to meet with Lawrence Liu. He told us not to tell David Cunningham, a friend of ours, or anyone else, that we would be on the flight until we arrived at the airport.

CHAPTER 2

Welcome to the Peoples Republic of China

A journey of a thousand miles begins with a single step.
~Chinese Proverb

A few weeks later, in March 1983, we embarked on our first trip to China. We left LA enroute to the Narita airport outside Tokyo and then onto Hong Kong, with a contingent of artists, two politicians, a zoo director, Lawrence Liu, two Lesser Pandas and a couple of Occidental employees. Cunningham never asked us why we were part of the entourage, but even if he had, we didn't know.

We spent two months traveling the country, meeting a great many people and visiting the OXY offices in Guangzhou and Beijing. Little did we know that this trip would be the first of fifty-seven trips we would take to China over the next nine years.

On the flight over, Liu began teaching us all a new game, which he called Chinese poker. The essence of the game was arbitrary with spontaneous rule making. Whenever there might be an advantage to Liu, he would introduce a new rule. Whenever anyone would challenge him—and our friend David Cunningham often did—he would reply that this was Chinese poker, and the rules were different. I nicknamed him "new rule Liu."

We had no idea at the time, but Liu was teaching us more than a game of cards. The flight and layover in Narita were comfortable for everyone except Warren Thomas who spent the night at the airport, sleeping with the two pandas in quarantine.

After a four-hour flight from Narita, we arrived on the mainland of China at Hong Kong, still a British colony at the time. The old Kai Tak airport, built on landfill, projected out into Hong Kong harbor and was infamous with pilots who considered it one of the most difficult approaches in the world. After making a slow, steep, low altitude turn next to a mountain, the pilot leveled out the wings and immediately lined us up with the runway. We were so low I could see people watching their television sets through the windows of apartment buildings below. They must all be deaf, I thought. I breathed a sigh of relief as we touched down.

From Hong Kong we were scheduled to lay over for one night and take the train into Guangzhou (formerly Canton) the next afternoon. We gathered outside the airport terminal and were bused to our hotel. The next morning, we boarded the buses again and left for Kowloon's Hung Hom train station to take the non-stop express run into the People's Republic. We were told the trip from the Hung Hom terminal to Guangzhou Station would take about three hours.

There were two daily non-stops to Guangzhou, and we were scheduled to take the 1:00 pm departure. Our polymorphous mix of artists, politicians and pandas boarded the train without incident. The train was clean, a combination of wood paneling and painted metal inside, and the various compartments had lace curtains on the windows. It looked slightly anachronistic, like an American train car from the 1950's. As soon as we were underway servers brought out hot tea and we settled in for the ride.

It took about an hour to pass through the countryside outside Kowloon, an area known to the British as the New Territories and cross the border into China at Lowu. From there we entered Guangdong Province and the country outside our window became increasingly rural. We passed rice fields and vegetable farms; their boundaries defined by a network of small levees. Farm workers labored in the flooded rice fields and oxen pulled plows through carefully tended vegetable plots. Occasionally we would see a gaggle of geese or a herd of ducks waddling en masse down a levy road, driven by a man with a long bamboo stick.

We sat enthralled, taking it all in and thinking little about the purpose of our trip. Lunch was cooked in an adjacent car over a wood-burning stove. We made small talk with our fellow guests and shared a meal with several of them. The food was delicious, a chicken soup with dumplings which reminded me of Jewish matzo balls and kreplach.

No one in our entourage seemed curious about our presence. Everyone was so taken by the exotic scenery that the conversation seldom strayed far from the experience of the moment. What is your purpose in coming? For the time being, we were awe-struck tourists and nothing more.

The filtered sunlight of early spring made the whole landscape seem magical. As we gradually approached Guangzhou, heading roughly northeast, the sun began to inch toward the horizon in the late afternoon and outside the left windows of the train we could see the light reflected off the water in the fields. As we reached the outskirts of the city, we passed more and more clusters of housing. Some of the homes looked very old. Small, walled compounds contained what looked like ancient, well-worn houses, drab and gray, with tile roofs.

Soon we passed over the Pearl River and found ourselves within the confines of the city. The view outside our window was no longer pastoral. Houses and buildings, both old and new, were packed together, cheek to jowl, along narrow streets jammed with pedestrians in gray or blue Mao suits, bicycles and tricycles laden with impossible loads, tiny gas-powered jitneys and diesel-powered trucks, and a few horse-drawn carts.

It was an incredible scene. How could so many people and vehicles fit into such narrow streets? It made Manhattan look deserted by comparison. Finally, passing across the eastern edge of the city, gawking all the way, we pulled into the Guangzhou Station. It was a little after four in the afternoon.

On the platform was a large delegation of Chinese officials, artists and a representative from the Guangzhou Zoo. As we stepped off the train, we were overwhelmed. There were hundreds of people on the platform, with food stands everywhere and people selling everything from lotus leaves filled with rice and various meats to fresh fruit.

The welcoming party greeted each of us, one by one, and we gave and received a business card at each introduction. We had been told that it was impolite to receive a business card and not take at least ten to twenty seconds to study it. The smell of the place was very different from what we had ever experienced before, exotic and pungent.

After a short welcome speech, Mr. Shi, who was the Deputy Mayor of Guangzhou, invited us all to a banquet to be held that evening. Mr. Shi was dressed in a blue Mao suit that I had only seen before in magazines and films. In this context I realized it was more than a symbol of proletarian modesty, it was actually a very comfortable and practical way to dress. Loose fitting, it had lots of large pockets and its cotton fabric was perfect for the hot and humid climate.

A moment later, as if on cue, everyone began shaking hands. The whole group of Chinese nodded their heads and said, "nee-how" to each of us. We quickly learned that this meant "hello," and reciprocated. We all shook hands, smiled and then boarded a large van they had brought for us. There were three other smaller vans for the welcoming delegation. All the vans were of Japanese manufacture, well-worn and several years old. As far as we could tell, everything in China seemed well worn.

The streets were teeming with people and bicycles; it reminded me of an ant farm. As we drove through the streets the sea of people would open up in front of our vans and close again behind us. After a short ride to the Dong Fang hotel we parked, got out and shook hands with everyone all over again. We were learning quickly that the Chinese have many protocol rituals that seem redundant and tedious to most westerners.

* * * * *

Our room at the Dong Fang Hotel was very plain, with drab walls. It was sparsely furnished with double beds, a small wooden console mounted between them, two chairs, a small, low table, and a wardrobe. The console between the beds was replete with several mysterious switches and was built in a style reminiscent of bad American furniture from the fifties. The bathroom had a tile floor which had not been scrubbed in a long while. There was a bathtub, with a hose attached to the water tap, and no shower.

For some reason, that console attracted Sheldon's attention. Some of the switches were unlabeled and others had Chinese captions. Sheldon had an inquisitive nature, especially when it came to electronics or small electrical appliances, and he tried them all. He decided to take a look at the wiring inside and determine the function of the various switches. He took out his small leather bag with a set of miniature tools. After about fifteen minutes of removing multiple screws from the console, he found a very sophisticated miniature microphone.

He was familiar with these types of devices. Years before, he had been in the electronics business and had sold similar devices to the FBI. Our first reaction was to laugh at the audacity of it, but we weren't totally surprised. We looked at each other silently, knowing that it would be a mistake to disturb any of the electronics. Sheldon reassembled everything and then we went out into the hallway to talk.

We decided that we would try a little test and see if the microphone was working. We wanted to be as subtle as possible, but we wanted to make sure. In 1983 it was virtually impossible to get Western over-the-counter medicines in China. We went back into the room, and Sheldon said to me, with great emphasis, "Sweetheart, I am really sorry. For some reason I forgot to bring the TYLENOL. I know you need it for your BACK PAIN. Maybe we can find some." After his little performance, we made small talk as we changed clothes and prepared for the banquet.

* * * * *

The next morning, we met with our group and Lawrence Liu, and we were taken to an artists' studio and met with several of the Chinese artists and our group exchanged art with them. It was very interesting. The artists got along very well, both sides were very eager, because ours was the first group of American artists to visit China. We actually met China's most favorite artist, Liu Hi Sui. He was 90 and very honored and respected throughout China.

That afternoon we had a ceremony at the Guangzhou Zoo where we officially exchanged the Lesser Pandas, we had brought from the United States for the Pandas that were going to be shipped back to Los Angeles.

After the visit to the zoo and the panda exchange, the vans reappeared and we found ourselves in a caravan again, driving from place to place until we arrived at an adult recreation center. Sheldon found the center decidedly uninteresting. We had been told that we were not to go anywhere without a guide, but I wasn't surprised to see him slip out the door. I just hoped he would find his way back.

More than an hour passed, and I was so relieved when Sheldon returned. Our Chinese guide was a bit perturbed and instructed him not to go out again on his own.

When we got back to the van, he quietly told me he walked for several blocks, looking in shop windows, fascinated by everything he saw. After a few minutes he came to a Chinese apothecary, where to his surprise one of the clerks spoke a bit of English. He asked him about purchasing some Motrin and was told there were many Chinese herbal medicines that would have a better effect. He said the only western analgesic available was aspirin, and even that was rare. He had never heard of Tylenol.

Later that night we were taken to another banquet. As we stood in the foyer of the immense restaurant, Sheldon asked our guide if he could tell us where we might purchase a pain reliever for me. He smiled and said that it was just a coincidence, but he happened to have something with him. With a little flourish, he pulled a large bottle of Tylenol out of his pocket, like a rabbit out of a hat.

* * * * *

Before we were seated for dinner, we had a brief time socializing and met a number of people. One of them was Keith Anderson, the manager of the Guangzhou office for Occidental Petroleum. Keith wasn't hard to find. He was a big man with red hair, a ruddy complexion and freckles. In a sea of small, dark-haired Chinese he stood out like a beacon. He told us that he had received a communique from the Oxy office in Los Angeles that we would be arriving and offered to help us in any way he could. He then asked us to meet him for lunch the next day.

Our Chinese hosts had arranged the dinner seat assignments to alternate between Americans and Chinese. The tables were set with China (what else!), chopsticks (forks for the wimps) and three glasses: one for beer, a second for a sweet red wine, and a third—a small liqueur glass filled with a clear liquid.

The small one, as Sheldon would soon learn, was for a Chinese version of Kentucky white lightning called Moutai, not to be confused with Mai Tai. If you put one of those little Mai Tai cocktail umbrellas in a glass of Moutai, the wood would probably dissolve. What a difference a vowel can make.

Moutai, is made from sorghum, and to the uninitiated tastes something like gasoline. It was famously used to welcome President Nixon on his historic trip to China in 1972.

Soon after we were seated a Chinese official proposed a toast of friendship. He was holding the little glass of Moutai and indicated that we should all do the same. He made the toast and downed the glass in one gulp, saying loudly "gan bei!"

Fortunately, women are not expected to participate in this male display of machismo. I glanced over at Sheldon, who did not normally drink alcoholic beverages, and saw he had emptied his glass so as not to insult our hosts. He started to cough and the Chinese official next to him just smiled, waved his hand, and his glass was filled up again.

The food at our banquet was incredible. There were twenty-one separate courses, and all the first courses were molded or assembled into various shapes, like edible sculptures.

There were various meats, vegetables, fish, crustaceans, and several creatures I had never seen before. Every time a new dish was served the Chinese person next to me would pick out the choicest morsel and put it on my plate. Somewhere around the fifteenth course I thought I could eat no more. Up to that point I had tasted everything, even those delicacies of indeterminate origin. Sometimes it just best not to know.

Unfortunately, the next course was considered by our hosts to be particularly special, a highlight of the banquet. It appeared to be an immense slug, the size of a sausage. It was slimy looking, and for a moment I thought it might still be alive. I was told it was a delicacy and only served at very special banquets, since it was very expensive. They assured me it had been cooked. What an honor, I thought, as I contemplated putting a piece of the oversized gastropod in my mouth. I took a bite and it tasted just as it looked. I couldn't get it down. My host thought I was a bit demented when it came to food. Who wouldn't delight in such a delicacy?

By the end of the banquet, we were stuffed with rich food, and I realized Sheldon was drunk from the Moutai. Not wanting to insult our hosts, he had slammed two more shots and the combination of the potent alcohol and jet lag had left him woozy. We were ready to be taken right back to our hotel and just fall into bed. This turned out to be wishful thinking.

As we walked—slowly—back to the restaurant's foyer, we were diverted from the rest of the group. Before dinner we had been briefly introduced to the City Architect of Guangzhou and the Deputy Mayor. They were waiting for us. Through a translator it was explained that they had planned an after-dinner tour of the city for us, so that we could look at potential sites for a roller rink. I looked at Sheldon and knew he was trying his best to look thankful.

They took us all through the city, pointing out sites they thought suitable for roller skating complexes. After about an hour of driving, Sheldon was really very woozy and having a hard time concentrating, but we knew it would be insulting to complain. Finally, we drove to the White Swan Hotel, which was the newest hotel in Guangzhou, located on the river.

The architect that was with us had designed the White Swan Hotel and proudly wanted to show it off. We were ushered into a private lounge with couches and started talking about the hotel. I have a degree in architecture and was interested in the design and construction. I didn't realize that by now, Sheldon was really feeling the effects of the

Moutai until he got up to go to the bathroom and was unsteady on his feet. I was relieved when one of the Chinese went with him to make sure he didn't fall and get hurt and could find his way back.

When he returned it was obvious he was in distress. Finally, one of the officials acknowledged this, and through the interpreter he indicated that he had something that would relieve his dizziness. Reaching into his pocket, he pulled out a bottle of Tylenol.

We never found out whether the Chinese realized that we had set up a test for them, or whether they were signaling that they knew exactly what was being said between us in our private conversations. The more time we spent in China, however, the more respect we gained for the Chinese and their talent for surveillance.

The next day Sheldon woke up determined not to repeat the experience of the night before. He had to learn how to survive a banquet, perform the customary toasts and retain the use of enough brain cells to function socially. He later learned the Chinese trick of replacing Moutai (it's a clear liquid) with water and pouring the real stuff out on the floor. Over the ensuing years he became quite an experienced Moutai drinker and could gulp down nine or ten shots at a sitting. He eventually got to the point where he could engage in a Moutai drinking contest with our Chinese hosts.

But the morning after the banquet, he had cotton mouth and a dull headache as we left the hotel in the late morning for the Guangzhou office of Occidental Petroleum to see the Great Redhead, Keith Anderson.

* * * * *

If the night before had seemed disorienting because of alcohol, this day would seem equally disorienting but for different reasons. It wasn't clear to us why we were meeting with Anderson. We had vague instructions from Dr. Hammer to keep our eyes open and report back to him, but what were we looking for? When we arrived, Anderson asked us a series of questions. What was our relationship with Occidental? With Dr. Hammer? We told him as little as possible which was easy, of course, because we knew next to nothing.

At one point in our conversation, he pointed to the light fixture on the ceiling above us. When Occidental rented the office, the Chinese had installed the tenant improvements. When the construction was finished and Anderson took possession of the keys, he dropped by one Friday evening with another Oxy employee, an American. No one was in the building. While they were standing under the light fixture Anderson commented that the paint color on the walls was not what they had selected. Monday morning when they returned, the office had been repainted.

"Welcome to the People's Republic of China," he said. We smiled at each other but didn't mention the Tylenol incident. Then, lowering his voice, he looked right at us and informed us that we were being used, both by Occidental Petroleum and the Chinese government. Anderson then told us that Occidental and China were embroiled in a difficult negotiation regarding a joint venture to build and operate a large, open-pit coal mine in Shaanxi Province. Our presence in China, he said, was somehow related to this negotiation. We looked at him with blank stares. We had no idea what he was talking about. But we were beginning to think that we might be pawns in a big game.

The Oxy office was on the top floor of the Dong Fang Hotel which, by Chinese standards, was very opulent. In those days every foreign company that had offices in China was required to hire Chinese citizens, and the Chinese would always put in one or more informants who would report to the Ministry of Public Security.

As we were leaving the office, one of Oxy's Chinese employees followed us into the hallway and said in English, "The Journey of a thousand miles begins with the first step—and you both have taken the first step." It was just another inscrutable message on a trip that was, for the most part, inexplicable.

We left the Oxy offices in deep thought, but it was so exciting to be in China, that we figured that whatever happened the experience would be invaluable.

CHAPTER 3

Balloons, Ballons, Ballons

"But the true voyagers are only those who leave. Just to be leaving; hearts light, like balloons..."

~Charles Baudelaire

Before we left on our trip, we had decided that we would bring something to China that would make a good impression; something surprising and out of the ordinary. Since we were in a business that catered to children, we decided to bring balloons. We had packed two thousand of them, all imprinted with our logo, "World on Wheels."

In the United States, if you went for a walk and approached a strange child with a balloon, people might think you were a child molester. Not so in China. The children there were not conditioned to fear strangers. We walked out into the streets of Guangzhou with a camera and a bag full of balloons and sought out every child we could find. The result was an unexpected joy.

Near the Oxy office was a small park with children everywhere. We picked out a nearby group and approached a little China doll, a girl about five or six years old. She was chubby with long pigtails and wore pants that were split up the middle in back. As we learned, Chinese children at that age have the back of their pants slit so they can urinate in the gutters, if necessary. She looked up at us with wonder in her eyes and her mother, aunt and uncle and all her friends looked on also. We were unlike anyone she had ever seen.

Sheldon blew up a red balloon and I squatted down and handed it to her. Her eyes went wide. Putting her hands to her mouth, she squealed with absolute joy. She had never seen a balloon before. Suddenly there was a mob of children surrounding us, squealing, and laughing. I tied the balloon with a long piece of string and the little girl went running through the park, balloon in tow, with a mob of children behind her. I felt like the Pied Piper. We spent a joyous afternoon blowing up balloons to the delight of children and adults alike and then retired to our hotel, exhausted.

* * * *

The next day we asked Lawrence Liu if he could take us on a private driving tour of the city. We wanted to see it in the daylight—and Sheldon wanted to see it sober. He arranged a car and driver for the three of us. As we moved slowly down a one-way street, Sheldon spotted a crudely drawn sign, the only one we had seen in English. It said "Computers." He asked Lawrence to stop the car so we could visit the store. Sheldon was something of a computer expert and was curious to see what they were selling. The car came to a stop and Sheldon asked if we could have fifteen minutes to look. Liu laughed and said of course, we could have all the time we wanted.

We expected the car to wait, but after we got out, it became clear that Liu planned to leave. Sheldon looked at him through the open window and told him we didn't know where we were, much less how to get back to our hotel. Liu just smiled an enigmatic smile and said,

"I'm sure you won't have any trouble." At that, the car drove away, and a swarm of people closed the gap behind it. We were left standing in the middle of the street.

We had already been told that foreigners were required to always have a guide with them and were forbidden to go out alone. Sheldon had already been reprimanded. As we would later learn, the guides served a dual purpose—they protected state security and they kept tourists from being swallowed up in the confusing complexity of the city.

Without such a guide we felt free but vulnerable. There were no cabs, no comprehensible public transportation, no street signs in English, we had no map, and no one spoke our language. After pondering this for a moment, we walked over to the computer store.

The computer sign was very crude, handwritten on a large, thick sheet of rice paper and tacked to the facade of the store. The store itself was tiny and staffed by three adults and two small children. They had a couple of personal computers of unknown provenance—probably Hong Kong—and a few miscellaneous components. We were gestured to sit down and offered a cup of tea. We heard the word "qweilo" (round-eyed barbarian) mentioned a few times, but mostly they just stared silently at us.

We sat there uncomfortably for a few minutes. The children were playing quietly in one corner, so we blew up two balloons and gave one to each child. This simple gesture changed the whole attitude of everyone in the store. We were instantly given the status of visiting relatives.

One of the shopkeepers, it turned out, spoke a bit of English after all, but went out to get a friend who was more proficient. He not only brought his friend, but some fresh Chinese pastry for us, too. The new person was a retired pharmacist who had taken English courses, and we were able to communicate fairly well. Meanwhile there were now about fifteen kids in that tiny store, all wanting balloons.

One of the Chinese clerks asked us to take off our shoes. We then followed him into a side room where we met six people who were translating English computer books into Chinese. They could not speak English, yet they were laboriously working through operating manuals and reference books, with well-thumbed English Chinese dictionaries spread out on the table. They were writing out the translations by hand.

If you have ever read the instructions to a Chinese consumer product or toy manufactured in the eighties, you can guess what the quality of the translation was like. Only in this case it was a bad Chinese approximation of good English syntax. It was an excruciatingly slow process, letter by letter, word by word. As we would learn, however, the Chinese are a patient people.

We eventually made our good-byes and left. On the street once again, we wondered how we would get back to our hotel. We stopped passersbys on the sidewalk and pronounced the name of our hotel. People would respond by taking us out into the street and pointing—unfortunately in different directions—so we chose a course arbitrarily and began walking.

After a few minutes we passed a large, old building and heard music. It was a waltz. Curious, we went in. It was a roller-skating rink, full of kids skating on an old terrazzo floor. The skates were antiques, some with bamboo bindings, but they were functional, and everyone was having a fun time. People smiled at us and were exceedingly polite, but no one spoke English. We took some photographs, waved politely, and left.

We were enjoying ourselves and temporarily forgot our anxiety. We stopped at shops up and down the street, looking at things both exotic and mundane. As we continued to wander, we noticed it was starting to get dark. A sense of apprehension returned, with the realization that we were strangers in China and could walk all night and not find our hotel. We didn't know that, in fact, we were safe from crime, as no Chinese at that time would have dared harm a foreigner. But coming from Los Angeles, we were concerned about being out, alone, in a strange city at night.

As we stood on the sidewalk, considering our options, a large, black, Chinese-made car suddenly pulled up next to us. A burly Chinese man emerged wearing a black leather jacket. He smiled at us, and in broken English told us to get in. The man didn't threaten us but looked determined. We stood there frozen for a moment, wondering what to do. Were we in danger? We started to question him. We asked who he was and what he wanted. He just kept repeating in broken English, "please get in car."

Finally, we decided that we had little choice. Further, this man seemed to know who we were. Maybe it was less risky to go with him than be stuck in the middle of a strange city after dark. We reluctantly got in the back seat. The man in the leather coat sat in the front with the driver and off we went.

At first, we drove in silence. But after a couple of minutes, Sheldon couldn't stand it anymore and leaned over the seat to ask them, again, who they were. As he did so, he noticed they had a tape recorder turned on, ready to record everything we said. We were really surprised, but later found out that this was common practice when dealing with important businesspeople. After all we were there on behalf of Armand Hammer, a man with whom the Chinese intended to do serious business.

In a few minutes, the driver pulled in front of the Dong Fang Hotel, stopped and we got out. The man in the black leather jacket, smiled silently and shook our hands. The car then drove away with the leather-jacketed man sitting impassively in the front seat. We stood there for a moment, contemplating what had just happened. Had we been followed? How did he know where to find us? Admittedly, we stood out in a crowd, but it was a big crowd.

Turning around to face the hotel entrance, we could see Lawrence Liu waiting in the lobby with a wry grin on his face. He motioned us to come inside. "I wondered when you would return," he said, but his words didn't ring true. If he had truly wondered, then why was he in the lobby at that precise moment? He asked us to follow him to a nearby room for a meeting with some unnamed Guangzhou officials—who just happened to be waiting for us. It was all too convenient.

* * * * *

Liu led us to a group of expectant officials who were gathered in a large room, the perimeter of which was lined with heavy chairs upholstered in a variety of fabric patterns, none of which matched. There we were seated, side by side, in what appeared to be a giant living room arranged by a really bad decorator and served green tea in beautiful porcelain cups.

He introduced us to the delegation, and according to the custom we had recently learned, everyone exchanged business cards, scrutinized them for the obligatory twenty seconds and sat down. He then asked us to introduce ourselves to the delegation and tell them what our purpose was in coming to China. Although this was somewhat unclear, Sheldon gave a short extemporaneous talk, explaining why we were there.

As he began to speak, with Liu translating, an elderly woman suddenly came into the room with an envelope and gave it to one of the Chinese officials. He opened the envelope and pulled out what looked to be color photographs and passed them around the room for everyone to see. Everyone, that is, except Sheldon and me.

We ignored the small commotion and Sheldon continued his little speech, telling the group how happy and excited we were to be there in China, and that our business in the United States was a healthy form of recreation for children of all ages. We were interested in expanding our business into the People's Republic of China.

Everyone smiled as Sheldon spoke and returned the photos to the man who had distributed them. He put them back in an envelope and a discussion ensued. It was entirely in Chinese. Liu, apparently, would explain something, the officials would respond, and the cycle would be repeated. We had no idea what the topic was, much less what was said.

At intervals, the Chinese officials would look at us and smile again, then Liu would look at us and the conversation would continue. It was bizarre. We sat there politely, like two mannequins. This went on for a couple of hours until some understanding seemed to be reached, everyone suddenly stood up, shook hands, and left.

Liu announced to us that we had made a good impression and if we kept up the good work, we would have a great future in China. We asked him what the pictures were about, and he pulled one out of his pocket. It was a photo of us blowing up balloons and giving them to Chinese children. He was evasive and vague when we asked what the meeting had been about.

A bit perturbed by all this secrecy, Sheldon asked him why he had left us alone—and who was that man in the leather jacket? He replied with an old saying from Chairman Mao, "The journey of a thousand miles begin with the first step" and he looked at us and said, "You have just taken your first step." The Chinese, it seemed, were masters of the indirect reply.

* * * * *

During our two-month stay in China we traveled to many cities and the balloons became an unexpected source of joy and a wonderful way to connect with the people of China. They also ended up being an excellent public relations tool for us and Dr. Hammer's business goals in China.

When we arrived in Beijing, we decided that we would experiment by walking over to Tiananmen Square and see if we could interest anyone in a balloon. Tiananmen Square is very large and can hold over one million people and there were kids everywhere with their families. Just as we had done in Guangzhou, we walked up to a family, which usually consisted of a mother, father, aunt uncle, grandparents and one child. Sheldon blew up a red balloon, I tied it with a long ribbon, and handed it to the little girl. The wonder that came into her little face could make your heart burst with joy. Before we knew it there was a multitude of people around us, many children all reaching toward us with anticipation. We stayed for over three hours and must have blown up a hundred balloons or more. We were exhausted, but the joy has lasted for many years.

At one point we realized that we were being watched as we spent those three hours in the Square. We walked over to the Peoples Monument to Freedom, and we were standing on it, giving out the balloons, and a red guard came over and shook his finger and directed us off the monument. Years later in April of 1989, we saw the first inkling of what was to come in Tiananmen Square with the vision of dozens of youths clothed in black swarming over this monument.

Another time as we were driving through the country with our group of Western artists, about fifty miles from Shanghai, we passed through a village whose houses were made from mud. It seemed like we had stepped back five hundred years in time. We asked our guide if we could stop, and of course at first, he refused; but in China if you are persistent, but subtle, using face and dignity for whomever you deal with, you can prevail, if you use logic… sometimes. The Chinese mind is very complex, their thought processes are different then westerners.

The guide alone could not make that decision because the bus driver, although he had no official capacity, was a person and we were in the Peoples Republic of China, and the bus driver was one of the people. After fifteen minutes of discussion and negotiation, the guide and the bus driver finally agreed we could stop. We were not allowed to purchase anything with our FEC's (Foreign Exchange Certificates), and we were to stay together with the guide and not wander off by ourselves. If we saw some food that we wanted the guide would pay for it and it would be charged to us later in some way.

We got off the bus and Sheldon and I (not for the first time) wandered away from the group. We found some children and started blowing up balloons. Within a short period of time there were over one hundred people surrounding us, and not all were children. We were in the middle of this group and they crowded in. At first, I got a bit apprehensive, but the looks on their faces were friendly. Everyone wanted a balloon; you would have thought I was a genie that just came out of a bottle. Their hands started stretching out to touch me and our guide who had come looking for us became alarmed, but he was at the edge of the crowd and could not get in.

Finally, after many people gently put their hands all over us, the crowd parted like the red sea, and an old man with a long beard and bare feet came through. It was obvious he was an elder and very respected. It felt like we had taken a time machine to another century. He was smoking a pipe, and everyone got very quiet. He pointed to the yellow balloon that Sheldon had just blown up and motioned that he should trade the balloon for a drag on his pipe.

Sheldon got a bit concerned, as he was not sure what was in that pipe, but he also did not want to offend him. So he bit the bullet, gave him the balloon, and took a deep drag on the pipe as he lit a match over the pipe bowl. Everyone cheered, and in a short period of time Sheldon realized he had just smoked some opium. We continued to give out balloons, with Sheldon in a dreamy haze, to shouts of joy and wonder.

After we returned to the bus, Sheldon told the English-speaking guide that he was sure he had smoked opium. In a very somber way, the guide informed us that opium was illegal in China and that no Chinese citizen would smoke it. Sheldon apologized and said he must have mistaken, and it was only tobacco he had inhaled. The guide saved face and we continued on.

By the time we got back to Beijing, news of these strange foreigners that were handing out balloons to the children all over the countryside of China preceded us, and we were invited to the Ministry of Culture for a discussion with the Minister and his assistants. We entered a very nice room, which had several couches, and we were served tea. The minister though his interpreter, told us that they had received reports of our activities and were pleased with our efforts. He said that most foreigners that visit China have business activities they are involved in and spend only as much time as necessary or tourists who have programmed activities.

We explained to him that our business dealt with children, and we felt we had a special responsibility toward their welfare. He invited us to a banquet that same night. They served twenty courses of exotically prepared dishes and then had us blow up balloons for each of the twenty people that attended the banquet.

The next day the China Daily (the propaganda daily party paper) ran a picture of us giving balloons to the kids and an article regarding our activities.

In one dramatic balloon encounter, we traveled to a small city in Northern China, and were blowing up and handing out balloons to a group of about thirty adults and children. All of a sudden, a young man about twenty-five came running past me and suddenly grabbed the balloon out of my hand and continued to run down the lane. Four middle-aged women from the group run after him, caught him and started beating him with sticks and their hands and yelling at him in Chinese. He fell to the ground covering his head and one of the women took the balloon and brought it back to me.

Through a person who spoke a little English, she apologized for the young man's bad manners, and told me that he was mentally backward and that we should not think that the people of the city were not very appreciative of our efforts.

Distributing balloons was one of the most pleasurable experiences we had in China. It also worked out very well for Dr. Hammer and Occidental Petroleum, as they were in the midst of a very difficult and impossible negotiation with the Chinese Government to open an open pit coal mine, (the largest in the world, in Shanxi Province.) Since we were partners with Dr. Hammer, our efforts toward trying to bring about the modernization of their roller skating centers, was considered a benefit to the children, whom the Chinese realize is their most important asset. It was a show of good will for Dr. Hammer.

* * * * *

After two months in China, we left for home. The trip had been a feast for the senses, a daily banquet of sights, sounds and smells. Yet, there was a subtext. Something was going on below the surface that we could neither see nor understand. It was clear that we were along for the ride not just as tourists, but as pawns in someone else's game.

CHAPTER 4

The Adventure Begins

The ox moves slow, but the earth is patient.
~Chinese Proverb

Soon after we returned to the United States, Dr. Hammer called us late one night at home to ask how our trip went. He asked about our experiences with the various Chinese officials we had met and how we liked the country. After a few minutes of small talk, the conversation turned to the Occidental employees we had met. Dr. Hammer wanted to know what we thought of each of them, whom he mentioned by name. We gave him our opinions and did our best to answer his questions, but our knowledge of these people was superficial, at best.

Of all the people we had come to know, we knew Lawrence Liu the best, simply because we had spent the most time with him. But that was not saying much. Liu was a cipher to us, as elusive as the wind. As for the others, we knew even less. Keith Anderson and the other expatriates seemed more curious about us, and why we were in China, than we did about them. They suspected something. But we were truly innocent. We were there to have a good time and perhaps lay the groundwork for a future business. Our report to Dr. Hammer seemed like a small price to pay for such a grand adventure and if we had been used in some mysterious way, so be it. We spoke for about an hour, Dr. Hammer thanked us and said good night.

Two weeks later we received a call from Richard Chen, who told us that Occidental had received a letter from the Ministry of Sports in Shanghai. The letter said that Shanghai wanted to modernize its roller-skating rinks and invited us to return and discuss a joint venture. To help expedite this matter, Chen suggested we meet with Mr. Yu Xue Wen, a Chinese national, who had recently been hired by Occidental to manage its Beijing office. Mr. Yu happened to be in Los Angeles for a visit.

We arranged a meeting with Mr. Yu for later that day. He was about 5'3" tall and appeared to be in his early forties. He spoke heavily accented but understandable English. At the time he had the title of Manager of Chinese affairs for Occidental Petroleum in Beijing and was responsible for the coordination of meetings between Oxy executives and Chinese officials. He was especially proud of the fact that he had personally arranged meetings between Dr. Hammer and the Premier of the People's Republic, Chairman Deng.

At our first meeting together, Mr. Yu was dressed in a polo shirt and jeans and was trying very hard to look like a hip Angeleno. Richard Chen, who sat in on the meeting, was more formally dressed in suit and tie. The two of them had distinctively different styles, not only in their dress but in their personalities. Mr. Yu was outgoing and assertive. Mr. Chen was quiet and impassive.

As the meeting progressed, Mr. Chen said little but seemed to communicate an unspoken secret with Mr. Yu. He would smile a knowing smile at him, and Mr. Yu would smile back. Mr. Yu told me that there were many business opportunities in China and that he was looking for partners who could develop those opportunities. He said that since we were old, trusted friends of Dr. Hammer, he would like to know if I had an interest in pursuing a business venture.

Mr. Yu carefully explained that as long as any potential venture did not conflict with Occidental Petroleum's principal activity, which was energy development, he was authorized to pursue any opportunity he wanted. "I have the full consent of both Dr. Hammer and the Chinese Government," he said. Richard Chen nodded his head, in silent assent to what Mr. Yu had said.

He was gracious and we seemed to get along well from the very beginning. We agreed to work together and immediately started to plan our second trip to China.

* * * * *

The next evening Dr. Hammer called us at home again. He asked if we could come over to his Beverly Hills estate right away, and afterwards tell no one that we had met. In particular, he did not want Richard Chen to know.

We pulled into the circular driveway of his Wallace Neff designed Beverly Hills home and were surprised to be greeted at the door by Dr. Hammer himself. He ushered us into the French-inspired home and into his mahogany paneled den.

As soon as we sat down, he launched into a story, telling us how he had started his trading business with the Russians, his friendships with Lenin and Stalin and his regret that now, at his age, it was unlikely he could do the same with the Chinese. He quoted Napoleon, who said that "when China wakes the world will shake."

He was nostalgic that night. "I wish I was forty again." But he offered to put his resources at our disposal. In return he asked that we report to him in secret what we saw and experienced in China.

We left his home with the same question that had plagued us since the beginning. Why us? At this point there were two possible explanations for Dr. Hammer's interest in us.

First, we wondered if he needed someone to create goodwill for Occidental Petroleum. Negotiations on the Oxy-China coal mining venture had been bogged down for months. Perhaps we were supposed to create a chain of roller rinks for Chinese children with the support of Occidental, and in the process demonstrate Oxy's commitment to the children of China. Perhaps we were just an expensive public relations gesture.

Second, we wondered if we were supposed to be Dr. Hammer's trusted eyes and ears in China. On the face of it this seemed logical, as he had asked us to fill this role. But this seemed unlikely, too. We were hardly the kind of moles one reads about in spy novels. We knew nothing, were never briefed, had no specific assignment, no experience in industrial espionage--in fact, we're not even naturally suspicious.

The truth would turn out to be far more complicated. Slowly, incrementally, we would be drawn into a complex web of relationships that included Occidental Petroleum, the Chinese ministries of state and public security, the FBI, Chinese organized crime and a whole cast of unlikely characters. It would be a wonderful, painful, exhilarating, exhausting experience—as complex as China itself.

This was the beginning of the adventure.

* * * * *

On our second trip to China in June of 1982, we were hosted by the Ministry of Sports. The OXY people had told them that we were interested in building modern roller-skating rinks for the children.

When we arrived in Beijing Mr. Yu and Ms. Zhang (a senior interpreter for the Chinese government) arranged a meeting with officials from the Sports Ministry in Beijing. We met and talked for about three hours and were invited to lunch. It was the usual banquet and when the meal was finished, the Sports Minister told us that they had an immediate project.

We were taken to the Capital Gymnasium, which was next to the Temple of Heaven on one of the main streets in Beijing. The Capital Gymnasium was the largest in Beijing, with several floors encompassing a sports complex. They took us up to the third floor, a space of about 35,000 square feet, overlooking the Temple of Heaven. They said that we could have that space and that they would do a Joint venture with us to develop it. We were overwhelmed. It was like getting space on Wilshire Boulevard in Beverly Hills.

They requested we create a letter of intent, which would be acceptable to both parties and that we would sign at a formal ceremony in the Great Hall of the people. We were beyond excited and immediately started to put together a document, that briefly stated what our responsibilities would be, and what the Chinese responsibilities would be. It started with the phrase, "This letter of Intent is entered into in the spirit of good will and mutual trust between the parties."

Ms. Zhang translated the document into Chinese and it was sent to the Ministry of Sports. Mr. Yu told us that he had received a call from the Ministry of Sports in Shanghai. We had visited with them on our first trip to China, and they wanted us to do the project in Shanghai first. He requested that we come to Shanghai as soon as possible.

Mr. Yu told us we should go and that he would take care of the Beijing Sports people. We could sign the Letter of Intent when we returned to Beijing. So off we went to Shanghai where we were met by officials of the Ministry of Sports.

They had reserved rooms for us in the Jiang Jang Hotel and had prepared an itinerary for the day. They took us to several locations, and each one was better than the last. We seemed to have our pick of places to build our first rink. We also toured some of the existing rinks. There were forty-five rinks in Shanghai. The largest was the rink in the Peoples Park, where an average of five thousand people skated every day. The largest grossing rink in the United States was five thousand skaters a week.

We chose an existing community center that had an outdoor rink and was located in the city center that we would renovate. We met with the manager of the center and an architect from the Shanghai architectural society and started laying out some preliminary plans.

We were fascinated with Shanghai. It was much more crowded than Beijing, the food was different, and they spoke a different dialect, Shanghainese.

We were visiting the Ministry of Sports complex when Sheldon noticed an empty room filled with snooker tables. He picked up a cue and shot some balls. He was soon joined by a jovial Chinese who picked up a cue and started playing with him. Sheldon was not a great snooker player, and it seemed neither was his opponent. They played two games and seemed evenly matched.

They were about to start the third game when we were called to meet with some sports officials. The young Chinese smiled at us and then cleaned every ball on the table with expert shots. He didn't miss one shot. Yes, we were snookered, and not for the last time.

We finally sat down with the Sports Ministry people and negotiated the Letter of Intent. It was identical to the one we had created for Beijing. We all agreed. We now had two projects, from the two major cities in China, with the Ministry of Sports, Beijing and Shanghai branches, our future was secured. We were elated.

A banquet was arranged for the signing ceremony that night. We went off to the telex office to message the Sports Ministry in Beijing that we would return in a few days and were very enthusiastic about signing a Letter of Intent to do a joint venture at the Capital Gymnasium.

About three hours before the banquet was to be held for us, we went back to the telex office to see if we had received a reply back from Beijing.

The reply read as follows: "Dear Mr. and Mrs. Krechman, we have received your telex and wish to inform you that we no longer have any interest in doing a joint venture with you in Beijing. Please do not contact us any further. Signed the Ministry of Sports.

As you can well imagine, we were dumbfounded. We immediately assumed that if the Ministry of Sports in Beijing, wanted no more to do with us, their branch in Shanghai would feel the same way. We sat in our hotel room for three hours waiting for the message we believed would come, that the banquet was canceled and our arrangement with the Shanghai Ministry of Sports had ended.

At about 6:30 there was a knock on our door, and it was the driver from the Sports Ministry. He was there to take us to the banquet. All our fears were groundless. We arrived at the banquet with about twenty-five people. We drank Moutai, toasted everyone and with video cameras recording the moment, we all signed the Letter of Intent.

* * * * *

It was suggested that we visit the city of Hangzhou, so the next day we boarded a train from Shanghai for the twelve-hour trip—one of our many excursions exploring China over the years.

Hangzhou is a city with a one of the largest man-made lakes in the world, West Lake. Centuries ago, there was an Empress who lived in Beijing at the Forbidden City. She liked the city and decided to build a lake there. She also decided that she would like to travel to that lake by water. It's about 2500 miles from Beijing to Hangzhou, so over many years she built a waterway called the Grand Canal, which flows from Beijing to Hangzhou and empties into West Lake. It's been said that the only two things you can see from space is the Great Wall of China and the Grand Canal.

When we arrived in Hangzhou we were greeted by our guide, a young man from the Foreign Ministry. Sheldon has always been interested in computers and he and the guide started talking about the technology. When the guide told us that Hangzhou had started to build a computer center and that there were already Chinese companies producing computer products, Sheldon asked if we could visit one of the factories. He just nodded.

We were taken to the West Lake Hotel, which was one of the original hotels built on the lake and were given a lakeside room. As I was sitting at the desk in the room looking out over the picturesque lake, I started to write a letter, just as a cockroach walked slowly across the top of the desk and across my letter. I couldn't help wondering if the Empress had ever seen a cockroach on her visits.

Our guide took us to lunch at one of the local restaurants. Hangzhou is famous for its eel, and we had eel stew. The sound of it was very strange, but it was delicious, and we acquired a taste for eel.

We walked around for miles. We visited the zoo, which was very primitive, compared to our zoos in the United States. It was very large, and they had two Giant Pandas, which for us was very unusual. We also saw some dogs outside the zoo, German Shepherd variety. This was the first city we had come to where we had seen dogs. In Beijing, dogs were eaten as a delicacy, and the Chinese are too concerned with their own survival, to take care of large animals, unless they have a productive use.

Our guide came to get us that afternoon to take us to the Yi Ling Temple, which is a very famous tourist attraction. The Temple grounds are large and as usual in China, there were crowds of people. It was like being in an amusement park, except instead of rides and games, there were temples with incense and huge statues of Buddha, in a variety of poses, colors, shapes and sizes. There were monks everywhere, in white robes and fresh food was being sold at hot food stands. On one side of the Temple grounds was a mountain with large foothills and carved out of the stone in several places where gigantic statues of Buddha. It was like being in South Dakota at Mount Rushmore. We were completely awed by the temple and its wonderful grounds. There are wonders like this all over China.

The next stop was the tea plantations. Hangzhou is known for its long green tea and the production of silk. Tea in China is like wine in the United States. There are countless varieties, and they all seem to have some medicinal value. The long green Hangzhou tea is known as long life tea.

The silkworm production was fascinating, and very unusual. By the time we finished our private tour, it was late, and we all were hungry. Our guide took us back to our hotel and Sheldon asked again, if we could visit a computer factory. He just smiled and said goodnight.

We had a lovely evening. We walked through the center of town, and had dinner at a local restaurant, which was always interesting, because no one spoke any English and we were the only round eyes in the place. We had to point to what we wanted, but everyone was very friendly, and the meal was fine.

The next morning, our guide called and said he would be at our hotel in fifteen minutes, and we were going to a computer factory. Sheldon was so excited. We dressed quickly and met him out front. There were two Chinese made automobiles and three new people—two were drivers and one was a representative from the computer factory.

The factory was located on the outskirts of Hangzhou. We walked up to the second floor and were met by two women who looked like laboratory workers in white coats, hats and shoes. We were taken into a room that was very clean and asked to put on white coats, nylon gloves, white hats and special shoes. We were told that this was a clean area, and that anyone that walked through the factory, should have as little dust as possible.

Carole Sumner Krechman and Sheldon Krechman

The factory was an assembly line, mostly women, with fluorescent overhead lights and long tables. They were assembling personal computers. The line was hardly mechanized, and everything was being done by hand including the soldering of certain parts. Everyone was very friendly and after touring the factory, we were invited into their conference room for some tea and conversation.

The conference room had a long table that sat about 20 people and the chairs were full. They told us through an interpreter that we were the first foreigners to visit this factory which was only about two years old. It was the first computer factory to be constructed, and they said that Hangzhou would someday be a computer center, like Northern California. Sheldon told them of his long history in the electronics business and that he was looking for some opportunities in China.

We spoke for about one hour and just as we thought the meeting was over, the doors to the conference room opened up and several people came rushing into the room, with microphones, TV cameras, and cables. It looked like network news.

Everyone jumped up and started talking and people were giving directions. The table was moved, and chairs were rearranged, as we sat there looking at all the activity. Finally, the interpreter came up to us and told us that what was going on was very unexpected. It seemed the local TV station had picked that very day and time to do an hour long special on the computer factory and it was just a coincidence that we were there. They said they knew it was an imposition, but would we mind joining in the program with them?

Of course, we went along with it. We all sat down at the table after it had been re-arranged by the TV people and would you believe, we were the stars. We realized it was a setup and later found out it was for propaganda purposes.

They started with a monologue, that we didn't understand, and no one interpreted for us. They started asking us questions, which were interpreted for us. The questions were innocuous. How long have you been in China? What cities have you been to? What do you think of Hangzhou? What do you think of the computer factory? Have the local people been friendly and cooperative? What do the American people think of the Chinese people? Were we concerned about the violence in the United States?

This went on for a while and after a bit, they ended the video, and started to pack up their equipment. We asked if we could have a copy of the video. No one said a word and they kept packing up. We finally asked our guide if he could get us a copy. He just looked at us and didn't answer. He drove us back to our hotel and we asked him again. He just smiled.

The next morning our guide picked us up to take us to the train station. We thanked him for the tour, and when we arrived at the train station, he handed Sheldon a large envelope with the video tape.

When we came out of China to Hong Kong, we had the tape converted from PAL to the US standard and were very curious to see it. When we finally played it, the video was great, but they cut out all the audio, so the tape was silent. We were later told that they had aired the tape on TV stations all the way to Shanghai.

* * * * *

On our return to Shanghai, as we were getting off the train Sheldon accidentally knocked me in the neck and shoulder with a suitcase, he had pulled off the luggage rack. My neck was twisted, and I was in a great deal of pain and discomfort. Since we were guests of the Ministry of Sports, they sent over a sports medicine individual who massaged my neck and shoulder, but to no avail.

Fortunately, one of the local people who were instructed to look after us, was the wife of an OXY executive who was working in the LA office, but his family was still in Shanghai. His mother was a doctor. I called his wife and told her the pain I was in, and she immediately had her mother-in-law come to our hotel room. The doctor had me remove my blouse and she took out what looked like a small hammer with sharp points at the end. She lightly hit the hammer in several places on my neck and shoulders and it lightly broke the skin. She then took some small glass jars and lit a match in the jar to remove the oxygen and then suctioned each jar on my neck and shoulders, where she had broken the skin. Next, she put in several acupuncture pins, and I sat quietly for an hour. At the end she removed the glass jars and the pins, and the pain was completely gone. It was a miraculous cure and our first, but not last experience with Chinese medicine.

* * * * *

Armed with our letter of intent, we traveled back to Beijing, in high spirits. We resolved to find out just what had happened at the Beijing Sports Ministry. We gave Mr. Yu a copy of the Letter of Intent and asked him for an explanation. He told us that both organizations were part of the same Ministry, and that he had no idea why the Beijing Sports Ministry had changed their mind. When we asked him to please inquire he said it was unnecessary and we should forget the entire matter and concentrate on doing business in Shanghai.

And then, surprisingly, the Sports Ministry in Beijing invited us to a meeting. They said they were very interested in the modernization of their roller skating centers and they wanted to introduce us to a bank in Hong Kong, who might finance our ventures. These were the same people that had taken us to the Capital Gymnasium and sent us the telex in Shanghai. Not a word was spoken about our previous meetings. It was like it just never happened.

China was always a place of mystery and unanswered questions. Wheels within wheels within wheels.

We traveled to Hong Kong and met with Mr. Nelson Chao, Chairman of the Sin Hua Trust. We later found out that the Sin Hua Trust was a Hong Kong front for the Bank of China. We were ushered into a large conference room with a table so wide you had to push any papers over to the other side by reaching as far as you could. Mr. Chao asked us to sit opposite him, so he could look into our eyes. The first thing he asked us was where we were from. When we replied, "Beverly Hills, California," he looked at us, smiled, and said, "Nice place to live."

We had an hour-long conversation and we both realized that he was sizing us up and of course his secretary was taking notes on what we had to say. At the end of the conversation, we asked him what the possibility was of funding our ventures. His response was, "The ox moves slow, but the earth is patient." He then ushered us out and thanked us for coming and said goodbye.

After several false starts, months of negotiations and dozens of adventures, we abandoned all hope of building a chain of roller-skating rinks in China. Through a convoluted series of events, we instead became involved in a large and complicated joint venture with the Chinese to build an office and hotel complex in downtown Beijing. We called our company World China Trade.

CHAPTER 5

Chinese Medical Miracles

Nature, time and patience are the three great physicians.

~Chinese Proverb

We spent over fifteen hundred days in the Peoples Republic of China, in every season, in every month of the year. The only health precaution we took for the first ten trips, was gamma globulin shots. After that we came and went as if we were going to Santa Barbara.

We drank the water from the taps, we ate food from stands along the streets and roads throughout China, and except for the first trip, where Sheldon and I both got a very bad bronchial cough and flu type symptoms, we never got sick except for some unusual incidents.

At that time, before you entered China from the United States, you would receive a pamphlet that would advise foreign travelers on many things. Under the area of health, the pamphlet explained that should a traveler get sick for any reason whatsoever they should make arrangements to leave China immediately and travel to Hong Kong where proper medical treatment was available.

It said that China was a third world country and that their medical treatments were antiquated, and the traveler would take their lives in their hands if they received medical treatment in the PRC. They also warned about taking any Chinese medicine or herbs, because they had not been tested or approved by the American Medical Association.

I first experienced the wonders of Chinese medicine when I injured my neck and had my first acupuncture experience in Shanghai which completely relieved the excruciating pain. On a subsequent trip, it was Sheldon's turn to experience the Chinese practice of medicine.

We had met a Chinese family in Shanghai with whom we became friends. Zev was the manager of an electronics plant that produced radios. It was very similar to Sheldon's father's business, who was a pioneer of radio and TV manufacture in the United States. For Sheldon, it was like old times and he and Zeb had a lot in common.

Zev and his family lived in a very small apartment. His wife was pregnant, and they invited us for dinner. It was not the usual practice for a Chinese citizen to invite a foreigner to dinner at his house, because there were always other people that would report to the Party Leaders about any strange occurrences happening within their purview. A foreigner coming to dinner was a strange occurrence. That's the way a communist country keeps control of the people. Everybody reports on everybody.

Mr. Yu had suggested that since electronics was the future, we should visit Zev's factory and see if we could work out a Joint venture relationship. Zev was very receptive to the idea and Sheldon was excited about touring a radio manufacturing plant.

It was January and very cold in Shanghai. We all dressed warmly and arrived at our appointment on time. The factory was not just one building, but a series of buildings in a complex that was surrounded by a twelve-foot chain link fence. It had an entrance where a guard sat in a small cubicle with a gate that he would open if you were approved to enter the complex.

Zev greeted us with a group of four other factory officials and they took us on a tour of most of the complex. It was very familiar to Sheldon since it looked like one of his father's radio factories in the early 1950s. There were long benches with seats on either side and an assembly line of hundreds of people, wiring and soldering by hand and assembling radios.

There was a more modern building and when we asked to tour it, we were told that it was unavailable for a tour at that time. (Zev later told Sheldon, in a weak and trusting moment, that radios were not the only product that was manufactured at the factory, but the other products were of a military nature, and he could not discuss them.)

We spent about two hours walking through the complex and really enjoyed the tour. The factory however, had little or no heat and the buildings were not insulated very well. If was drafty, and cold. It had just started to snow. The Chinese were all bundled up with layers of clothes, and they all had heavy long underwear. You could almost see your breath on the inside of the building. We were grateful when we were ushered into a large conference room, which was as usual, filled with couches where we all sat and were served some tea. The conference room was heated, which I think did just because we were there.

We started as always with both sides saying positive things about each other's country, and then discussing each other's experience. Sheldon had a lot in common with them and they were very pleased at his knowledge of electronics and the manufacture of radios. We were really enjoying the tea. It was hot and delicious, and was a special red tea, that you drink in the winter. It's very strong and very robust.

After drinking two or three cups, Sheldon had to go to the bathroom. Zev told him that they did not have any facilities for guests and the only men's bathroom was the one used by all the employees, and he was concerned. Sheldon told him he grew up in old factories and not to worry. Just point him in the right direction.

Several minutes later Sheldon returned to the conference room. We all gasped. His face was white, and blood was pouring from his finger. He was in shock. Zev jumped into action. He took off his belt and put it over Sheldon's wrist and pulled it tight to act as a tourniquet. Then he and another official from the meeting took him by the arms and I followed them down a flight of steel stairs to the factory infirmary.

What had happened was that when he entered the men's room, there were four toilet cubicles. The door to each cubicle was metal, with a sharp edge and rusty hinges. There was a hole in the window and the cold air was coming through and the cubicle doors were rattling. As he stood there doing his thing, he put his right hand on the door jamb of the cubicle. Suddenly there was a large gust of wind and the metal cubicle door slammed shut on his index finger. That was when he realized he had crushed it.

As we entered the infirmary, I remembered a story that was told to us at the US Embassy in Shanghai, about a woman who had her hand caught in a car door. She was taken to a Chinese hospital and given treatment. Her hand got much worse and infected and by the time she had gotten back to Hong Kong, part of her hand had to be amputated. (That's the story they tell you to make sure you don't receive any treatment in China). It was obvious that I was really scared and very worried.

We were met in the infirmary by a woman in a white outfit who immediately sat Sheldon down and examined his finger, which by now was beginning to throb and hurt, and looked just awful. She washed it off with some disinfectant and took down a large bottle of Chinese medicine from a shelf. It was white and had a paste like consistency. She spread it thickly over his injured finger and then wrapped it with a thick layer of gauze.

She then put about eight acupuncture needles in various parts of his body, gave him a spoon full of black thick liquid and had him lay down on a cot in the infirmary. She suggested we let him rest for a while, and we went back up the stairs to continue the meeting.

About a half an hour later, to my utter amazement, Sheldon returned to the conference room. He said he felt a little lightheaded, and that his finger was throbbing, but less than before and he felt okay to continue the meeting. By the time we got back to the hotel, the throbbing and pain were gone, and he had just a slight sensation in his finger.

The following week, I made sure that Sheldon did exactly what the woman had told us, including taking a spoonful of the black liquid, (she gave him a small bottle) every morning and every night. His finger felt tender, but he had very little, if no pain. At the end of seven days, he took off the gauze and with the exception of a very thin scar, his finger was completely healed.

For several years prior to going to China, Sheldon had suffered with a recurring problem with his wisdom teeth. He had never had them removed and it seemed once a year he would get an infection in the lower right or left wisdom tooth. It would start slowly and build up and within a very short period of time, he would have massive swelling on one side of his jaw and very intense pain. It would incapacitate him to such an extent that it was impossible to work. He would suffer through a week of agony until the infection subsided.

One day in Beijing during the construction of our hotel project, the right side of his jaw started to hurt. I was concerned when he told me because I knew what was going to happen, but this time we were in China, without the benefit of our dentist. I asked Mr. Yu if he would take us to the Capital Hospital near the Beijing Hotel. When I told him the problem, he said that he also had a tooth problem that he had been neglecting—a pain in one of his left molars.

He told us that we could not go to the Capital Hospital because we were not Chinese citizens, and that I would have to take Sheldon to the expatriate foreign infirmary for treatment. The reputation of that place was terrible, including the fact that they did not have any dentists. I insisted that Mr. Yu arrange for me to take Sheldon to the Capital Hospital, and he kept telling me that it was impossible. I informed him that my experience in China had left me with the feeling that nothing was impossible if you had the right Guanxi (a Chinese term that loosely means you know people who owe you favors.)

Finally, after three days of arguing and Mr. Yu making whatever calls necessary, he told me it was all arranged. By that time, Sheldon's jaw was swollen, and he was in considerable pain. Mr. Yu also had a swollen jaw, and I could see that he was also in pain, even though he refused to admit it.

Lily, Mr. Yu's wife, came to the office and drove the three of us to Capital Hospital. It was a very large complex and when we entered, I saw several patients who were dressed in stripped outfits, similar to the way prisoners used to dress in the United States. We entered a building and walked up the stairs and there was a long hallway with at least fifty women and children waiting their turn for dental work. The main room was very large with about fifty dental chairs, almost side by side. Each chair had a patient (lots of kids), and the dental technicians were mostly young women.

At the end of the large room there was an alcove, where there was a dental chair and an older man with a white outfit. We walked directly to the alcove and there were seven people on a bench and a woman in the dental chair. She took off the sheet protecting her, stepped down and Sheldon was motioned to sit in the chair. Mr. Yu told me that he was the first foreigner ever to be admitted into the Capital Hospital.

Sheldon laid back on the dental chair. Mr. Yu told me the older man was one of the most respected dentists in Beijing and was the dentist for the top leaders in China. He smiled at Sheldon and had his assistant bring him a tray of dental tools that had just come out of the sterilizer. He probed very gently and looked into his mouth and then one by one each of the seven people sitting on the bench, got up, one at a time and each one looked in his mouth also.

Then he took out a small bottle of very dark thick liquid like paste and with one of his dental utensils, packed a thick white piece of cotton like string with the paste, and gently packed in down between his gum and the infected wisdom tooth. He then smiled and through an interpreter told Sheldon to keep it in until 6:00 pm that night.

Then Mr. Yu nervously got into the chair. The dentist had him open his mouth and each one of the seven people got up and looked into Mr. Yu's mouth. Finally, they all started to discuss Mr. Yu's condition, at least that's what we think they were discussing. Finally, everybody nodded their agreement. Mr. Yu was not consulted. The dentist put several acupuncture pins in Mr. Yu's face and a few other places on his body. Attached to the pins was a series of small wires, leading from a box that generated slight electrical pulsing DC current.

Mr. Yu had to have two root canals, and the dentist worked on him for about an hour. Mr. Yu looked relaxed and except for having to keep his mouth open (which was not unusual for him) he did not look uncomfortable at all. When he was finished, he told us that he had felt no pain at all through the procedure and even after it was complete, and except for a small tingly sensation, he was okay.

The dentist gave Sheldon three bottles of different liquids and told him that after 6:00 pm, he could take out the absorbent string. He was instructed to wash his mouth out three times a day for thirty days with the three different liquids. One for the morning, one for the afternoon and one before bedtime, and not to wash his mouth out with water after using the liquid for at least one hour. We were also told that since we were foreigners, we would have to pay foreign rates for the treatment and the bottles of mouth medicine. The total sum was the equivalent of $3.50 U.S.

As instructed, at 6:00 pm Sheldon took out the string and used the mouth medicine, and by the next morning the swelling was completely gone. He used the mouth medicine for the next thirty days, as the dentist directed.

In all the years that followed, Sheldon never had another incident with his wisdom teeth. It's hard to argue with a culture that has been practicing medicine for thousands of years.

CHAPTER 6

Guanxi

Guanxi: *an individual's social network of mutually beneficial personal and business relationships.*

The transition from roller-rink entrepreneurs to big-time real estate developers was accomplished over time through a Byzantine process of manipulation, incentive and behind-the-scenes transactions. Through a series of introductions and inducements we were linked up with some of China's most powerful players and positioned, unknowingly, to serve the interests of various state agencies. The catalyst for all of this was the inimitable Mr. Yu.

By our third trip to China in 1983, we had formed a California corporation and called it World China Trade. Richard Chen would receive stock and become a director along with Dean Lee, another Oxy employee in Beijing. Dean was an American citizen whose family lived in Orange County California but worked in Beijing under the direction of Richard Chen. We agreed to pay Mr. Yu a salary and cover necessary expenses, such as rent, car and driver.

We raised start-up funds from a group of investors, mostly friends, and filed the corporation papers. Sheldon was listed as chairman of the board, I was Vice Chairman, and Mr. Yu was designated president. This made Mr. Yu the very first Chinese citizen to be an officer of an American Corporation—something which gave him great status in China.

Now that we had a company, we needed offices. In the eighties all foreign companies in China had their offices in hotels, the most prestigious of which was the Beijing Hotel. It was located on the corner of Chauhan and Was Fu Jing which at that time was like Rodeo Drive in Beverly Hills with high end stores and food shops.

When the Chinese government constructed the first office building in Beijing, not far from the Beijing Hotel, Oxy moved its offices there. The old Oxy offices had been located in the Beijing Hotel, in three interconnected rooms. Mr. Yu arranged for us to take over Oxy's former space.

Along with Oxy's former office, we inherited, Ms. Zhang, a former Oxy employee. She would become Mr. Yu's assistant. We gave her the title Manager of American Affairs. Ms. Zhang spoke excellent English and had been one of the top interpreters for high officials of the Chinese Government.

Our funds were limited, so when we moved in, we decided to purchase our office furniture at a modest local store, rather than import it from Hong Kong. Mr. Yu and Ms. Zhang had a place in mind, so we all piled into our little company car, a vintage Datsun, and headed out. Finally, after about an hour, we stopped in front of what looked like a second-hand thrift shop.

Inside the shop was a jumble of chairs, desks and various types of cabinets piled up in stacks. There seemed to be no particular order and every piece was different from the other. It was a far cry from the typical American furniture store, with its carefully arranged merchandise.

I have a good eye (and an architecture degree), and I went through the store, carefully examined each piece, and picked out the best furnishings for our use. Outside the little establishment a large group of people had gathered, staring at us, gesticulating and laughing.

Shameless gawking is socially acceptable in China. We smiled at them, and they all waved at us.

After I had picked out the furniture, Mr. Yu and Ms. Zhang started the bargaining process. We could not understand the words, but the gestures told the story. The negotiation started out calmly but gradually became heated. The crowd outside had something to say about the transaction, too. At one point Mr. Yu and Ms. Zhang started to wave their hands, and the level of everyone's voices rose considerably. This went on for about twenty minutes.

Finally, Mr. Yu, with an angry look on his face, stalked out of the store and motioned for us to follow. Outside the store Mr. Yu told us, in a very calm voice, that the manager was being very unreasonable about the price of the furniture. We later found out that a lot of that negotiation was just a show for us. We waited outside for a few minutes and then we followed Mr. Yu back in the store.

Meanwhile, it seemed that the crowd outside had become very involved in the negotiation, and everyone had a different opinion, including our driver. After another twenty minutes everyone started to smile, and Ms. Zhang took out a wad of bills from her purse and paid the store manager. We were told the total amount of the purchase was between $150 and $200 dollars. The purchase included several desks, chairs and file cabinets.

That afternoon the furniture was delivered by two Chinese men in their seventies. These two septuagenarians looked exceptionally fit, with lean muscular arms and trim physiques. We were curious to see how they had brought the furniture, so we followed them down to the street. There by the front door were two tricycles with wood platforms on the back, each piled high with furniture which had been tied down with hemp rope. These two old men had pedaled the huge load clear across town and were now preparing to carry everything up to our offices.

The rooms were on the corner of the fourteenth floor and had an impressive view of both a main boulevard, Chan Yan Avenue, and a secondary road, Wau Fu Ging Street. This was a prime location, near the center of the city and Tiananmen Square. It wasn't fancy—nothing much was fancy in Beijing in the eighties—but we were very pleased. Our new furniture was quite utilitarian, even though the style and finish quality were far inferior to anything available in the United States. As the last piece was brought in, two young men appeared. A few furnishings had been left over from the Oxy offices. The two men carried it away.

Later that afternoon a man from the hotel management came to our offices and was introduced to us as an assistant manager. Mr. Yu got into a long discussion with him but did not stop to interpret. After he left, Mr. Yu told us that there would be an additional charge for our rooms. It seems that since the young men had removed the leftover furniture (which apparently belonged to the hotel) and taken it to the basement, we would be charged for storage. We would also be charged extra for the "space" our new furniture was taking up. The whole situation seemed ridiculous, but Mr. Yu said, "This is China." It would turn out to be his all-purpose answer for every inexplicable circumstance.

Mr. Yu had procured our furniture, but we were responsible for securing a copy machine, typewriter, computer, and assorted office supplies. None of these items were available in Beijing at the time and would have to be purchased in Hong Kong.

Unfortunately, there was an import duty of two hundred percent of the original purchase price on any office equipment brought in from outside China. We told Mr. Yu that since our funds were low, it was not possible to purchase these items and pay the import duty, too.

Mr. Yu told us not to worry. He said we should purchase them anyway, bring them through Chinese customs and declare nothing. He told us his "guanxi" was strong enough to deal with any customs' problem. We were neophytes, but we were already beginning to learn the importance of guanxi. Guanxi translates roughly as "favor." Guanxi is the lubricant that keeps the wheels of the Chinese system turning. In the US, it would be called a kickback or bribe. We were already the beneficiaries and the victims of guanxi.

All foreign corporations in China are required to hire local Chinese employees to work in their offices. This has a dual purpose. It helps the local economy, but more importantly it guarantees the Chinese government inside access to every foreign business. When you hire a

Chinese employee the government sets the rate, which in most cases is slightly below US standards.

The salary is paid not to the employee, however, but to the Chinese government. In 1984 the salary range was between $500 and $1,000 per month, depending on skill level and responsibility. The government would keep most of the salary and then pay your employee the average local rate, which ranged between $25 and $100 per month. In this way, you paid the government a handsome sum to spy on you.

Because the salaries that employees actually received were so low, foreign companies like ours were expected to supplement wages by dispensing guanxi in the form of gifts, trips to Hong Kong and Foreign Exchange Certificates. This was strictly illegal, of course, but routinely done. The amount of guanxi a person received was a quantitative measure of that person's social status and financial worth. The entire country is run by means of these under the table payoffs.

Mr. Yu, we soon learned, was a master of guanxi. Yu handed out favors that garnered him immense power. For example, one of the scarcest commodities in Beijing was housing. There was a chronic shortage and housing construction was going on everywhere. Despite the shortage, however, if you could get an apartment, it was cheap. The law of supply and demand didn't operate in China.

If you had the guanxi to get it a new apartment in a high rise, the cost was five dollars per month. They were considered luxury apartments, although by US standards they were downright primitive. A typical new apartment complex was ten or twelve stories high, had intermittent steam heat controlled by some state bureaucracy, and elevators that stopped at every third floor. The Chinese government assumed that people could easily walk up or down two flights of stairs and therefore saved money by skipping the extra openings and doors.

Apartments in Beijing averaged 600 square feet divided into three rooms. The rooms consisted of bare cement floors, walls, and ceilings and one light bulb per room which dangled from the ceiling on a cord. Each unit had a tiny kitchen area with two unregulated gas burners (i.e., on or off), a cold-water tap, a small toilet area with a flush hole but no fixture, and a floor drain where you could stand and pour water over yourself that you had heated on the stove. Guanxi determined who got these apartments and on which floor. If you had good guanxi you might get an apartment on a floor which the elevator served.

Mr. Yu was powerful enough to arrange apartments for people he favored. He lived in a new building himself and had two apartments across from each other. This took considerable guanxi. One of the apartments was unusually large and had two bedrooms, a den and a living room. In his apartments he had silk rugs, a real toilet fixture, a refrigerator (which was quite rare) and an electric water heater (a tremendous luxury).

How Mr. Yu acquired so much guanxi we didn't know, but however he acquired it, the importation of smuggled goods would be a major test. We agreed to go to Hong Kong and purchase the office equipment. The rest would be up to Mr. Yu. He instructed us to wrap the cartons as though they were gifts and cross the border passing through the green flag line at customs for people who had nothing to declare.

We purchased the equipment In Hong Kong including a water heater for Mr. Yu's other apartment. We returned to Beijing with stacks of cartons wrapped like birthday presents, with paper, ribbons and lots of tape. They were all piled on a big luggage cart that groaned under the weight.

As we approached customs, we looked for Mr. Yu, but he was nowhere to be seen. Nevertheless, we headed for the green flag line as instructed, pushing the cart. The customs official looked at the pile of cartons and asked Sheldon what was in them. He told him the cartons contained used toys for the children of Beijing.

It was a ridiculous lie and I thought for sure we would be arrested on the spot. The officer made a gesture and was soon joined by reinforcements who began picking at the packages. Through a few small holes they could clearly read the labels on the cartons. They asked us to wait a moment and walked away to conduct a small conference.

Soon a customs official came over to talk to us. By this time a small crowd of curious onlookers had gathered. The official asked Sheldon to open the cartons. With a queasy feeling in his stomach, he told him he'd rather not—they were so full of toys, and they'd be difficult to repack. He asked Sheldon to follow him. I watched in panic as they took Sheldon into a small room where he repeated his lie to two more officials. They made a telephone call, had a long conversation with someone, and then lectured him on the illegality of bringing in equipment and not declaring it. They said the penalty was very severe. By now, Sheldon was in a near panic too.

After what seemed like an eternity, Sheldon returned to the customs counter. I was still standing by the cart, and worried sick as one the officers followed behind Sheldon and spoke to the counter agent in Chinese. The agent then turned to us and said in English that everyone had agreed it would be too inconvenient to unpack the boxes, and gesturing with his hand, waved us through.

We were both weak kneed and perspiring, and thinking evil thoughts about Mr. Yu, but greatly relieved. Yu was waiting outside in a van. "I told you not to worry," he said. He had let us suffer, of course, so that we would appreciate the power of his guanxi.

* * * * *

Our office was all set, we had several Chinese ministries interested in business with the United States and we were talking to several US companies wanting to do business in China. We thought we are all set, and then we found out about sponsors.

A few days later we were visiting the law offices of Graham and James, a large international law firm with a branch in Beijing. Their resident lawyer was a woman named Sally Harpole. Sally spoke fluent Chinese and was an old China hand. We told her about our new offices, and she asked us many questions—what our business was, who were we dealing with and most importantly, who was Mr. Yu Xue Wen? We explained to Sally that we were a new business and had taken over the old Oxy offices in the Beijing Hotel. Our purpose, we told her, was to develop businesses between the United States and the Peoples Republic of China, an exquisitely vague but true statement.

She was amazed that Mr. Yu was President of our corporation. Sally had been in China for years and said it was unheard of for a Chinese citizen to leave the employ of the government and become an officer in a U.S. corporation. She was also very surprised to hear about our new offices. She told me that there were many US companies waiting for months to find office space. The hotel rooms at the Beijing Hotel were especially coveted. When we told her the rent we were paying, she just laughed and said it must be a mistake—it was a fraction of what other companies were paying.

When we stood up to leave, I gave Sally our private phone number. She immediately sank into her chair, her face revealing her utter amazement, and concern. It seemed that we had only one of two private lines in the entire Beijing Hotel. She told us to sit down. Some very sage advice followed.

She said we were novices and should keep our eyes and ears open; that things would change and what appeared to be reality would shift again and again, until we were totally confused. The Chinese agenda, and we could be sure they had one, would proceed with or without our knowledge or consent. Then she asked us a question: Who was our Chinese sponsor?

Sponsor? We didn't know what she was talking about. Sally then proceeded to explain that every foreign company doing business in China was required by law to have a sponsor. She said that ordinarily it was impossible to even rent an office without an official, government approved sponsor.

One of her functions as an attorney in Beijing, was to take foreign companies through the approval process. It ordinarily took anywhere from six to eighteen months to complete, at considerable cost. Sally was in the process of obtaining approvals for three companies each with gross revenues in excess of 100 million dollars per year. Our company was brand new, had not even conducted any business and we were already installed in the premier office space in Beijing, with our own private telephone line.

Sally explained that getting a sponsor was no easy task, and the more important your sponsor, the more influence or guanxi one had. We asked her who the best sponsor for us would be, and she said the Ministry of Foreign Trade. She also added that getting the Ministry of Foreign Trade as a sponsor would be out of the question. They only sponsored companies like General Motors or Boeing. We would have to settle for a sponsor much lower in the hierarchy, and she would be pleased to offer her services for that purpose.

She added that because of Mr. Yu and his guanxi this task might be easier, but not much. The cost to get a minor sponsor would be around $20,000, plus whatever additional guanxi payments that might have to be made to the various ministries. She also said that even with Mr. Yu's guanxi, it would take four to six months to accomplish. Her advice was to start the process immediately, as the Chinese government could swoop down at any time, close our office and order us to leave the country.

We thanked Sally for her time and told her that we would speak to Mr. Yu and get back to her regarding her services. We explained that Mr. Yu was supposed to be taking care of all of our bureaucratic necessities, and perhaps he had already acquired a sponsor for us but had neglected to tell us. We left, determined to ask Mr. Yu who our sponsor was the moment we got back to the office.

When we returned, Sheldon walked directly over to Mr. Yu's desk, where he was comfortably ensconced in his enormous chair, and asked him if we had a sponsor. He asked what sponsor we wanted. Sheldon took this to mean "no," and replied that he wanted the Ministry of Foreign Trade, the one who could help us the most. Mr. Yu responded that the Ministry of Foreign Trade—know by the acronym MOFERT—would be the logical choice, but they only sponsored very large companies.

When Sheldon further prodded him on how we can have this office and be doing business in China without a sponsor, he looked utterly unconcerned. Then Sheldon said we should go through the process or hire Graham and James to help us.

Sally Harpole had raised our anxiety level and we were worried that we wouldn't be able to conduct business properly until we had a sponsor. The wasted time could be costly. Mr. Yu said that if it was important to us, he would arrange everything. He then picked up the phone, placed a call, and carried on a short conversation in Chinese.

An hour later two Chinese men showed up, sat down with Mr. Yu and had a fifteen-minute conversation. When they had finished talking, Mr. Yu asked us to join them. He introduced us and explained that the men were officials from MOFERT. At that, one of the men stood up and produced a single piece of paper, handed it to me and asked if I could fill it out on the typewriter. It was an official form, written in Chinese and English. It required a minimum of information.

I filled in our name and address and the purpose of our business. We then signed it, as did Mr. Yu, and handed it to the official. The man from MOFERT then took out his seal and stamped the document. Immediately, the two men stood up, shook our hands, said something in Chinese and left.

After they had gone, we asked what the next step was. Mr. Yu said all was finished and furthermore there would be a banquet that night to celebrate. We just stood there, amazed.

That same evening, we were honored by MOFERT with an extraordinary banquet. There were twenty-five courses, lots of speeches and much drinking. The room was full of important people, all of whom came with only a few hours' notice. We were seated next to the former Mayor of Beijing, Yi Long Ki. Yi had been Chairman Mao's personal secretary on the Long March and was a man of immense prestige. Sheldon was asked to speak to the group and after several drinks of Moutai, he was more than ready. He made a long speech about how very happy we were to be in China, how we loved the Chinese children and how much respect we had for the Chinese people. Mayor Yi rose, picked Sheldon up and hugged him. Everyone was drinking, except Mr. Yu, who never drank.

Mr. Yu had very strong guanxi indeed. In China guanxi is more important than any law or regulation. It is a true measure of personal power. The foreign corporation which fails to understand this will not survive for long. To give and receive guanxi is a delicate transaction, one that requires an intimate knowledge of the subtleties of Chinese power brokering.

The next day we went to see Sally and showed her a copy of our sponsor agreement. She was absolutely speechless but told us, after a while, to be very careful. She was convinced the Chinese had some secret agenda for us and our company. She was right.

CHAPTER 7

Americans in China

*I hear and I forget, I see and I remember.
I do and I understand.*

~Chinese Proverb

One of the goals of our company, World China Trade, was to connect American businesspeople with their Chinese counterparts. We made several successful connections, but there were also mishaps with Americans who personified the derogatory term, "ugly Americans." Here are three memorable stories of our adventures with Americans whom we introduced to China.

In the early days of our company, we met an impressive young man, Strauss Zelnick, at a party in Beverly Hills. He was a rising star at Bertelsmann Music Group, which at that time was a division of Bertelsmann, the huge German media conglomerate. He and Sheldon hit it off right away because at one point in time, before I met Sheldon, he was a music manager and handled such diverse talent as Herbie Hancock, the Iron Butterfly, an early heavy metal rock group, and

Black Rock Aransas, a southern rock group whose members were friends with Bill Clinton. When we told Strauss we had just started a company in China, he asked us what kind of music they were playing there. I flippantly said, "It's Chinese to me." We laughed, but then he said he was really interested in learning what the music scene was like in the People's Republic, and he would like to join us on our next trip to China.

He was an adventurous young man and convinced his company to buy him a ticket and he joined us on our next trip to Beijing. The fascinating thing was that he had done some research about underground music under Mao, and what was going on in the music world in China. He took us to two places outside our normal haunts. There was a small music festival and Strauss knew were the musicians hung out to jam and we followed along. He and Sheldon were thrilled to listen to new music created by young Chinese musicians.

Later they escorted us to an underground art museum in a bombed out building that still had bullet holes in the walls from the "Cultural Revolution" when free thinking and creating did not exist in China under Mao. But the reality is that we humans are all the same, and we bonded with food, and music 8,000 miles from home.

It was eye opening and very cool to witness this underground world of musicians and artists, an experience we would never have had if we hadn't met the young ambitious Strauss Zelnick. It was no surprise to Sheldon and me that he went on to become a vice president at Columbia Pictures, then president of 20th Century Fox, and then back to Bertelsmann as CEO of BMG Entertainment. Today he has his own media company.

* * * * *

We looked at many industries that might be advantageous for connections between American and Chinese business. One of those was the silk industry, and as it happened, Mr. Yu had connections with the Silk Ministry in China.

Through Bob, an old friend and customer of Sheldon's who was in the printing business in Los Angeles, we met with a large garment company that purchased silk and other materials throughout the world. The company was owned and operated by two bothers named Burt and Arnold. Burt had a very aggressive personality and a large ego, since he and his brother had built a sizable business and had made a great deal of money. Arnold was much more laid back and more of the technical part of the business, where Burt was the outgoing sales type.

After several meetings convincing them that we had influence in China and could connect them to the proper factories, they agreed on an arrangement for us to bring them to China and make introductions. The deal was they would pay us $10,000 as an advance fee and then we would get a sizable commission on any silk goods they purchased from China. Bob also decided to travel with us. He too had paid us an introduction fee to printers in China and had become an investor in World China Trade.

Going to China in the early 1980's was not as simple as having a U.S. passport and hoping on a plane. You first had to get a Chinese visa. The visa office was located at the Chinese Consul in Los Angeles, and it was a laborious task to obtain. You had to go in person, then wait, usually for an inordinate amount of time, first to receive an application, then to fill out the application and then wait to have it approved. It asked all kinds of questions and approval usually took six weeks or more.

Sheldon and I had been given multiple entry and exit visas, and therefore did not have to get a new visa, every time we went back and forth to the PRC. But we should have realized that we might have some difficulties when we brought Burt, Arnold, and Bob to the Chinese Consul. It was not very modern, and most of the Chinese spoke with a broken accent and usually took care of the Chinese people before the foreigners.

When we arrived, there were several people in front of us and Burt got very irritated. He started to complain in a very loud and boisterous way that he was not used to being treated this way. He insisted that we try and pull some strings to hurry the process along. We were mortified when he was very rude to one Chinese official, that he took to be an errand boy, who was in fact the secretary to the Vice Consul.

Sheldon took Burt outside the building and tried to explain that his attitude would create problems for us and that they could refuse his visa application. He responded that they should know who he was, an influential businessman, and that they were just ignorant people from a third world country. Sheldon managed to calm him down by reminding him that if we could arrange for him to purchase silk directly from China and not though his old Hong Kong sources, where there was a big commission, he would save a great deal of money, and that even though this was a tedious process, it was well worth it.

He continued to be unreasonable, so Sheldon left him outside and came back inside the Consul. We asked to meet with the Vice Consul, who was a friend. He told us that China was not interested in dealing with rude barbarians, and that Burt's actions had created a negative impression. We told him that business was business, and that Burt could be a major importer of silk. We asked if he could let his brother Arnold take care of the visas for both of them. He invited Arnold into his office.

Arnold apologized for his brother's actions and told the Vice Consul that they were very sincere about doing business with China and that he would personally make sure that his brother behaved himself in the future. The Vice Consul agreed to let Arnold apply for both visas. The applications were processed, but we noticed that Burt's had a special Chinese notation that we did not understand.

In preparation for our trip, we explained to Burt, Bob and Arnold that China was not modern and that they should bring items like toilet paper, handwipes and any medicine or over the counter drugs they might require, since many items were not available in Beijing. Burt had a lot to say about that, but we ignored most of it. We were hopeful that once we arrived, he would be overwhelmed and act accordingly. Luckily, he and his brother traveled first class and we traveled business class.

We arrived in Beijing and started to go through customs. Unlike U.S. customs, Beijing was much more laid back, and the attitude of the Chinese customs inspectors was genial and friendly. Not so with Burt. Their attitude changed rapidly, and they inspected everything he had, in a very somber fashion. He of course was as usual loud and rude, and after his custom inspection, he was taken to a private room and questioned for about half an hour. He came back subdued, and we felt that the Chinese had in their own way accomplished what we could not do.

We had red flag limousines used for dignitaries, waiting for us at the airport. These Chinese made autos had red flags above each headlight and taillight, hence the name. We were whisked away to the Beijing hotel where we met with Mr. Yu and our Chinese office staff and had a grand dinner in the Chinese restaurant in the hotel. We were shown to our rooms and the trouble started again.

Burt said his room was not acceptable, and he rambled off a litany of complaints. It was dirty, there was no shower, just a bathtub with a hose for the shower, the TV had only Chinese programs, the food was lousy, and he wanted his money back because we had cheated him. His brother finally prevailed on him to calm down and we all went to sleep

The next day, we met in our office and attempted to lay out our plans for the day, which included a trip for Burt and Arnold to visit large silk factories and a trip to the printing plants for Bob. Burt stormed in livid. He went on a tirade on how he hated this country and its ignorant people, he should never have come here in the first place, we had taken advantage of him, and he insisted on leaving the country immediately. In deference to Burt, I must say that he was not the first who went off a bit after arriving in China. We had another occasion where we brought two partners from the largest accounting firm in the world and they ended up having a fist fight in the lobby of the Beijing hotel, over potential power. So, we tried to calm things down with Burt.

Mr. Yu retired to his office with the darkest look I had ever seen on his face. He was so angry I thought that Burt might be in personal physical danger. Sheldon went in and tried to explain to Mr. Yu, who had lost considerable face over this issue, that Burt was irrational and that he should not take it personally. Mr. Yu told Sheldon that he was always personally monitored and could be severely criticized for Burt's errant behavior, and that before he would allow himself to be humiliated, he would take whatever drastic steps necessary to resolve this situation with this arrogant, and stupid foreigner. He added that they would not let Burt leave the country and if he continued on, he would have the Public Security People restrain him.

Sheldon and I were at our wits end. We decided to have a talk with both Burt and Arnold. Without mincing words, we told them the facts and warned Burt that his actions could not only hurt him but all the rest of us. We explained that this was a communist country, and the people we were dealing with could eliminate him in a variety of ways, and that we could do nothing about it. We also told him that he could not leave the country, until permission was given. We left and his brother Arnold spent over an hour with him. Finally, they came back to the office, Burt apologized to Mr. Yu and said they were ready to visit the silk factory. By that time none of us wanted to go with him, but I reluctantly agreed to the task and off I went with Burt and Arnold.

Sheldon had the easier assignment and went with Bob to tour one of the printing factories. But it wasn't without drama. The factory manager was very cordial, and they were served lunch in the factory dining room. Bob was gracious, and very knowledgeable in the printing business. He gave the Chinese several ideas, which they were grateful for. Bob had an interesting sense of humor and throughout the visit would make comments, that unfortunately the Chinese could not comprehend.

Near the end of the day, all the factory employees were ushered into a room. The manager introduced Sheldon and Bob as honored guests and asked Bob to make a few comments. He didn't want to criticize, since the factory was old, with ancient equipment and few modern methods, so he decided to lighten up the conversation with some humor. He told the group that he had enjoyed the tour, but somehow, he had gotten printing ink on his pants. He knew that as a printer, it was impossible to tour a print plant without at some point getting ink on yourself.

It was meant as a statement that would bring him together as one of the group. The room got very silent. There was no laughter, no smiles, just somber faces. What happened was they felt he was complaining, and that they had made a serious error in allowing him to get his pants dirty. They felt responsible and the manager was concerned that he could be criticized.

They offered to buy him new pants, clean his pants, or whatever they could do to remedy the situation. Bob had unwittingly made a serious gaffe and trying to explain it was just a joke, only made it worse. When they arrived back at the office, Mr. Yu informed them that the manager had called and was sending a written apology, and they insisted on buying Bob a new pair of pants.

When I returned with Burt and Arnold, to everyone's amazement, Burt was a totally different person. He was full of smiles, and he went around shaking hands with everyone. He was very impressed with the silk factories. They had treated him with cordiality and respect, but most of all he was offered high quality goods at very reasonable prices. All he could talk about was how terrific everything was and what a long and prosperous future he would have with China. He told everyone what a magnificent job I had done, and it seemed that what started to be very negative was turning into a positive.

But the Chinese have long memories and Burt had insulted them. The remainder of the week went very well, with lots of banquets and several meetings with silk factories. Burt and Arnold were leaving the next day, and there was a farewell banquet, hosted by the Silk Ministry. Burt made a speech, had several samples to take back to the United States, and was well satisfied with the trip in general. All the unpleasantness seemed to have been forgotten.

We all decided to go to the airport to say goodbye. The flight Burt and Arnold were taking was CAAC (Chinese airlines). The flight was off to Hong Kong, where they would board a United flight back to the United States. We said our good-byes and they boarded the airplane. Mr. Yu suggested that we wait until the flight took off before we returned to our office.

About fifteen minutes went by and we saw Burt being escorted off the airplane by a Ministry of Public Security official. Arnold was told to stay on the airplane, and it took off without Burt. We were very concerned, because we saw on Mr. Yu's face that he was aware of just what was going on.

Burt was taken to the Ministry of Public Security and his belongings were searched. They found several antique Chinese coins, which were illegal to take out of China and some photographs that were taken in an area that the Chinese had strictly forbidden. They allowed us to see Burt and he was very shaken up. His old bravado and arrogance were gone—he was plain scared.

We asked Mr. Yu to take care of this and have Burt released, but Mr. Yu said there was nothing he could do. We were sure he was in on the whole thing. Burt denied having anything to do with the coins and the photos. Meanwhile the Chinese told him that he would have to stand trial and perhaps go to a Chinese jail. He was frantic when they would not allow him any phone calls. Finally, after two days, they told him they were dropping the charges and put him on a flight back to Hong Kong. Mr. Yu had a satisfied smile on his face, still claiming he knew nothing about it.

* * * * *

It was January and we had been in Beijing for a few days with another friend and client, Saul Leonard, who was a partner in the international accounting firm of Laventhol and Horwath and was the partner in charge of the hotel division. His purpose for the trip was to investigate the possibility of building a China business for his firm. Saul was always a polite, courteous and respectful businessman wherever he went. This time our cringe worthy moment was with an OXY employee.

One morning, Mr. Yu told us that we all had to go to Benxi the next day. We all wondered where Benxi was, and Mr. Yu explained it was in Liaoning Province, which was located in northern Manchuria, not far from the North Korean border. He added that Dean Lee from OXY would accompany us on the trip to investigate business opportunities. The mayor of Benxi was a friend of Mr. Yu and Dean Lee. The city also had, what they considered a natural wonder, the Caves of Benxi. It turned out that the Caves of Benxi, was like one of the eight wonders of the world. We were excited and so was our client.

It was about twenty degrees Beijing and Mr. Yu told us that it would be still colder in Benxi. We had an 8 am train and Mr. Yu hustled us into the car, and we raced to the train station. One million people per day go through the main train station in Beijing. It is a vast complex of trains, tracks, buildings and immense fresh food stands, selling everything from vegetables, fruits (the fruit in Northern China is very meager), nuts, rice, and more items.

It was extremely confusing and mobbed with people and animals, who were sitting, standing, and sleeping. Dean Lee told us that at any one time, day or night, there were more than 300,000 people in the train station. We ran for the train, holding on to each other so as not to get lost in this mass of Chinese humanity. We arrived at a train and started to board when Mr. Yu frantically shouted, "Get off, it's the wrong train." We all jumped off and Mr. Yu sent his assistant racing away toward the right train, which unfortunately happened to be on the other side of the station, while we ran after him.

We got to the proper train, all out of breath, and we realized that Mr. Yu's assistant had gotten the train to wait for us. (Guanxi).

This train looked like something out of an old Russian movie. It was like being on the Siberian Russian Railway, which as it turned out, it actually was. We had a private compartment as did Saul. It was very modest, but comfortable with down feather pillows and mattresses. The dining car was also very modest, with a coal burning stove in the middle of the car. Lunch was a hot soup made of snake and chicken, with vegetables and noodles. The train had stopped at a small station and the dining car cook, purchased several items that were rice and vegetables wrapped in lotus leaves, from an open stand and we were also served that.

The bathrooms on the train were another matter. They were dark, cold and grimy. The odor was very bad, and I used my Handi Wipes over my nose and mouth when I went in, which was as little as possible.

At 8:00 pm through a speaker in our compartment, a dialog started and lasted for about thirty minutes. It was in Chinese, but Mr. Yu had told us they broadcasted the party line with Chinese propaganda every morning and evening.

We arrived in Benxi at 5:00 am the next day, and when we stepped off the train, it was twenty degrees below zero. We were all glad Mr. Yu had prepared us and we had dressed in our warmest gear. Waiting to greet us, was the mayor and three other city officials. Benxi is a small industrial city of about one and half million people. One of their main industries was the manufacture of steel.

We drove through the city, and it was snowing, but because of their industry, it was bleak and grimy. We arrived at the City Hall complex and as we got out of the car, Sheldon and I noticed an outdoor roller-skating rink, opposite the City Hall complex. There were about a hundred teenagers roller skating outside, in below zero temperatures. These kids were smiling and laughing and having a wonderful time. It was a delight to see them.

We went into the City Hall and were ushered into a large conference room. We sat at long tables and there were several Chinese sitting opposite us. Each one would get up and come to the table, sit in front of us and tell us, with the help of an interpreter what industry he was in, facts about his particular factory, and what he had to offer in a joint venture, or sale of a product. It ranged from pottery, to steel, to the distribution of beer, wine, and clothing. They kept coming in a seemingly never-ending stream. They were all very cordial and polite and no one spoke any English.

The room had no heat. You could see your breath and there was frost on the table legs. They were dressed in a much more rural manner then the people in Beijing. They all had long woolen underwear and several layers of clothes under the blue or gray Mao outfits.

We were all dressed warmly with layers of clothes, and it was the first time I could remember wearing gloves inside a room. As the temperature changed, you either added or took off a layer of clothes. This procession of the managers or directors of the different industries went on for about three hours, and then it was time for lunch.

We moved to a large dining room and there were several tables filled with people that were invited to our lunch. We sat at the head table, with the mayor and other city officials. We started toasting with Moutai almost at once. Benxi made their own Moutai, and it was like mountain brew. The Moutai had a slight yellow color to it, and it was much stronger the Moutai we drank in Beijing. Everybody was toasting, and it was so cold that the Moutai felt good going down my throat into my stomach.

They served at least twenty courses. The food kept coming—vegetables, meat, poultry, fish, noodles, rice, soup—and each dish was more delicious than the previous one. We were drinking, wine, beer,

Moutai, tea, and it just went on and on. Everybody was finally getting a bit woozy and happy. They started to sing and laugh, and we all had a very good time.

After lunch we were shown to our room for a rest. It was so hot, we had to take off most of our clothes. The heat was hardly ever used except in very extreme circumstances, but as we were honored guest, they turned it on full blast in our room for us. We had to open a window, to get the room moderately cool.

The bathroom was very interesting. The hot water was only available two hours per day from 7:00am to 8:00am and 8:00 pm to 9:00 pm. When you first turned on the faucet, the water came out like a black lagoon. When you wanted to drain the bathtub, you had to pull a cork plug out of the side of the tub and the water would run across the floor of the bathroom to a drain on the floor near the door.

We had a very nice nap and slept off some of the alcohol we had been drinking at lunch and were ready for the afternoon session. We sat in a much smaller room and the meeting was attended by only seven or eight people. The city manager and the city's chief architect also attended this meeting. They brought out a large model of a hotel project, and a set of plans and specifications. They had worked very hard to develop the model and plans. Their goal was to develop a hotel complex for tourists to come to Benxi and visit the Caves of Benxi. I was excited and spent a long time reviewing the plans and giving advice as to how to modernize them. But we all realized that to build a twenty-million-dollar hotel for foreign tourists, in a city without an airport was not very realistic.

After spending the afternoon reviewing and discussing the potential development, they took us to a local live theater. It was terrific, and very entertaining. It was filled with local people and the entrance price was the U.S. dollar equivalent of thirty-five cents. The first act was a group of acrobats. There were ten of them and at the end of the act, they were five or six high in a pyramid, with burning torches. Then came a group of roller skaters who skated on a tabletop. Then came the magicians. It just went on and on for three hours. We received a lot of stares. Most of these people, if not all, had never seen a gweilo (round eyed barbarian) before.

The dinner that night was like our earlier lunch—a great amount of food and lots more drinking and carrying on. Dean Lee seemed to take a fancy to the mayor's daughter and was dancing with her. I was a bit concerned, and I didn't want any unforeseen difficulties to arise. We finally all retired to bed and were told that we were going to visit the Caves of Benxi the next morning.

We were put in a van the next morning and drove for about two hours in the countryside that looked like we were in the middle of a Korean War movie. It was bleak and cold, and we were passing snow covered hills, with little vegetation. We finally arrived at a small building in the middle of some snow-covered mountains and were given a small brochure and a cup of tea.

We then walked out of the building on a path for about half a mile and came to a large mountain with two huge steel doors on the bottom. It reminded me of the movie, *Ali Baba and the 40 Thieves*. Two of the people with us each took a large steel latch and opened the doors.

Inside was an incredible sight. The temperature was about 65 to 70 degrees, and they told us that was the average temperature inside the cave, regardless of the season.

The ceiling must have been at least fifty feet high and there were colored lights facing up toward the ceiling which has stalactites, some of them ten feet or more, facing down from the top. Inside there was a lake, which was crystal clear, with some small boats on it. We got into one of the boats and they started to row us deep into the cave. As we rowed, the width of the lake got smaller, and the ceiling became lower and lower. We saw endless stalactites and stalagmites, of incredible colors, widths, and dimensions.

The crystal-clear lake had fish of many colors, that we were told were blind. You could actually see down to the bottom of the lake floor, which had all types of unusual rock and life forms. The only light was a string of colored lights that had been strung with just a few wires, along the side of the lake. We rowed for about half an hour and finally came to where they had stopped excavating to enlarge the lake area so that boats could pass through. They said that the lake went on for miles and miles and they were not sure how long it was or where it ended.

It was like one of the eight wonders of the world. Little by little they were excavating and extending where the boats could go on the lake inside the mountain. We were all very impressed and thanked them very much for taking us into this wondrous cave.

Mr. Yu told us that we were only ten miles from the North Korean Border and asked if wanted to see it. We said we certainly would. The border was just a stretch of land with a small crossing and guard house on either side. Each side had armed soldiers, and everything looked very peaceful. Sheldon asked Mr. Yu if we could go into North Korea. He replied that even though he had a great deal of Guanxi, North Korea was another matter, and that once we entered, we may not be able to leave. Sheldon asked if we could talk to the North Korean Border Guards. He said we could try. The guards on both sides knew each other and one waved to the other and we walked across to the North Korean side.

There was a language barrier, but communication was established. The North Korean soldiers gave us some tea, which was very different from the Chinese tea we had been drinking. We were told there was a small town nearby and we asked if we could go there. Mr. Yu said we were pushing our luck. We decided that it was not a good idea and returned to Benxi.

That night we had another banquet and started drinking and toasting when I saw Dean Lee disappear with the mayor's daughter. Our train was leaving late that night for Beijing, and when we finally found him with the mayor's daughter, it was obvious that both of them had too much to drink. Actually, that's an understatement as he could hardly stand up.

On the way to the train station, we had to stop the car for him to throw up. It seemed embarrassing to me, but no one else gave it much thought. The mayor and his group were all there to say goodbye and welcomed us any time in the future to come back to Benxi and its fabulous cave.

Before Saul left China, we had viewed many sites for hotel development, and had long meetings with potential joint venture partners, including the Beijing Hotel. He felt there was a great deal of potential for hotel development in China.

CHAPTER 8

From Roller Skating Entrepreneurs to Real Estate Developers

Good things are produced only through much grinding.
~Chinese Proverb

After Saul's trip to China, we decided that instead of attempting to build roller skating rinks, we would develop a hotel project in Beijing, which would be much more lucrative. We had come to realize that because the roller rinks would cater only to the Chinese population, who had only Chinese money (RMB) to spend, that could not be converted into Foreign Exchange Certificates (FEC), there would be no way to take the profits out of China, except in counter trade. Beijing, however, was ripe for real estate development and I had an idea.

From Roller Skating Entrepreneurs to Real Estate Developers

In the early 1980's there were only two modern hotels in Beijing that had been built by foreigners. One was the Jianguo Hotel, down the street from the venerable Beijing Hotel, and the Sheraton Great Wall, midway between downtown and the airport. The Jianguo Hotel was more strategically located but fairly small. It had been developed by Clement Chen, an expatriate Chinese from San Francisco. Chen brought in the Peninsula Group of Hong Kong to manage it, and the Jianguo was an upscale place beloved by wealthy tourists and corporate executives.

The Sheraton Great Wall Hotel was more of a tourist place, although it had its share of offices, too. Because there were no office buildings to speak of—and those few that did exist were mostly substandard at the time—and because of its location near the center of Beijing's business district, the Jinguo's hotel rooms were used as headquarters by several major foreign corporations and law firms. Both hotels, of course, were joint ventures with government agencies, without which nothing can be accomplished in China.

My architectural background came into good use, and I developed a unique concept for a mixed-use project that included a first-class hotel with several restaurants, apartments for foreign businessmen and offices for foreign corporations.

We had never developed a hotel project before, but the word impossible was not in our vocabulary. We had spent quite a lot of time in the People's Republic by then and had a clear idea of what the marketplace needed. We were encouraged by Mr. Yu, Richard Chen, and Dean Lee that our idea for a hotel project was an excellent one, and eventually our little company was guided into the real estate development business by our Chinese hosts.

In a nation in which there is theoretically no private property, securing a piece of land for a real estate development inevitably involves negotiations with some arm of the government. And with a bureaucracy as centralized as China's, you might expect some sort of clearing house with a register of available land and an efficient bureaucracy whose job it is to arrange for land leases. One of the advantages of communism, according to communists, is efficiency in such matters as the distribution of state resources. Of course, you might believe that pigs fly, too.

There is in fact no such agency and the process of finding available land, as we were soon to find out, is so complex and mysterious that it makes chaos theory look comprehensible by comparison. The acquisition of a land lease is an arduous process in which the goal is to wear down foreign investors. When the Chinese finally present you with the deal they had in mind in the first place, you are so thankful to have a piece of land—any land—that sheer relief overwhelms good judgment. All the hapless foreigner wants to know at that point is where to sign.

We naively assumed that our experience would be difference and that our diminutive master of guanxi, Mr. Yu, would be able to arrange everything expeditiously. Mr. Yu started to contact several sources and we began to meet many government organizations that had property that might be suitable for our type of project. This took many months and several trips back and forth from the U.S. to China.

It was a very frustrating experience. Mr. Yu would come to us and tell us that he had found an excellent property, and we would go investigate the site, meet with officials and spend endless fruitless hours in discussion and negotiation.

This routine, or something like it went along for several months. It was like playing horseshoes—you could get really close, but never quite get there. Each time Mr. Yu would bring us a property, we would get very excited, and he would tell us that this time it would be different. It always was a bit different, but the result was always the same, *no deal*.

We prepared endless letters of intent and would have banquets, and more meetings. We went from one side of Beijing to the other looking at properties, met with a multitude of people and we were getting weary and discouraged. It was like being on a roller coaster ride.

On one trip, we actually traveled to Shen Zhen to look for property. This was a new border city, next to Hong Kong, that the Chinese were building for the future. We traveled to Shanghai, but all with the same result.

Then one day Mr. Yu told us that he had located an excellent property and that we should go look at it. If we liked it, he would arrange for us to meet with the appropriate officials and begin negotiations.

The property turned out to be directly across the street from the Beijing Hotel. We could actually see the land from our office window. There could be no better site in Beijing. It was two blocks from Tiananmen Square on Beijing's main commercial thoroughfare, within walking distance to the Forbidden City, and adjacent to the hotel which had served as the main meeting place for businessmen and bureaucrats since the country had opened to the West. Not only that, but the parcel was also nearly vacant—bare land was rare in Beijing—and it seemed not to be coveted by any other foreign investor at the time.

It seemed too good to be true—which of course it was. The vacant lot was only being used by an old man who, for a few cents, gave donkey rides to children. The symbolism escaped us.

We were very excited. To call the property "prime" would have been an understatement. We began negotiations immediately and everyone seemed receptive to our proposal. The land was supposedly controlled by a state-owned shipping agency, although it would have been an odd place for a warehouse. Nevertheless, we spent many hours with various officials, sitting quietly while Mr. Yu negotiated in Chinese.

Over a period of several days, we ate together, drank together and made many speeches. We told everyone that we were thankful to have this opportunity and were honored by the friendship everyone had shown us. All of the social exchanges seemed genuine. Many foreigners were aloof with their Chinese hosts, but we never were. I assumed that we were making good progress.

Finally, the officials of the shipping agency indicated that we had a deal and suggested that we all celebrate at a banquet that evening. We toasted one another and the future of the project.

Sheldon was always asked by the Ministry to make a speech at these banquets. The speech was from our hearts. He would tell the Chinese how very much we appreciated the opportunity to come to China and be honored by so many people. He would also tell them that we were Jewish, and that the Chinese and the Jews had a long history together. A history that went back three thousand years. He would remind them of Kaifeng, a town north of Beijing that had a temple where Judaism was practiced by Chinese people for a thousand years. He told them the thing that the Jews and the Chinese have in common was merchant mentality.

We had come to China to build something for the children, because we thought, as the Chinese thought, that the children are the most important asset, as they are our future. Sometimes he would tell them of the ten lost tribes of Israel and that there is a theory in the Torah, that one of the tribes went east, and that it's possible that the Chinese are all Jews.

Mr. Yu would always tell Sheldon afterwards that he should not bring politics into the discussions. We would tell him that it is not political its life. He would tell us that Israel and China do not have any diplomatic relations. We would always remind him of the fact that the only two private aircraft allowed into China were Dr. Hammer's 727 Boeing and the Israeli jet that was owned by billionaire tycoon Shoul Eisenberg, who had his offices on the ground floor of the Beijing hotel. Mr. Eisenberg had been doing business with China for many years and he was an Israeli citizen.

We would always end the banquets with new friends. The Chinese really liked us because we loved their children, we ate with them, we laughed with them, and we wanted to be with them, unlike most foreign business visitors that were in China for as little time as possible, just to conduct business. Most did not mingle with the "common folk" as they say.

We agreed at the banquet that we would meet the next morning to sign the letter of intent and go forward with the project on that prime piece of property. That night we stayed up until 3:00 am writing and re-writing it. We arrived at the office early to prepare for the meeting and signing of the letter of intent. Mr. Yu met us and calmly said the meeting was off, the deal was over, and that the piece of property was no longer available.

We were shocked. We asked him why they changed their minds, and what if anything, we had done for them to back out. He said we did nothing wrong, they liked us, and were very happy to meet us at the banquet. He then looked at us, and said, "This is China, and the ox moves slow, and the earth is patient."

Mr. Yu liked proverbs, even if they were entirely irrelevant to the situation at hand. Oxen have no strategy and pursue no agenda. Americans are not patient. We didn't understand. But before we could ask any more questions, Mr. Yu announced that he had another property for us to see.

The second property was even better, he promised, although it was hard to imagine a site superior to the one we had just spent so much energy trying to acquire.

Nevertheless, we dutifully trudged across town to look at it. It wasn't as good as the first site, but it was the only one available—or so we were told—and we began the whole negotiation process all over again. After another round of meetings, dinners and a second letter of intent, the deal fell through.

This went on for several months. In a carefully choreographed process, we were subjected to a series of negotiations for a succession of properties and for each transaction we came incrementally closer to making a deal. Mr. Yu would bring a property to us and assure us that everything would be different "this time," but the result was always the same: No deal. Each negotiation was slightly different, as Mr. Yu said it would be, and each time we were allowed to achieve certain small victories—just enough to hold our interest and keep us in the game.

We crisscrossed Beijing, looked at twenty or so properties, attended a score of banquets and prepared endless letters of intent. It was an emotional roller coaster ride, designed to wear us down. In retrospect the manipulation is transparent but at the time we had little awareness of the psychological strategy to which we were being subjected. The Chinese are masters of the human psyche and know precisely how to keep you on the edge of the knife between despondency and hope.

Then one day Mr. Yu came to us and said there was another piece of property we should look at. It was located next to the Worker's Stadium, on the second ring road, midway between the Sheraton Great Wall and Beijing Hotel. We were nearly burned out but grudgingly agreed to go look at the site.

It was a large parcel and none of it was vacant. Most of the land was occupied by an old glass products factory and the rest by a ramshackle collection of tiny, conjoined, ancient looking houses. Building on the site would require major demolition work and the relocation of hundreds of people. The location was okay, but the demo and relocation work seemed daunting. The architectural preservation movement, which is so strong in the U.S., has few if any advocates in China. Most Chinese are free of sentimentality about such things. We made note of the site's facilities and location and returned to our room at the Beijing Hotel.

A few minutes after we arrived, Mr. Yu called and told us he wanted to bring a gentleman to meet us. His name was Wang Fu Shen. Mr. Wang was the man supposedly in charge of the glass factory property, although we later learned that he was a high-ranking officer in the Ministry of State Security. This group was the most powerful and feared agency in China, more ruthless and clandestine than its sister agency, the Ministry of Public Security. We agreed to see Mr. Wang and, in a few minutes, Mr. Yu and Ms. Zhang appeared at our door with him.

This was the first time we had met with anyone on such an informal basis. Usually, negotiations began with a series of formal introductions and long, almost ceremonial meetings. Mr. Wang simply sat down and with no formalities produced a site plan, unrolled it and began to describe the various possibilities for developing the parcel. He said, rather matter of factly, that the project had already been approved, a deal was assured, and then launched into a discussion of the dollar equity each side would contribute to the project.

Sheldon and I just looked at each other with a combination of boredom and detachment. We'd heard it all before. Why should this be different? Detecting our mood, Ms. Zhang looked at us and said, "This is real."

Ms. Zhang was right, and suddenly the pace began to accelerate. Mr. Yu came in the next day and announced that we had a competitor, Donald Nixon, the former president's brother. This was going to take a lot of guanxi, according to Mr. Yu. We had no way of knowing if this was true or not. They were undoubtedly playing Nixon as well as us, and we later came to doubt whether Nixon was a serious contender.

The Chinese wanted us to have this site—for reasons we would not discover until much later. But the drama was played out as though it were a genuine competition. Nixon's group was in town and supposedly had the backing of the central government—whatever that meant— and the mayor of Beijing. We had several meetings and Mr. Yu claimed to call in many favors.

From Roller Skating Entrepreneurs to Real Estate Developers

The guanxi was flowing. As part of the negotiations, we met with the Beijing branch of the Ministry of Public Security, formerly headed by a man named Li Ping. We later with Mr. Li himself, who was introduced to us as the coal minister. Whatever his title, he was enormously powerful, and we subsequently discovered he was closely associated with the Chinese espionage community. He went on to become the premiere of China from 1987 to 1998.

It was a very hectic week of high-level meetings but by Friday, Mr. Yu came to the office with a big smile on his face and announced that the deal was made. Our offer to put up an initial 3.75 million U.S. dollars had been accepted. As we would eventually learn, we were the hand-picked choice of the Ministry of State Security.

The following Monday we decided to go back and look at the site we had just agreed to develop. Our letter of intent with the Chinese included a pledge to construct several new apartment buildings to replace housing that would be lost, and we wanted to revisit the residential area.

We walked all around the property that morning and then decided to tour the glass products factory in the afternoon. The factory was still operating, as it had been for many generations, and its equipment looked as though it dated back to the turn of the century. It was a vast old brick building, and in one huge room, we came upon a sight I'll never forget. It was the electrical control room and it looked like something out of an old black and white Frankenstein movie. It was full of huge transformers, ceramic insulators, old analog gauges, and electrical switches. The whole room buzzed and crackled with energy of high voltage electricity.

Near the center of the room was a massive electrical switch, the kind that is shaped like an inverted tuning fork. It was at least five feet tall and painted bright green. Sheldon walked over and stood in front of it, fascinated. And then, in the blink of an eye, he put his hand on the lever and pulled it down. Instantly everything went dark, and silence enveloped the room. Mr. Yu nearly passed out. I chocked back a laugh while Sheldon stood there looking a bit dazed. Our tour hosts stood nearby, frozen.

Sheldon later told me he didn't know what came over him. He just had an irresistible urge to turn it off. Maybe it was the months of frustrating negotiations; perhaps it was temporary insanity. I laughed when he said one of the electrical workers who spoke a little English whispered in his ear, "I've worked here forty years and I always wanted to do that."

It took two days to restore power, not only to the glass factory but to the surrounding neighborhood. Fortunately, it didn't scuttle the deal. In China it pays to be a little unpredictable.

CHAPTER 9

Interlude: Our Daughter Comes to China

*As distance tests a horse's strength,
time reveals a person's character.*

~Chinese Proverb

Outside of our business dealings in China, we had many memorable occasions and grand adventures. And of course, there was always intrigue. One occasion that stands out is when our sixteen-year-old daughter Jolie came to visit us on one of our trips. It was the summer of 1986 (before the hotel project) and a very important milestone year for Dr. Hammer.

When we took off for our trips to China, Jolie stayed with her older brothers and sisters, but this particular time she asked if she could come and visit us. We arranged for her to fly to Hong Kong where she would stay with our Chinese Hong Kong friends, Eugenia and Ken Wai before joining us in Beijing. We had met Ken and Eugenia on one of our earlier trips to China. Eugenia was an interior designer, and Ken was a refrigeration engineer who was educated at Purdue University. Both Ken and Eugenia were from old Hong Kong families and were very well connected in the upper circles of the Hong Kong social and business life. We got to be very good friends, and always saw them whenever we would come in and out of Hong Kong.

We knew Jolie would be in good hands with them, but we were nervous about a sixteen-year-old year taking a trip to Asia alone and our nerves went into overdrive when we heard the news that there was a typhoon off the coast of Hong Kong, just when Jolie was supposed to arrive.

We were relieved that the plane was able to land, and our friends had a Rolls Royce limousine at the airport to pick her up and bring her to their house in Wan Chai. Jolie stayed with them for a whirlwind three days. She was escorted all over Hong Kong in limousines, taken to the best restaurants, and had a wonderful time. They then put here on the plane to Beijing.

We were in the midst of a very important occasion. Dr. Hammer was in Beijing, staying at the state guest house. Finally, after several years of difficult negotiations, his company, Occidental Petroleum and a Bank of China subsidiary, signed a $475-million loan to finance China's largest coal mine. At that time, it was the largest and most high-profile U.S.-Chinese joint venture aimed at more than doubling China's exports of coal.

The night Jolie was arriving in Beijing, a huge celebration banquet was to be held in the Great Hall of the People with over 1500 guests. Mr. Yu and Ms. Zhang were responsible for all the arrangements. Our office was a beehive of activity.

Many top Central and Beijing government officials would be attending, including Den Xiao Ping, a Chinese revolutionary leader, military commander and statesman who was then the paramount leader of the People's Republic of China. Ping famously said, "to get rich is glorious." He is considered by many to be the most significant political leader of the latter part of the 20th century, bringing China out of poverty, and changing the power of the world economy. Also attending was Li Pung who became the fourth Premier of the People's Republic of China in 1987.

To say this was a big deal celebration is a gross understatement. Jolie's plane was to arrive at 2:00 pm, but it was on CAAC, China's airline, which was not the most dependable of airlines. We arrived at the airport at 1:30 and by 4:30 the plane had still not arrived. Somehow it got diverted to Tianjin. They took everyone off the plane, which had made Jolie very nervous. The flight finally boarded on a different plane and arrived about 5:30 pm. Mr. Yu had gone with us and was now very anxious about the banquet he was responsible for, which was starting at 8:30 pm. He spoke to a few of the airport officials, and they went out to the plane, got Jolie off first, and brought her right to us without going through any customs' procedures at all.

We immediately got into our car, and as our driver rushed us back to the hotel, Sheldon told Jolie she would have half an hour to get dressed, as we were going to a banquet with Dr. Hammer and the Chairman of China, along with 1500 other people. She would be the only teenager.

Jolie looked shell shocked. She had flown through a typhoon, had three days of incredible luxury and Asian affluence, boarded a Chinese plane and landed in what looked like a field in outer Mongolia, then boarded another plane, landed in Beijing, and was escorted off the plane by Public Security people. But with a resiliency possessed only by the young, she rallied to the occasion and was ready to leave on time.

We arrived at the banquet, and were seated in the front table, right in front of the dais, where the top officials and Dr. Hammer were seated. There are no turkeys in China, so Dr. Hammer had brought over 250 for this special occasion. Every table got a turkey. There were many speeches and Jolie seemed to be taking it all in. Then came the pictures. We all posed, and she had her picture taken with the top Chinese officials in the country. Everyone complimented us about Jolie and Dr. Hammer was beaming.

In those days, China was very safe for foreigners. Sheldon and I walked the streets all over and mingled with the Chinese in every walk of life and everyone was always very pleasant to us. We left our hotel room door open; we left our valuables and money right on the dresser and no one ever took anything. We decided that we would get Jolie a room to herself, and she could come and go as she pleased, with access to our car and driver, or whatever she wanted to do.

We introduced her to our friend Joe Roseman who managed the Great Wall Sheraton Hotel. Joe had a son living in Beijing with he and his wife and Jolie struck up a friendship with him, that turned into a romance. Kip introduced Jolie to all his expatriate friends and in just a few days she had a whole group of chums. She started to learn a bit of Chinese and these kids went everywhere. There is no legal drinking age in China, so these kids were drinking large bottles of beer. She met kids from all over the world, whose parents were either government officials, or expatriates working for foreign companies doing business in the PRC.

It was actually very easy to have Jolie in China. She hung out with her friends and we never worried. She would join us for breakfast and sometimes dinner and was having a wonderful time.

About a week after being in Beijing, we decided to take Jolie to Beihai Park, where you can rent rowboats with a rower. A nice young guy took us out and he took a fancy to Jolie. Interestingly he spoke English, which he told us he taught himself. When we were finished, he invited us to his house for some tea. Jolie wasn't too interested, but we agreed because we thought it would be a good experience for her to see how the people live, and we drove him to where he lived with his mother, sister, grandmother aunt and uncle.

It was in the city in one of those places that was very old, with no running water, except for a spigot in the central courtyard. The units looked like they were made of mud and brick and inside the floor was old, cracked cement. The heat was a peat/coal small stove in the center of the room, but there was a sink, with a drain to a bucket and two gas burners. It was as clean as could be expected and we were graciously invited in.

We were served tea and fresh watermelon, which in the summer is sold in the streets. Only the young man spoke English and we spent about half an hour there. Sheldon asked to go the bathroom and was shown outside to a communal toilet. (The reason we ask people coming to China to bring Handi Wipes is that they can cover their noses.) After spending time in China, we got used to the lavatories, and it became almost natural. But this latrine must have been there for many years, and Sheldon was embarrassed that it was just too difficult to use. We left and went back to the hotel, where the lavatory facilities were much different, but still not up to our standards here in the United States.

The next day the young man showed up in our office, and Sheldon asked Mr. Yu if we could find him some employment. Mr. Yu said he would try, but nothing ever came of it and Jolie was not interested in a continued relationship with this boy. She was involved with her group of friends and was enjoying herself. Sheldon decided that he would try and help this young man, so a few days later he went back to the park, with our driver, who spoke a bit of English and asked for the boy.

It seems that no one knew of him, and he did not work at the park. We then drove to his home, where we had the tea, and the driver went in and then told me that the people who we met with, had never seen him before our visit. The young man had told them he was with the government, and we were honoring them with our visit. Sheldon asked Mr. Yu what was going on and as usual when it was a subject he didn't want to discuss, he just ignored him as if he hadn't asked anything. We never saw the young man again.

One day Jolie came to the office and said that a group of expatriate kids have decided to go to Beidaihe, a town on the ocean, for a holiday. It's a about a ten-hour train ride and the United States embassy had a house in the community. At first, we said no dice. She was only sixteen, we had no idea where Beidaihe was, and we were concerned about a group of teenagers traveling around China alone. Jolie of course pleaded and so did Kip. They told us that they would be escorted by US marines from the embassy, so we had no cause to worry. Those marines were in their early twenties, and I could well imagine what might happen. I asked Mr. Yu to arrange for the Ministry of Public Security to keep their eye on them and make sure they did not get into any trouble. He laughed and agreed and told me not to worry.

Jolie went off the Beihai for four days. We didn't hear anything, until Mr. Yu came to us one day and told us there was a slight problem. It seems that Jolie and her friends, including three marines, went over a wall into a public swimming pool late at night after closing and were swimming around and drinking beer at 2:00 am in the morning. The City officials seemed to be aware of them, most likely from the public security people, and streamed into the building, and found them. The marines' story was that they were there to protect the kids and had followed them, and the reason they were wearing bathing suits, was to make sure no one drowned. The kids had little to say. They were lectured by the Chinese and their respective parents, and the incident was forgotten, except by Mr. Yu who had a great laugh at the whole thing.

The night before Jolie was supposed to leave, I met a very interesting man in the lobby of the Beijing Hotel who introduced himself as Paul Kelly. That night at dinner, Paul showed up and sat down at our table. He told us that he was a private businessman, involved in the security business. Sheldon asked him what he did previously, and he said he was a secret service agent, and had accompanied Nixon and Bush to China. The waiter came by, and Paul ordered for us in perfect Chinese. He also spoke Hebrew and several other languages. This was the beginning of a very interesting relationship.

CHAPTER 10

Due Diligence

*If you want to find out about the road ahead,
then ask about it from those coming back.*

~Chinese Proverb

We signed the original letter of intent to develop the glass factory property for the hotel development project with BLIPU (Beijing Industrial Product Union) which was Mr. Wang's company. We would later find out it was a front for the Ministry of Public Security. The letter of intent, however, was just a prelude to the real negotiations, which would lead to a formal joint venture agreement—a very complicated and lengthy document. Our company, World China Trade was responsible for making the financial arrangements, which included finding a lender to provide construction financing. The Chinese, in turn, were to find an agency that would guarantee the loan.

At the suggestion of friends in Hong Kong, we met with Mr. Charles Wrangham, vice chairman from Standard Asia Charter Bank in Hong Kong to discuss if they would consider funding the construction loan. Mr. Wang had told us that the project would cost a maximum of twenty-eight million US dollars, based on his analysis. The first thing Mr. Wrangham asked for was a detailed budget so that he could determine if it was realistic.

We traveled back to Beijing and told Mr. Wang that the bank needed a written budget. Mr. Wang took out a piece of paper, wrote twenty-eight million dollars on the paper, then took out his chop and sealed it.

We explained to Mr. Wang that the bank would not accept that document, and what was necessary was a detailed list of the construction costs from start to finish. Mr. Yu then explained to us that Mr. Wang's word would have to be sufficient.

We traveled back to Hong Kong to meet again with Charles Wrangham. This time he invited us out for an afternoon on Standard Charters' yacht. It was a wonderful afternoon, and we met Sophia, Charles's wife and several other executives from the bank. We sailed through Hong Kong Bay and out to Lantau Island. We were wined and dined in a very elegant way.

We finally got to talk about business and Mr. Wrangham asked if we had received the budget from Mr. Wang. When Sheldon handed him the piece of paper, he started to laugh and could hardly contain himself, which is very unusual for an Englishman. When he regained his composure, he added that the budget of course, was necessary.

Through our Hong Kong friend Eugenia Wai, who was an interior designer, we had been introduced to Arthur Kowk, who owned Arthur Kowk Architects. I was very impressed with him and their award-winning projects, and we wanted him to work with us on the hotel. Arthur, with his knowledge of architecture and construction in China, was able to put together a proper budget, which the bank accepted.

We brought the budget back to Beijing and showed it to Mr. Wang. He took a fast look and said it was acceptable, signed it and put his chop on it. Then Mr. Wrangham asked Mr. Wang to guarantee that if there were any over-runs on the construction then the Beijing part of the joint venture would guarantee to provide those funds. Mr. Wang agreed, and later in the life of the joint venture it came back to haunt him, when Standard Chartered Bank asked him to honor that guarantee.

We also arranged with Arthur to help create a feasibility study. The study was necessary and would prove the financial viability of our project to the bank and its directors. (At least that's what it was supposed to have done).

We were clients of the firm of Laventhol and Horwath, an international accounting firm, and asked the managing partner in the Los Angeles office if they were interested. They were indeed very interested, because it would be the first study of its kind ever to be done in China and could position them as the experts in financial feasibility studies in the hospitality business in the Peoples Republic of China.

Laventhol and Horwath, had a sister office in Hong Kong and they arranged for the United States office and the Hong Kong office to conduct the study together. Mr. Wang and the Chinese side, refused to have the American firm involved and insisted that the British offices of Laventhol and Horwath work with the Hong Kong office to perform the study.

We flew to Hong Kong and met Jeff Parkinson from the London Office and then we all met with Sam Wong, the manager of the offices of Horwath in Hong Kong. The Chinese arranged visas for all of us and we flew together to Beijing to assist the Laventhol and Horwath people with the feasibility study.

When we arrived, the Beijing Accountants Bureau held a banquet for us, and told the Horwath people that they had already done a feasibility study on the project and were satisfied that it was financially viable. The Horwath people asked to see the study and, as usual, the Chinese refused. They said it was an internal Chinese document that foreigners were not able to see. The Horwath people persisted and said it would be very helpful to see this document, as it could be a base for the one they were preparing. The Chinese said they would like to oblige, but they could not because of the rules of China pertaining to internal financial documents.

The banquet went on quite late and there was a lot of drinking of Moutai. Jeff Parkinson came close to passing out and we had to carry him to his hotel room.

The next day was the start of the due diligence for the study. Our first stop was the office of British Airways. We had made an appointment with the manager, and he was expecting us. Jeff had a terrible hangover, was dragging his feet, and vowed never again to get into a drinking contest with the Chinese. He was trying to be a good sport, as the English like to be, and as he put it, "I over did it a bit."

We arrived at the offices of British Airways, which was located in the Jianguo hotel. The manager, who looked very haggard, brought us into his private office, and told us that his staff, with the exception of his assistant, was all local Chinese. He motioned us to whisper, as he pointed toward the ceiling, and made gestures with his hand. He then wrote on a piece of paper that his office was bugged with secret microphones and that we should be careful what we speak about.

The accountants asked several questions pertaining to the amount of tourism that came in on the British Airways flights, where they stayed, and what the expectations were for the future. His answers were very positive. We asked him how his relations were with the Chinese, and he told us, that they were excellent, and that the Chinese were very easy to do business with and very straightforward. As he was saying those words, he was shaking his head from side to side and pointing up at the concealed microphones.

We spent about an hour with him and as he walked us out to our car, he told us he was the fourth manager in four years in the Beijing office. The first two managers were relieved because of psychological reasons and the last manager had to be taken out in a strait jacket. He was completely paranoid, and obviously very frightened. He told us we should be very careful and that everything we say and do is written down and filed away, to be used against us if necessary.

He actually was correct about everything being written down. In every meeting, wherever you are, there is always one person taking copious notes. In fact, we were in several meetings throughout the life of the Joint venture where there was a person who read facial expressions, and after the meeting they would sit and discuss the foreigners and just how to manipulate them. It was interesting that the more you understood about what they were doing, the easier it was to deal with them. The Chinese always expected twists and turns and we were always perfectly straight and honest with them. It always confused them and worked to our advantage.

The next meeting was at the offices of JAL (Japan Airlines). We again met with the manager of the office. Since he was Japanese, he had a broader understanding of the Chinese then any western foreigner could have. In the early 1980s there was still a deep-seated friction between the Chinese and Japanese. It stemmed from the past and the rape of Nanjing, which was during the Japanese invasion of Manchuria. There was anti-Japanese literature all over Beijing, and the Japanese never mingled outside of business with the Chinese.

We were at dinners in the Great Hall of The People many times, and on one occasion, we had some discussion regarding Japanese products. One of the Ministers, poured a dish of sizzling rice over a large soup bowl and as he poured said, "Bombs over Tokyo." Mr. Yu referred to the Japanese as "Little yellow dwarfs."

We sat down in the manager's office and introduced ourselves, and he informed us that business was very good. There were many Japanese that wanted to come to Beijing for business and pleasure and that it would grow every year. He told us that JAL had made a strong commitment to China, and the future was very bright. There could be fifty more hotels built and they still could not keep up with the demand in the future. He was right.

The accountants asked him where his flight attendants stayed when they had to lay over in Beijing and how many room nights they used. He told them that JAL reserved several hundred room nights a year in advance. The Chinese also required that JAL pay for all those room nights a year in advance.

The accountants then remarked if JAL was prepaying the room nights, they must be getting a sizable discount. The Manager looked at us, and with a typical inscrutable Asian face, told us that the Chinese insisted they pay a twenty-five percent premium. Using a logic only the Chinese could understand, they were told that by pre-paying and reserving the rooms a year in advance, then the Chinese could not rent the rooms to anyone else; therefore, a premium was necessary. The Japanese paid it without a backward glance. It's obvious why they did.

One only has to look at a map of the world to see that Japan is just a tiny island, compared to the China giant.

We next visited CAAC the official Chinese Airline. The manager was very cordial. They served us tea and told us that they expected a bright future in tourism and that the Chinese Government was negotiating for the purchase of several new jet aircraft from the United States and France. They also said they had conducted a feasibility study with the Beijing Accountancy Bureau, and that it had come out financially viable for the next ten years. The accountants asked if they could see it or have a copy. We were told that it was an internal document and not available for foreign perusal.

The accountants stayed for four or five days and visited the three foreign joint venture hotels that were developed at that time. They spoke to the managers, and hotel personnel, and then visited the manager of the Beijing Hotel, where we were staying and where our office was. The manager told the accountants that the hotel was fully reserved for the next year and requests for reservations come in daily. They asked to see his reservation records and were told they were internal documents, and not available to foreigners.

We expected that the Horwath accountants would be getting frustrated, but both Jeff Parkinson and Sam Wong were familiar with the Chinese and realized that this was China and it would be an exercise in futility to try and understand.

The night prior to their leaving, there was another banquet hosted by the Beijing accountancy Bureau, and they got Jeff Parkinson into another drinking bout. The Chinese would start out by making a toast with Moutai and downing it in one gulp. One of the Chinese from the accountancy bureau would get up and make a toast and say GAMBAI, and he would down his shot glass, and then Jeff would get up and make a toast and he would down his shot glass full of Moutai. As he put his glass down, before you could blink an eye, a waiter would fill it again. After about eight ganbei cheers Jeff was glassy eyed, and I only hoped he wouldn't pass out. The Chinese, of course, were enjoying themselves immensely.

After the banquet, we took Jeff back to his hotel room. We then had a meeting with Mr. Yu and Mr. Wang regarding the outcome of the feasibility study. We told them that if the study came out negative, then the bank could refuse to loan us the construction financing. We also told them that the Chinese were not being very cooperative in refusing to share the studies they had done, as it was at least a basis for the Horwath study. Mr. Wang told us again that Chinese law prohibited the sharing of the Chinese study with foreigners. We had heard that story before, so we stressed that the most important thing was for the study to be positive.

Much later in the joint venture, we found out that Mr. Sam Wong, the Horwath accountant from Hong Kong was called later that night, by either Mr. Wang or another Ministry of Public Security official. He was told he should remember that he was a Hong Kong Chinese and that 1997 was not so far in the future, and that it was important that the study be positive. It was just a mild form of typical Chinese extortion.

The next day we drove the accountants to the airport, and as we approached, Mr. Yu gave Sheldon a large brown envelope and told him it was copies of the Bureau of Accountancy feasibility study. He also said since Sheldon was a foreigner, he could give it to the accountants without a problem. Jeff Parkinson, bleary eyed, thanked him and off they went.

The feasibility study was positive.

CHAPTER 11

The Architect, Saving Face, and Games

Even the highest towers begin at the ground.
~Chinese Proverb

Based on the feasibility study, we agreed to move forward to develop the joint venture agreement, which would be the body of the contract, to build the hotel complex. It was Sheldon's job to develop the draft, a tedious process with constant changes that ended up taking weeks and weeks and many sleepless nights. I was in charge of the design and construction of the hotel from the American joint venture side, so while Sheldon was working on the draft agreement, I focused on selecting the architects.

The Chinese insisted that the Beijing Design Institute be the primary architectural firm on the project. However, I had helped them realize that since they had little or no experience in the design of modern hotels, that a foreign firm was also necessary.

The firm I wanted to hire was Arthur Kwok and Associates. Arthur was from a very well-known Hong Kong family who originally came from Shanghai and had prospered in Hong Kong. They were in several businesses, such as banking and department stores. Chinese families in Hong Kong are like US corporations, with many and varied business entities and the Kwok family was one of the most prominent.

Arthur was very well known as an architect and had done many large-scale projects, such as hotels, racetracks, marinas and office buildings. Like all Hong Kong Chinese, Arthur wanted to do as much business in China as possible. 1997, the year Britain would hand back Hong Kong to Beijing, was coming and he felt that his position would be safer and more secure if he could do business at any level in China. Beijing was very important, as the top leaders were there.

I visited Arthur's office and several of his projects. I was very impressed with his excellent work, as well as his manner which would be a plus in dealing with the mainland Chinese.

I proposed to Mr. Wang that Arthur be selected. Mr. Wang refused. He was adamant that he wanted an American architect and not one from Hong Kong. We tried to explain to Mr. Wang that an American architect, who did not speak Chinese and who did not understand how to deal in the PRC would be useless. Mr. Wang as usual, was very stubborn and said that he would not deal with any Hong Kong Chinese, as they were as he put it "running dogs." He told us that he would not even sit at the same table with a Hong Kong Chinese.

Despite his refusal, I knew it was in the best interests of the joint venture to have Arthur Kwok involved in the project and I was determined to convince Mr. Wang of that fact. I explained the situation to Mr. Yu, who informed us that there was great resentment of the Hong Kong Chinese in the PRC, and it would be very difficult, if not impossible, to change Mr. Wang's mind.

I flew back to Hong Kong and met with Arthur and explained the situation to him. He was not surprised, as he knew better than us of the resentment between the Hong Kong Chinese and the PRC.

I asked Arthur to fly to Beijing and told him we would try and set up a meeting with Mr. Wang, and Mr. Lu Gong who was the architect and representative from the Beijing Design Institute. Arthur agreed and said he would also bring one of the architects from his office who had come from Beijing and had worked in the Beijing Design Institute.

We flew back to Beijing, and I met with Mr. Wang. I told him that we had made no commitment to Arthur Kwok, but that he had come to Beijing, just to sit down with Mr. Wang to discuss the possibility of his involvement in the project. Mr. Wang refused and reiterated his "running dog" litany and insisted on us bringing in an American architect.

We asked Mr. Yu to intervene, explaining that it was not polite to ignore Arthur Kwok. He was a respected architect and had flown all the way from Hong Kong to meet and discuss this hotel project. Mr. Yu agreed to talk to Mr. Wang and try to convince him. This negotiation went on for three days, as Arthur waited patiently. He knew China better than us.

Finally, Mr. Yu said that Mr. Wang would meet with Arthur on one condition—Arthur was to sign a document, that I was to prepare prior to the meeting. The document would state that in the course of our meeting the site of the hotel project would be discussed and shown to Arthur. In the event that the joint venture decided not to employ him, he would agree not go behind our backs and try to steal the project for himself.

This of course was ridiculous. Arthur Kwok was a Hong Kong Chinese that was always fearful that when he traveled to Mainland China, they could revoke his visa and not let him leave the country, not to mention that Mr. Wang was part of the Ministry of Public Security, the most powerful and feared Ministry in the country.

The purpose was purely to embarrass Arthur and make him lose face. It was as if they were calling him a thief and wanted him to acknowledge it by signing the document, and they wanted me to prepare it and have Arthur sign it, so that I would fully realize their position.

It's interesting to note the differences in the way Mr. Wang and Arthur Kwok lived. Mr. Wang lived in about 1000 square feet of space, he had some luxuries, such as a TV and refrigeration, and his heat was controlled by the government. In US terms, he lived like lower middle class at the best.

The Architect, Saving Face, and Games

Arthur Kwok lived in a huge estate on top of a mountain, overlooking Hong Kong Bay. Had several servants, a Ferrari, a yacht, limousines, and lived like a prince. He was a hard worker but lived in the lap of luxury. He was also very aware that when Hong Kong reverted back to the Chinese it would be under the total control of the Ministry of Public Security.

Arthur was smarter than most of the Hong Kong Chinese who traveled to Beijing flaunting their expensive clothes, fur coats and lots of jewelry in the faces of the mainland Chinese people. Arthur came in modest clothes, had a very subdued manner and was very respectful. Unfortunately, he could not speak Mandarin, only Cantonese and also had to have an interpreter.

We met with Arthur and explained the situation. He told us that this project was very important to him, and that he would sacrifice almost anything to be part of it, but the letter was a direct insult, and he would not be able to survive the loss of face. Therefore, he could not sign it.

We met again with Mr. Yu, and I explained Arthur Kwok's response to signing the letter and requested that we arrange a dinner, hosted by Arthur with Mr. Wang, Mr. Lu Gong, Mr. Yu, Ms. Zhang, Sheldon and me.

Mr. Wang refused and said that if Arthur Kwok would not sign the letter, then he would not even sit in the same room with him. I told Mr. Wang that he was being very unreasonable, that we had put a lot on the line for this project and that the least he could do is meet on social terms with Arthur Kwok. Mr. Wang finally agreed.

Arthur brought along the architect from his office in Hong Kong and as usual, no business was spoken at the dinner. There was a lot of drinking and toasting, and Mr. Wang was very social and political, and Arthur who lost only a bit of face was very humble. To our benefit the architect who came with Arthur knew Mr. Lu Gong and everyone got along very well. The dinner ended and the next day we met with Mr. Wang, and he said to me, "This guy Arthur is not such a bad guy at all."

We set Arthur up in the small anteroom next to our offices. I spoke to him at length about my concepts of what the hotel/apartment/office complex should look like and asked him to draw some very preliminary plans. We worked closely for about five days. He submitted his drawings and went back to Hong Kong.

Mr. Wang and his group decided that Arthur Kwok might be suitable as the second architect for the project, the first being the Beijing Design Institute. We agreed that each group should create a model for the project and then both models would be reviewed by our group.

I also had attempted to spend some time with Mr. Lu Gong, to give him some ideas on hotel architectural development, but he was very standoffish, and unfortunately did not speak any English. My creative ideas were very modern and commercial, and dealt with the flow of people, and how the project would operate as a mixed-use development. Mr. Lu Gong said that he fully understood the project and the Beijing Design Institute would build a model that would reflect what the Chinese considered to be the optimum way to construct it.

Sheldon and I returned to Hong Kong to pursue our negotiations with Standard Chartered Bank and within one week Arthur Kwok had completed his model. Mr. Yu had telephoned us and told us that the Beijing Design Institute had also completed their model.

We returned to Beijing with Arthur Kwok's model, which was made out of Styrofoam and had most of what I wanted—one overall structure with different buildings, that were all connected.

We met in our office and Mr. Lu Gong brought the Chinese model. It was built like a battleship and was very well put together with hard plastic and metal screws. Arthur's model was glued and precise, but nowhere near the effort that was put in by the Beijing Design Institute. The Chinese design unfortunately, was very old and not modern. They had three separate buildings not connected and it was not at all functional. Arthur's design was more modern, but still did not have what I wanted.

I stood in-between both models and started to verbalize what I was looking for. Since I don't speak Chinese, I started to take pieces out of both models, to show what I wanted and felt was best for the project. When I started to take apart the Chinese model, Mr. Lu Gong got very red in the face and Mr. Wang looked distressed. An argument started and everyone in the room got very upset. Undeterred, I continued to heatedly argue my point. Mr. Lu Gong was blustering in Chinese, and Mr. Yu was trying to calm down Mr. Wang. Sheldon, realizing the situation was totally out of control, calmly took my hand and we left the office.

Mr. Yu came out and said the situation was deteriorating rapidly and suggested that we go back to Hong Kong and let things cool down. When we arrived and told Arthur what had happened, he was not surprised.

Before this incident, I had found out that Mr. Lu Gong's idol was Frank Lloyd Wright. While in Hong Kong, I decided to try and find some books about Frank Lloyd Wright to bring back to Mr. Lu Gong, in an effort to make peace. I found several and purchased five of them.

When we returned to Beijing, I asked Mr. Yu to arrange a meeting with just me and Mr. Lu Gong, with Ms Zhang as the interpreter. When I gave Mr. Lu Gong the books and told him that my idol was also Frank Lloyd Wright, the whole atmosphere changed. We became friends and started to work together. Ultimately, Mr. Lu Gong accepted most of my ideas and concepts.

The joint venture agreed to employ Arthur Kwok and, as I suggested, divide the architectural responsibilities. The Beijing Design Institute would be responsible for the structural elements of the design and Arthur Kwok and Associates would be responsible for the interior and overall project design. The Chinese decided that the Beijing Design Institute would receive 51% of the fee and Arthur Kwok and Associates would receive 49%. (The unfortunate reality was that Arthur never received all of his fee and did at least 75% of the work.)

I shuffled back and forth from Beijing and Hong Kong, working with both groups, trying to create a functional and well-designed complex. It was an interesting experience. Arthur spoke only Cantonese, Mr. Lu Gong spoke only Mandarin, and I spoke only English. Through patience, determination, and years of experience in design and construction, I was somehow able to keep a balance between the two architects and develop an excellent, practical, and functional design.

* * * * *

Sheldon and I spent a great deal of time in Hong Kong, meeting with Arthur Kwok the Architect, Charles Wrangham the banker, and the Bovis people who were the construction supervisors on the hotel project. It was our responsibility to negotiate with these three entities, and there was a constant ongoing discussion of a multitude of issues that had to be dealt with.

We would socialize often with our friends Ken and Eugenia Wai. Ken was doing a major part of his business in Southern China, primarily in Guangzhou, where he had family. He had a great deal of knowledge and down to earth insight on how to deal with the mainland Chinese.

He related a story to us of one of his clients, Beatrice Foods, a large conglomerate out of Chicago, Illinois. In 1985 Beatrice negotiated a joint venture with the Guangzhou Ministry of Trade to modernize an existing ice cream factory. This factory had been in existence for decades, and its methods and machinery were extensively outdated.

Ken's area of expertise was in the machinery, and Beatrice Foods had hired Ken as a consultant to monitor the project as it was being modernized. The ice cream factory had a staff of existing employees, including the manager of the factory, who had been working there for over 35 years. He was very respected by all the employees and the city, as the factory had consistently produced a quality product through the years. And the machinery, although old, was always properly maintained and kept in good working order.

Beatrice management decided that this existing manager, was old fashioned, did not speak English, and therefore a new manager from outside of China would be necessary. Ken advised the Beatrice management that they should be careful that the old manager would not lose face.

The new manager came from the United States and was versed in the management of a modern ice cream factory, but certainly not versed in dealing in the Peoples Republic of China. He treated the old manager, who was now in a subordinate position, as an illiterate because he didn't speak English. The new manager however, only spoke a little bit of Cantonese.

The renovation and restoration of the factory was completed, and the new factory opened and started producing ice cream, the modern

The Architect, Saving Face, and Games

western way. But at the end of each day, some part of the new equipment would break down and it would take a day or two to solve the problem, so that the factory could resume making ice cream.

This went on for quite a period of time and Beatrice sent in several people who were engineers and machinery experts. They could not figure out the problem since each one seemed to be of a different nature and a different part of the machinery.

The City of Guangzhou was questioning the Beatrice management as to why this was happening and bringing forth the fact that prior to the restoration and modernization, the factory was producing ice cream on a daily basis with a minimum of difficulty.

Finally, the Beatrice people called Ken, told them of their frustration and hired him to investigate the problem and attempt to find a solution. He travelled to Guangzhou, and met with the new manager, who told him that he was really frustrated and didn't know what to do. Ken asked him if he had asked the old manager if he could help. He told him that the old manager would be of no use, since this was new modern equipment that the old manager was not familiar with.

Ken went to talk to the old manager and took him out for some tea. After some conversation, they realized they had friends in common in Guangzhou and they spoke about family and China. Ken asked him what he thought of this new equipment, and the old manager said that modernization was fine. When he asked what he thought of the new manager his reply was, "Patience is a virtue" and "A loss of face can be the beginning of triumph."

Ken traveled back to Hong Kong and spoke with the Beatrice management. He told them he had a solution that would remedy the problem. The solution was a maintenance and repair manual written specifically for the machinery in the Guangzhou factory. They agreed and said they would have the manuals written by professionals, but Ken suggested that the manual should be written by the old manager. They agreed. With input from the old manager, a manual was written, and the old manager got all the credit.

The old manager got his job back and was assigned an assistant from outside China with modern experience. The machinery in the factory began to work properly. The output and quality vastly improved, and the joint venture was a success.

Ken told us that the old manager was quietly, subtly and expertly, sabotaging the equipment every night in a different place and in a way that was undetectable, because he had lost a great deal of face, and in a quiet and patient way, he got his face back.

It was a story we took to heart throughout our dealings with the Chinese.

* * * * *

One afternoon we were shopping with Ken in Hong Kong, and we wandered into a bookstore. As we were browsing the aisles, Sheldon came upon a game of Monopoly that was in Chinese. The Board was identical and so were the pieces, but everything was printed in Chinese. Sheldon suggested that he buy the game and take it back to Beijing and play it with Mr. Yu and his family. Ken laughed and said, "You are going to bring in the ultimate capitalist game to a communist country." Then he told Sheldon to be careful.

We brought the game to Beijing and when Mr. Yu invited us to dinner at his apartment, Sheldon brought it along. Mr. Yu's two sons were very happy that he had brought a game, and with Mr. Yu interpreting, Sheldon explained how to play Monopoly. They played for about three hours and when Yi Yu, Mr. Yu's nine-year-old lost all his houses, he started to cry. But they had fun and Mr. Yu asked Sheldon to leave the game with him.

The next night he invited us to his house again, and this time there were three of his friends who were from the Ministry of Public Security. The Public security people never had business cards and seemed to always wear black leather jackets.

Mr. Yu was a great cook, and we had a wonderful dinner. He then took out the Monopoly game and they all sat down and started to play, with Mr. Yu explaining the rules. It became obvious after a while, that this was not just a friendly game, as all the players were very serious. Sheldon realized he should be careful and not try and win the game, since he had some experience playing Monopoly.

The Architect, Saving Face, and Games

As the game progressed, Sheldon realized he was playing with some sharp and determined players. He reassessed his thinking and tried his best to win. They played well into the night, and it was without a doubt the most serious and determined Monopoly game I had ever witnessed. There was a great deal of negotiation and arguing but since it was all in Chinese, we would only see the final result. At about 6:00 am the next morning they finally finished. Sheldon was second from last. We were all exhausted, the men shook hands, and one of the three men took the Monopoly game with him. We never saw it again. This turned out to be the first of "disappearing" items.

CHAPTER 12

The Art of Going Slow

"A journey of a thousand miles begins with a single step."
~Chairman Mao

The long and frustrating search for the property to build the hotel (which we realized in retrospect had been pre-ordained from the start) and the obstacles and subterfuge during the due diligence process were merely preludes to the misery that was about to come—the joint venture agreement.

After several months and many trips to Hong Kong, we managed to convince Standard Chartered Asia (SCA), to underwrite the joint venture. This was a difficult process that took many months to accomplish. Working cross-culturally is never easy, and every step in the loan process required voluminous documents in Chinese and English, and endless explanations of bank policies that are commonplace in the West, but almost unknown in China during the eighties. Charles Wrangham, the bank's managing director, probably had little idea what he was getting into—and neither did we.

It was our job to draft the joint venture agreement which would be the body of the contract. Through their sources, the Chinese had received copies of the contracts of the first two joint venture hotel projects that had been developed in Beijing and we used them as templates for our agreement. We sat for many days and hours drafting our new agreement. We naively thought that once we negotiated the agreement, the final contract would just be a brush up on the grammar and a few items that we had neglected to address. We were dead wrong.

There were very few computers available, and Sheldon typed all the pages on an old electric portable typewriter. Then he would review them with Mr. Wang, the Chinese from Chongqing, our sponsor MOFERT (the Ministry of Foreign Trade), officials from the mayor's office of the City of Beijing, and the Beijing Lawyers Guild. This was a long and arduous process, with all items carefully discussed, and because of all the people involved, changes were made constantly.

Every night Sheldon and I would go over the changes that the Chinese had made that day. Every time we thought we had agreed on an item, the Chinese would change their mind and we would have to discuss it again. We began to realize that part of their process was to try and understand as much as they could in the most basic terms, and the other part of the process was the process itself. We drank tea all day, we ate lunch together, we had dinner together, the cast changed all the time, and we continued to negotiate.

The Chinese did not believe in boiler plate documents. They wanted to understand and agree, at least in principle, to all the details of what they would be responsible for and all the details that the American side would be responsible for. Unlike western contracts, the Chinese wanted little documentation as to what legal remedies either side would have if either side did not live up to their respective responsibilities. Their philosophy was that when and if a dispute came up, the parties, in good faith would negotiate, agree, and try to solve them to mutual satisfaction. At the time, this philosophy seemed to make good sense.

Sheldon typed the agreement sixteen times. Each new draft would have to be translated into Chinese and then Mr. Yu and our office staff would go over the documents to assure that the Chinese and English were identical. (We later found out that Mr. Yu lied to us and there were critical elements in the joint venture contract that were different in the final analysis).

When we finally completed the agreement to everybody's satisfaction, it was reviewed by our sponsor MOFERT, the most powerful Ministry dealing with foreign trade.

A banquet was planned in a special room in the Great Hall of The People, to celebrate the completion of the agreement and to have a signing ceremony. There were several top Chinese leaders at the banquet, and it was very festive. The food was outstanding, with twenty-five courses of a wide variety of food. The Chinese would always alternate seating between the Chinese and foreigners. When the courses were served, the Chinese seated next to a foreigner would always pick out the choicest morsel of food with chopsticks and put it on the plate of the foreigner sitting on his right. That of course was not a practice with Mr. Wang, who took the choicest morsel of food for himself.

After the last course (we had learned to eat sparingly with the beginning courses) one of the Chinese got up and started to sing. This was not the first time we had experienced this. Joe Spielberg, who was a managing partner at Leventhal and Horwath (the firm that did the feasibility study) joined us at the banquet. Knowing that the Chinese often get up and spontaneously perform, he brought along his clarinet, and after the singing he got up and started to play Jewish folk songs. I am sure this was the first time that Jewish music had been played in the Great Hall of the People.

The Chinese really enjoyed it, and, on an impulse, I got up and took Mr. Wang by the hand and before we knew it, we had fifteen to twenty people dancing the Hora around the room. We danced for about an hour and it was a really memorable occasion.

* * * * *

Now we had to negotiate with Mr. Wang (BLIPU) and the City of Chongqing to finalize the joint venture contract. We had foolishly assumed that after we had spent so much time and effort on the agreement, even having an important banquet and signing ceremony, that the finalization of the contract would be easy, with a few minor changes and would not take a long time to complete.

But the Chinese have mastered the art of going slowly, and it was as if we were starting at the beginning. Each item was carefully examined and, in most cases after hours of discussion and negotiation, had to be re-written. Sections of the contract that we had gone over for hours in the agreement stage, were changed.

The process took several weeks, and every day Sheldon was once again typing and re-typing sections and pages of the contract. The next morning, he would hope that after the translation into Chinese it would be complete, but there were always a few more changes and it would have to be re-typed again.

He was responsible for all the editing, and the final draft would be incorporated into the contract verbatim. And because the electricity was intermittent, it would interrupt his typing on the old portable and he would often have to start over again.

At one point, we came upon a section that we had all agreed upon and was of a simple nature. Sheldon made the mistake of commenting on that fact and that we could move along to the next section. The Chinese looked at him, smiled to each other and then spent at least three hours on the section. It was their way of saying that one should never hurry the process.

Finally, we came to an agreement in principle about the structure and terms of the loan. The only thing left was to reduce our final understanding to writing and review the draft. For all practical purposes, the wording of the contract had already been agreed upon and recorded in the minutes of our meetings. What remained was a straightforward job of transcription and formalization.

Sheldon flew to Hong Kong where the bank prepared the final contract and had a professional translation service prepare copies in Chinese. He then brought the contracts back to Beijing, where Mr. Wang insisted on having the contracts translated a second time. None of the local translators, unfortunately, had experience in dealing with the nuances of legal contracts.

Charles Wrangham and two of his colleagues flew to Beijing a day later and were met by two lawyers from the China office of the international law firm, Graham and James. On a Monday morning we joined the three bankers, two lawyers and our employees, Mr. Yu and Ms. Zhang. We all met around a table in our offices at the Beijing Hotel with Mr. Wang and his associate, Mr. Li representing the Chinese side.

Along the perimeter of the room sat several other Chinese officials, two clerks who took notes, and a representative from the Beijing Municipal Government. Nothing gets done in China except by committee.

We thought the meeting would be uneventful, as we had already agreed on every important point. And so did Mr. Wrangham, who opened the discussion with a few pleasantries and then asked the Chinese if they had any questions about the contract now that it had been translated (twice!) and they'd had a chance to study it. We were not prepared for the answer. Mr. Wang calmly replied, "We will start with the first word on the first page."

It was the beginning of an excruciating process that would take ten days. Mr. Wang was not unlike an orthodox Rabbi studying the Torah. Every verb was parsed, modifier explained, and noun defined. But the goal in this case was not enlightenment. The process was designed to wear us down. It was like dripping water: word, by word, by word, the hours and days went by until I had a roaring headache.

It took us four days to review the vocabulary of the text, and with a great sense of accomplishment we finally arrived at the end of the process late one evening. Everything we had agreed upon was in the contract, and the Chinese understood every word. That night we went home and got a good night's sleep.

The next morning, we reconvened and Mr. Wrangham, with the relieved demeanor of a man just released from prison, optimistically asked, "Now that you fully understand every word in the document, are there any clauses or issues you would like to discuss?" The question was a mere courtesy, as we had already spent months hammering out the particulars of our loan agreement. What could possibly be left to discuss? Mr. Li spoke up and said very quietly, "We will start at the first word on the first page."

* * * * *

The banking agreement was full of boilerplate clauses, standard legalese that is a part of every banking contract, worldwide. Mr. Li and Mr. Wang wanted to jettison all the boilerplate, most of which contained language that protected the bank in case of a default. Mr. Wang considered these protections "superfluous." They were asking, in effect, that the bank agree to lend the money on a handshake without any recourse should things go wrong. Perhaps these protections were only symbolic, anyway. China had no independent legal system for litigating civil disputes.

We didn't fully realize at the time how dependent we were on the goodwill of our joint venture partners. If the Chinese, for any reason, decided to default on the loan, there was little recourse. They lived up to their contracts not by force of law or fear of litigation, but out of simple pragmatism. The Chinese wanted American businesses to invest in their country—and bring with them dollars, expertise, and technology—and they knew that the price of that investment was a semblance of genuine, legal obligations.

As we eventually discovered, Mr. Wang and Mr. Li, had more nefarious things in mind for our joint venture than just the hotel development, and were fighting for as much ambiguity in the contract as possible, in the hope that they could exploit it later on. However, in terms of their own rights, they wanted as much specificity as possible. Although this strategy was utterly transparent, they acted as though it were perfectly reasonable. The Jews invented the word "chutzpah" but the Chinese were its living embodiment.

After endless arguing over clauses the bank could never agree to remove, Mr. Wrangham reached his limit. He stood up one afternoon and announced that he was going back to Hong Kong and the deal was over. A silence fell over the room.

With the relaxed demeanor of someone who had real power, and knew it, Mr. Wang began to tell a story. He directed Mr. Wrangham's attention to the days when his bank had an office in Shanghai during the Cultural Revolution. The bank had an English manager and fifteen employees in an office building downtown. They had attempted to leave the country when the city was in turmoil with militant Red Guards marching in the streets. The Ministry of State Security, however, imprisoned the bank employees in their own headquarters and refused to give them exit visas. They were not allowed to leave the building for fifteen months. Mr. Wang had been a powerful figure in the Ministry then, and still was.

The story was a cautionary tale, a not-so-subtle threat that Mr. Wrangham wouldn't be allowed to leave the country until he capitulated. The chastened banker sat down. Having settled nothing, the conversation turned to the interest rate the bank would charge.

Wrangham had offered the bank's best rate, .75 percent over HIBOR (Hong Kong Interbank Rate, similar to our prime rate). The Chinese wanted .25 percent over HIBOR. A two-day argument ensued. Finally, Mr. Li announced that he had received an offer from the Bank of Tokyo for .25 percent over HIBOR. This was a shock to us, as it was the first we'd heard of it. Mr. Wrangham asked if there was a written offer. Mr. Li said, yes. It was in his briefcase at that very moment.

It was critical for World China Trade that Standard Chartered get the loan because our investment funds were coming from Union Bank in Los Angeles, who was at that time owned by Standard Chartered, and it was a condition for us to borrow our equity. It certainly put us in the middle, but what else was new.

Mr. Wrangham asked to see the document and Mr. Li refused. A tense silence fell over the table. He insisted again on seeing it. More silence. At that point one of the men who had been sitting quietly at the perimeter of the room slowly rose and spoke. He was from the Ministry of State Security. He announced in heavily accented English that it was not necessary for Mr. Wrangham to see the document and that there would be no more discussion at the table regarding that issue. End of conversation.

Mr. Wrangham, his associates and lawyers, all got up and left the table. There was nothing more to say. This wasn't negotiation, it was blackmail.

Later that night we sat with Mr. Wrangham, who said never in his life had he been in a negotiation like this but that his bosses in London had a long-range view of China business and this just comes with the territory. He wondered if the Chinese would really stop him if he tried to leave the country.

* * * * *

We thought it was all over. Sheldon and I went back to our room and tried to figure out if we had any options left. It seemed to us that the Chinese strategy depended on a certain behavioral consistency on our part.

As far as the Chinese were concerned, all westerners shared certain traits and tended to react in predictable ways. Americans, in particular, were impatient and easily frustrated. When confronted with negotiations that proceeded at a glacial pace, and demands that were patently unreasonable and self-serving, Americans tended to break down and give away many, if not most, of their bargaining points. The prospect of enormous profits in the awakening economy of the world's most populous nation motivated people to make the deal—no matter what.

But what if we weren't predictable? What if we did something entirely unexpected like Sheldon's unexplained impulse to turn off that switch at the glass plant. It shut down a huge factory with hundreds of workers for two days. It was an expensive indulgence, but the Chinese were more bewildered than angry. The Chinese have more impulse control than the strictest Puritan ever had. It was an act so utterly unexpected that it short-circuited the normal system of rewards and punishments. There was no punitive response, not even an official reprimand.

During the whole course of our negotiations, Sheldon and I had shared almost every meal with our Chinese associates. Business was never discussed on these occasions and sharing food was always an amiable and good-natured social exchange. Mr. Li and Mr. Wang would joke with us, and we would pass food back and forth serving each other, as is the Chinese custom.

It occurred to Sheldon that our meals played an important symbolic role in the on-going process of cementing our joint venture agreement. To the Chinese, a shared meal is a symbolic act of great importance, a cultural trait they share with the ancient Jews. In spite of the hardball tactics of our formal meetings, the meals had an independent purpose that was unrelated to the content of the negotiations.

Hospitality to guests was a social responsibility that is deeply rooted in the Chinese psyche. To be inhospitable to an outsider, particularly in the context of forming a partnership with that person, would be a significant loss of "face." And that was when Sheldon had a stroke of genius. "What would happen, if I refused to eat with them? What if I went on a hunger strike?"

The next morning Sheldon arrived at the meeting and announced to Mr. Li and Mr. Wang that he would not eat a single morsel of food until they changed their position. It was like dropping a bomb. They were horrified. Mr. Wang said that he would get sick, and they did not want to be responsible for the damage it might do to his health. Their concern was genuine. Sheldon reiterated that they were behaving unreasonably and that he would not eat until they changed their minds. He said this with a sober face, although I thought the situation was somewhat comical.

That day at lunch, and again at dinner, he sat silently at the table, refusing to eat anything. Everyone passed food around and encouraged him to eat. As a special inducement they prepared his favorite noodle dish, but he refused it. In the meantime, I was secreting away food in my bag, which I sneaked up to our room. I had no intention of letting Sheldon starve.

This went on for three days and every day we would meet with Mr. Wrangham and make no progress. The Chinese were getting increasingly frantic about the supposed hunger strike, and Sheldon would play it to the hilt. Whenever he was around them, he would act faint and have dizzy spells at the negotiating table. Finally, they sent someone from the ministry of health to visit him. The earnest medic tried to explain that his fast could damage his health and since we were honored guests, it would cause them great embarrassment. Sheldon simply stated his position and refused to eat.

On the ninth day of our negotiations, and the fourth of his hunger strike, there seemed no way to break the deadlock. Mr. Wrangham had reached the end of his rope and wanted a resolution. We met in his room and discussed the situation. He said that he would consider anything that would break the impasse, but not to reveal this to the Chinese.

The next day Mr. Wang repeated, verbatim, what Mr. Wrangham had said in our private discussion. That night we went to visit him in his room again, and Sheldon pulled out the console between the beds and found a microphone. We explained to him that he was in China and should have expected the room to be bugged. We left him looking weary and downcast, and headed back to the office.

As we entered the office, Mr. Wang and two of his Ministry of State Security thugs were waiting for us. Sheldon kept up his act, and stumbled, as if from weakness. The two thugs took his arms and forcibly sat him down on the couch. Unbelievably, Mr. Wang straddled his legs and sat down on his lap, facing him. He had brought some dumplings, and he proceeded to force feed Sheldon. I couldn't believe what was happening, and ordinarily I would have been very angry, but the whole situation was so farcical that all I really wanted to do was laugh. I watched as Sheldon dutifully ate the dumplings and then he started to talk.

Sheldon told Mr. Wang that we would guarantee that the documents would be valid in both English and Chinese—as this had been a sticking point earlier in our discussions. It wasn't a particularly timely or meaningful offer, as the negotiations had already moved on to other more difficult issues. They asked Sheldon what he meant. He was honest and said he didn't know, but if it would end the stalemate, we were willing to do it. He was operating on pure intuition. It seemed like the face-saving concession they needed, although it gained them nothing tangible.

Sheldon's hunch turned out to be right. He had done the one thing they had never expected, and it worked.

In short order, the interest rate was settled, and the boilerplate clauses accepted. The last item was the banks legal fees. It ended with Mr. Wrangham thinking that he would prevail by letting the Chinese decide what the fees should be, instead of presenting the bill which at this time amounted to over $150,000. Mr. Wrangham stated to the Chinese that he felt they were fair and honorable in their dealings and that they were aware of what the banks legal costs were. Therefore, he said he would leave it up to Mr. Li to decide what the joint venture would pay to the bank for their legal costs.

Mr. Li, in his Chinese way, told Mr. Wrangham that he felt that there should be no payment at all, because all foreign lawyers were parasites and hindered the business relationship between parties interested in doing business. We finally settled at $15,000 dollars.

The deal was agreed upon; however, our ten days of misery was not over.

* * * *

After we had signed our joint venture contract, and the proper entities gave their approval (all one hundred of them), the Chinese side of our joint venture put half of their required equity in RMB (Chinese currency) which was equivalent to 1.875 million US dollars into our account at the Bank of China Beijing. Per our agreement, we were also supposed to put up 1.875 million US Dollars. Union Bank in Los Angeles, who agreed to loan us our equity, would not issue any funds until we had secured the financing for the construction of the hotel project, which was being funded by Standard Chartered in Hong Kong. The Chinese would not negotiate for the construction or financing until our money was deposited in the joint venture bank account. It was a classic Chicken and egg situation.

When we told the Chinese and Mr. Wang that we did not have the funds and at that moment the bank would not release the funds, Mr. Wang became very upset. He told us that we had agreed in writing to deposit these funds. All the approvals were in place, the contract was signed, and we were not living up to what we had agreed upon.

We explained to Mr. Wang that our equity was conditioned on Standard Chartered Asia providing the construction financing and until that was in place, we could not get any funds released. Mr. Wang said that the joint venture's negotiating position with Standard Charted bank was compromised, because they knew that unless the joint venture took the loan from them, we would not have our equity infusion.

There was much consternation, and they called a meeting with our joint venture board members from Chongqing, representatives from the mayor's office, officials from the Ministry of Public Security, and Dean Lee and Richard Chen from Occidental Petroleum.

It seems liked much face would be lost over this issue, since there were so many agencies and governmental authorities involved in this transaction. The meeting was held in our offices in the Beijing Hotel, and it was one of the few times that there was not a lot of translation, just a lot of glaring at us. We got the sense that everyone was on the spot. This joint venture seemed to be very important to a great many people and this apparent breach of the agreement, caused a great deal of concern.

After a while we all went down to dinner. There were at least fifteen of us, including two children belonging to one of the officials. It was not uncommon for children to be brought to some of our meetings. Sheldon went to the hotel store and bought two small toy airplanes and gave them to the children. At dinner everyone was very cordial, and as usual, no business was discussed.

After dinner we went back to our offices and continued our discussion. It seemed that Richard Chen and Dean Lee from OXY were on the spot. They both started to sweat as the questions poured out at them. Mr. Yu was more relaxed, and it seemed he was not part of the interrogation. At least that was how we read the situation, because they were speaking Chinese, and nothing was being translated.

Finally, Sheldon and I came up with the idea of an escrow account, where the funds would be held and automatically released when the construction contract was finalized. We told Mr. Yu our idea and he brought it into the conversation.

The Chinese had never heard of an escrow account and the whole concept had to be explained to them. There was a great deal of silence and then they continued in loud voices to interrogate Richard and Dean. It turned out that the concept of escrow in their minds, was mistrust. They resented the idea and we finally told them there was no other way.

They agreed, but of course that was just the beginning. The next day we flew to Hong Kong and met with Charles Wrangham and told him what had transpired. We explained that if the bank did not accept and place the funds in an escrow account, then the joint venture would be canceled and the Chinese would probably have negative feelings regarding the bank, because of the issue of mistrust.

We got on a three-way conversation with Union Bank in Los Angeles, and they agreed under certain terms and conditions. Standard Chartered said that the funds would have to be placed in their bank in Hong Kong.

We flew back to Beijing and had a meeting with all concerned. The Chinese agreed to accept the escrow, but the funds would have to be placed in the Shenzhen branch of Bank of China. Shenzhen was a comparatively new mainland Chinese city, right across from the Hong Kong border territories. We called Mr. Wrangham and he said that was not acceptable. The funds had to be placed in Standard Chartered Bank in Hong Kong. Here we were in the middle again, but what else was new.

We argued with the Chinese for two days. They said they have gone as far as they could by accepting the whole escrow concept, but they had reached their limit. The funds had to be deposited in the Bank of China, Shenzhen branch or they would cancel the Joint venture.

Once again, we flew back to Honk Kong, met with the Mr. Wrangham and told him that the Chinese were threatening to cancel the joint venture. He said the bank was already out on a limb and that if the funds went into China, it would be too big a risk for the bankers in Los Angeles.

He invited us out to dinner on the Standard Chartered yacht, and we had a great time. He told us he really wanted to make this deal, but there was only so far he could go. He asked us to go back to Beijing and try again to convince Mr. Wang and the Chinese group. By this time, we were exhausted. We felt like Ping Pong balls, bouncing back and forth between Hong Kong and Beijing, but we agreed.

We flew back to Beijing for yet another meeting where nothing was resolved. The Chinese seemed very calm, very much different from Mr. Wrangham in Hong Kong. We finally got Mr. Yu away from the group and had a heart-to-heart talk. We realized that we had to solve this problem, or the joint venture could be terminated. Then I had an idea. What if the funds were put into the Bank of China in Hong Kong?

Mr. Yu brightened up and said he would try to sell the idea to the Chinese. After about a day, they accepted, and we flew back to Hong

Kong to meet with Mr. Wrangham again. He said the idea had some merit and he would try and convince his bank to accept.

Thankfully, the bank agreed, and we flew back to the United States to arrange the transfer of the funds to Standard Chartered, who in turn would make the escrow deposit.

We then flew back to Hong Kong and notified the Chinese and the Bank of China that Mr. Wrangham and Sheldon had decided to personally bring a cashier's check to the Bank of China Hong Kong Branch.

The next day with a cashier's check in hand, they walked over to the bank and were met by the manager and high officials of the bank. They first asked to see Sheldon's passport, to verify his identity, then asked to see a copy of his visa and a copy of the signed escrow agreement. They checked Mr. Wrangham's identity, and his credentials, and after a very tedious hour, they said that everything had checked out and they could continue with the transaction.

They presented the cashier's check, and bank examined it and made some calls to verify its authenticity. That took another hour. They did serve them some tea while they waited.

The bank officials finally said everything was in order, but unfortunately, they could not at that time accept the check and Sheldon and Charles should come back in two days. Trying to figure out the Chinese psyche, could drive anyone crazy. They returned in two days and the transaction was complete.

The last step was for our board of directors to ratify the contract. What was supposed to be a mere formality got us expelled from China.

CHAPTER 13

Expulsion from China

"Fuck you, fuck you, fuck you."
~American proverb

It was the middle of summer and it had taken months of long and tedious negotiations to finalize the joint venture contract. Everything had been agreed upon and all that was left to formalize it, was to hold a board of directors meeting to ratify what we had agreed upon and then deliver the documents to the Chinese governmental agencies dealing with these matters. The meeting was to take place at our offices in the Beijing Hotel.

At the same time, I had invited several people from the Natural History Museum of Los Angeles, including Craig Black, director of the museum, and his wife, to join us in China. I was on the board of governors and had gotten to know Craig well. His father had been a missionary in China, and he had grown up there, so he was very excited to return. But he was even more excited because the museum was very interested in being the first in the United States to show treasures from

China that nobody had seen. By now we had been in China for over three years, and we had excellent connections with the right people.

While I was busy hosting our visitors from LA, Sheldon attended the board meeting to ratify the joint venture contract, a "simple" formality. After three weeks of going at it day and night with bankers, lawyers, Chinese officials and the like, we had agreed on all the issues, and we had a written agenda for the board meeting. All the key parties were now present including Richard Chen, who was on our board and also working for Dr. Hammer as his Vice Chairman. The meeting itself was, in effect, just a transcript of what we had previously agreed to for an official record.

The Chinese side was not happy with us at that moment because we had insisted on several checks and balances. The most important was our insistence that checks written on the joint venture account over $500 had to have agreement and signatures from both sides. The meeting was progressing and around two hours in there was an item introduced on the agenda that was not previously discussed or disclosed to us.

In our joint venture contract, we had agreed that half of our investment, which was 1.875 million US dollars, would be released from escrow at the start of the project. Six months after this initial contribution, we were to have a board meeting to decide mutually when the next payment would be due. In fact, that is the way we set up our funding with the banks and our investors.

This new item was a bombshell, and it was the first time that an item was introduced that had not been disclosed and agreed upon prior to the meeting. Mr. Wang stated through an interpreter that the second installment was due three weeks after the first installment was received. This was not what we had agreed upon and was not what was stated in the English version of the contract, nor was it stated in the Chinese version—at least that's what Sheldon thought at that moment.

He questioned Mr. Wang and told him that the item was not on the agenda and that it should not be discussed. He added that that item was mentioned in our contract and that the details were far different. Mr. Wang, through the interpreter, told Sheldon in his inimitable Chinese fashion that it was Government law that dictated how foreign investment was to be funded in a joint venture relationship. We had been through this before. When the Chinese want to change something, they always use the excuse that it's a law. Unfortunately, these laws were not written down anywhere and seemed to be verbal at the best.

Sheldon brought out the contract and they argued for a while. Then Richard Chen said that it was unnecessary to argue. Since the item was not on the agenda, it would not be stated in the minutes and therefore it was a waste of time to deal with the issue at the board meeting.

They went on to discuss several other items, but the atmosphere was filled with tension. The meeting finally adjourned at about 1:00 am and Sheldon returned to our room. I was still awake, and he updated me on what had happened. Exhausted, we both fell asleep, until the phone rang at 3:00 am.

It was Mr. Yu. He told Sheldon that it was very important that he come back up to our office and sign the minutes of the meeting as the deadline for the consummation of our contract had been reached. Sheldon asked him if the minutes were translated into English. Mr. Yu said no, but he should just sign the Chinese version and then it would be translated into English the following day.

Sheldon explained that he was weary and could not sign the Chinese minutes without understanding what they had to say and that would come from the translation. He told Mr. Yu that he was concerned about the item that had come up during the board meeting and that he was not comfortable signing the minutes until he had a chance to thoroughly review them. Mr. Yu insist that Sheldon come up immediately, and that he had no choice and must sign those minutes tonight.

Sheldon became very upset and told him that he was going back to sleep and that we would deal with this in the morning. Mr. Yu said if he didn't come to the office, then he would come to us and get those minutes signed. Sheldon became very irritated and told him that if he came down, he could wait outside the door all night, and hung up the phone.

About twenty minutes later, the phone rang again and this time it was an official from the Ministry of Public Security who spoke English. He informed Sheldon that he was being an obstructionist, and that since the Ministry of Public Security was a partner (this was news to us) that he was ordered to come to the office and sign those minutes.

Sheldon reiterated what he explained to Mr. Yu. He was an American citizen trying to do business in the Peoples Republic of China and that he would not be intimidated by him or his organization. He had the responsibility of American investors and would not sign those minutes until he had thoroughly reviewed them in English, and had an independent Chinese verify that the English and Chinese versions were identical.

The Ministry official became very angry in a Chinese way, which is not raising your voice but threatening in an obtuse way. He informed Sheldon that our visas could be pulled, our status in the country could be at question and that it was to our benefit to sign those papers now. I have to admit we were very nervous. Here we were in a Communist country having an argument with the Chinese KGB. But Sheldon stuck to his guns and refused in as polite a way as possible. It's very important to save face in China—that alone is a long learning experience.

After a short night with little sleep, we were both up early. I had planned a tour of the Forbidden City with Craig and his wife for a private walk-through of the acres of treasures. As I headed to meet them, Sheldon headed to our office determined to resolve the impasse.

I spent the day with Craig and his wife selecting what we wanted to bring back to the United States for the first major exhibition of Chinese treasures at the museum. It was a fascinating day. I wish that we had mobile phones at that time, because I would have taken pictures of this huge, cavernous space in the Forbidden City with ancient treasures that went back thousands of years.

It was also my birthday and the Chinese had planned a huge party for me that evening at the Temple of Heaven, a masterpiece of architecture and landscape design that was built in the fifteenth century. The emperors used to have their parties at the top of the five staircases and the views are spectacular. This was where my party was being held. Among the many dignitaries were Dr. Brown who was Chair of the Natural History Museum, and his wife.

While I spent a glorious day at the Forbidden City going over treasures and making lists, unbeknownst to me, Sheldon had a knockdown, drag out fight with Mr. Wang, and I wasn't around to calm him down. Here's what happened.

When Sheldon arrived at the office, everyone was very quiet and somber. The fact that my birthday party was that evening, and our office and Mr. Yu were helping the museum people to forge a relationship with their Chinese counterpart at the Forbidden City, complicated matters.

Sheldon asked Mr. Yu if the minutes had been translated into English and he grudgingly informed him they had. Usually, the translated minutes were typed correctly and gone over minutely before presented to us. This time they were hand scrawled on some small pieces of paper, that were torn and smudged. Sheldon sat down and read through them, and wouldn't you know it, the item that was not on the agenda, that Richard Chen told him would not be in the minutes, was indeed there and stated that everyone had agreed upon it.

Sheldon told Mr. Yu that he would not sign those minutes and they would have to be changed. Mr. Yu became very upset and said his personal safety and that of his family was at risk if Sheldon didn't sign those minutes. Sheldon explained to him that our deal with the bank called for at least six months before we had to come up with our final payment. In the new minutes, it said the payment was due in three weeks. If we were unable to make the payment, then we could lose our initial payment of $1,875 million and our investors would skin us alive. It seemed to make no difference to him about the American Investors.

Sheldon then went to one of our Chinese employees and asked him if that item in our Joint venture contract was the same in the Chinese and English versions. He hemmed and hawed, and with a very sheepish grin (Chinese always laugh when they are put into difficult positions) told us they were not, and the Chinese version of the contract was similar to what was on the board agenda.

Sheldon was furious. He confronted Mr. Yu and asked him if he knew there was a difference. He admitted he did and had lied about it. When Sheldon asked him why, he said because he knew we wouldn't agree to it.

At that moment in time, Sheldon didn't trust any of the Chinese, and he knew he had to stand his ground. He asked to have a meeting with Mr. Wang to try to settle this issue.

Expulsion from China

Mr. Wang and a few of his cohorts showed up. Sheldon started to discuss the issue, but Mr. Wang was very stubborn and refused to bend in any way. Sheldon told him that if the language could be changed in some way that would give the US side some protection, he would consider it. Sheldon was adamant and forceful. This went on for hours. He tried to call our attorney in Los Angeles but could not reach him. (In those days you had to reserve a call to the US, and it took between 3-6 hours to get a call through).

The Chinese had several different people come to the office to try and convince him, but it just ended up in arguments. Finally, two large Chinese showed up, and it was apparent from their demeanor that they were thugs from the Ministry of Public security. They took Sheldon into the inner office and tried to intimidate him to sign the documents. They told him he was obstructing the joint venture, and that there could be severe penalties and repercussions, if he did not comply.

Sheldon explained that he was an American citizen and not subject to Chinese law. We were trying to do business and had been lied to. We had a responsibility to our US investors, and certainly would accept and listen to a compromise but he could not sign the documents the way they were written. They continued to harass Sheldon and things got very ugly. They sort of forced him into a corner of the room and put their fingers hard on his chest and said, "You will sign those documents right now with no further hesitation."

At that moment something snapped. Sheldon thought to himself, *I am an American from a free country, and no one has the right to force me to do anything against my will*. He knew if he succumbed to their intimidation and threats, he would be useless in any dealings with the Chinese in the future. He turned to them and in a very loud voice that was heard by everyone, said, "Fuck you, fuck the Chinese Government, and fuck the Ministry of Public Security. I will not sign those minutes the way they are written." He then pushed them aside and stormed out of the office yelling, "Fuck you." I don't think anyone had every said that to the Chinese Ministry of Public Security. Sheldon became a legend in the banking circles of Hong Kong.

That night at my birthday party, all of the Chinese officials, including Mr. Wang and the two thugs Sheldon had said fuck you to were there, along with the entire party from the Natural History Museum and several dignitaries. Except for the extreme tension, it was a wonderful party. The Chinese went through the evening as if almost nothing had happened.

We returned to our room and again at 3:00 am we received a call from Mr. Yu telling us to meet in the office first thing in the morning. When we arrived at our office Mr. Wang and the Ministry of Public security were waiting for us. They informed us, as they aptly put it, that it would be in our best interest to leave the country immediately. I wanted to stay but it was obvious we were in a mess.

When we told them we would leave, they asked us where we were going. Sheldon told them to Hong Kong to tell the entire story to Charles Wrangham at Standard Chartered Asia. They told us we could not do that because it would screw up the joint venture. We told them that the bank had read the contract and approved it with the English version, and they had a right to know, since they were lending the joint venture over $20 million dollars.

After they left, Mr. Yu told us if we didn't leave immediately, there was going to be trouble. And even more ominously, he said if Sheldon came to the border, he'd be shot. He also told us we'd have to designate somebody as our representative to sign the documents the way they were and added that we were no longer welcome in China. We designated our attorney, Joe Brightman. We prepared to leave the next day, and left Joe to sign the board meeting notes ratifying the contract.

We had real concerns that the Chinese might not let us leave the country, since you cannot leave China without a stamp from the Ministry of Public Security on your passport. But to our great relief, they didn't stop us and soon we were headed back to LA wondering if we'd ever see China again.

CHAPTER 14

Back in the Game

"No words spoken when leave."
~Chinese Proverb

We returned home and consoled ourselves with the fact that the hotel project would proceed. The land deal had been made, the designs had been semi-approved, and we communicated regularly with Mr. Yu on the progress. We were also sending materials and supplies from the U.S. for the construction. We hadn't told anyone we had been thrown out of China. While we were back in the US protecting ourselves, we were also looking for new projects, and fortunately Dr. Hammer was always trying to connect us to people who were looking to invest in China.

One day we got a phone call from Richard Chen saying there were a couple of guys who were interested in investing in the hotel, or building something in China, and that Dr. Hammer suggested we meet with them. A couple of days later, the two guys, who happened to be Donald Nixon (Richard Nixon's brother) and John Dean (who a few years earlier had served time in Federal prison for his role in

Watergate) showed up at our home in Beverly Hills. The investment opportunity for the hotel was closed, but we started to talk about other potential opportunities. We liked John and soon met his wife, and the four of us became friends and often socialized.

We were also doing a lot of PR around the hotel and that's when we got a call from Jerry Speyer, one of two founding partners of the New York real estate company Tishman Speyer, which controls Rockefeller Center. We had met him two years earlier when he was trying to build an office tower complex in Shenzhen with American Express's name on the building. Shenzhen was officially made a city in 1979 and was on the verge of becoming a modern metropolis that links Hong Kong to China's mainland. We agreed with Jerry that the office tower was an excellent opportunity, but he was stymied by a lack of progress.

Jerry sent us tickets to meet with him in New York. We had a great conversation about how we could help him. We told Jerry we had already put together the Asia Hotel project which was starting construction, and he was enthusiastic that we could work on his project.

We started to put together a proposal, and John Dean was going to be one of the investors. Sheldon and I figured it was a good thing for us to work on since we were stuck in the United States, and we had to figure out how we were going to get back into the good graces of the Chinese, because Mr. Wang was a very powerful man. (Unfortunately, the project never came to fruition. When Tiananmen Square happened a few years later, we were in the middle of the hotel's construction, and we had to focus ourselves on making sure that didn't go down the drain.)

About three months into our expulsion fate stepped in. I got a call from HUD, the Department of Housing and Urban Development of the United States. "Mrs. Krechman, we understand you're building a hotel in China, and we're putting together a group of women in construction—developers, architects, and designers—to take them to China. We would like you to lead the delegation."

Sheldon was still stinging from our being thrown out when I told him about my invitation. I really saw this as a windfall and a chance for us to get back into the game, although he wasn't quite so sure. He did agree though that since I was leading a delegation of well-known women from around the globe on behalf of the United States HUD department that included the Deputy Director, plus a representative from the State Department and a representative from security, it was highly unlikely that they would throw me out of China. I accepted the invitation.

* * * * *

On January 20, 1985, six months after we had left China, I headed to LAX for my flight to San Francisco where I was meeting the group to fly to Tokyo where we would spend the night and then go on to Beijing. I had booked an early flight from LA so that I would have plenty of time before our flight to Tokyo. Well as it turned out, it was Super Bowl Sunday, and it was the first time that the game was being played in San Francisco. Everyone must have booked early flights too. We taxied away from the gate and then sat and sat on the tarmac in a very long queue of planes. We were not moving at all. I was getting really nervous, and I kept looking at my watch.

Finally, out of desperation, I called over the flight attendant and told her I had a strange request. I explained that I was on my way to meet a group of twenty women from HUD in San Francisco to fly to China, and if I missed my flight, it would be a disaster because I was their leader. No one else in the group, not even the Deputy Secretary of HUD, had any experience in China. I told her I didn't know if there was anything she could do but maybe there was a way we could jump ahead of all these planes. I didn't think anything would happen, but the next thing I knew our plane was moving out of the queue into the front.

I got to San Francisco barely in time to get to the international terminal to meet my group and board the plane. When we arrived in Tokyo after our 11-hour flight, all the women collected their luggage. They each had several bags with many changes of clothing. As they gathered their belongs, I was still on the TSA side waiting for my bag. After waiting some time and it still hadn't arrived, we left the airport. I figured eventually they'd find my luggage and get it to me.

I was wearing a comfortable jumpsuit which I had selected for the long flight, some weird designer thing, and I realized I couldn't wear that for the rest of my trip. After spending the night in Tokyo, we had plans to go to a very nice little Japanese town called Narita, just to give the group a flavor of Japan. We would spend the night there and then leave for China in the morning. When we arrived in Narita, I bought myself a pair of black tights, a black skirt, a black shirt, a jacket, a T-shirt, some toothpaste, and a little bit of makeup. And that's what I wore the entire ten days of our journey.

I swear to this day that the Chinese did this to me as a test. I traveled throughout China with these women, all dressed to the nines. And then there was me. I looked like a Chinese lady dressed in my black clothes, that I washed at night. After visiting many locations in China, we finally got to Beijing. It had been six months since I had been there.

Beijing was going to be our last stop and I brought the women to the site of the old glass factory to show them what we were doing. The glass factory had been demolished and there was now a two-story office building on the property. We had bought materials in the U.S for the hotel which were shipped in containers to China by boat. The work crews had unloaded all the materials and then used the containers to build the office. And who was there to greet us? Mr. Wang himself. He was very gracious and excited about meeting these women. And he was very kind to me.

And then low and behold, that very afternoon, my luggage was delivered to the hotel. In it was my red Chanel suit, just in time for a big banquet that was being hosted for us by Betty Bao Lord, an international bestselling author, and her husband Winston Lord. At that time, he was the United Nations ambassador to China. They were very charming and so excited about hosting us for a very special evening.

The group went home, and I stayed on to talk to Mr. Wang. I told him Sheldon had to come back and help get this project done, and we had new things we wanted to do in China. What did we have to do? That's when he asked me if I could get him airplanes for the airport he had built on Hainan Island, which with its tropical climate, beautiful beaches and forested, mountainous interior, had excellent tourism potential. Yes, he had built an airport and didn't have any planes.

As it turns out I knew somebody in LA who bought used planes, so I told him we could work on making that happen. A month later, Sheldon was allowed to return to Beijing. Mr. Wang met him at the airport and took him to the hotel and into our office and lifted him up in joy. I had stayed in LA to find the airplanes. We were able to buy 747s, 720s, and several smaller planes and shipped them off to the island, which made Mr. Wang very happy.

And that is how we maneuvered our way back into China.

CHAPTER 15

Interlude: The Station Wagon

"Nothing in China is ever as it seems to be."

The Monopoly game that disappeared after we had taken it to Mr. Wang's home, was child's play compared to the disappearing station wagon.

In the early 1980's in China, the only transportation was by cab or car and driver. The cars were all Japanese small to medium sedans, that only held four at the most—three in the crowded back seat and one in front. The only larger vehicles were vans, which were prohibitively expensive to bring into China, if allowed at all. The going customs rate was two hundred percent of the value of the automobile, and of course there were little or no parts available for American automobiles.

We were bringing business people to China and we were always cramped for space in the automobiles. Back in LA, we had a Mercury

Interlude: The Station Wagon

station wagon that Sheldon had souped up with a very large four-barrel carburetor and some other modifications, including the elimination of all smog devices (that increased its performance.) The car was five or six years old at that time and was loaded with full power, leather seats, a sunroof and all the amenities. When Mr. Yu came to visit in the United States, we would use this vehicle.

We decided that we would sell it to our company, World China Trade, fill it with all kinds of parts and send it off to Beijing. We painted the sides with our company name, World China Trade, and Mr. Yu was responsible for arranging shipment to China.

After a great deal of paperwork and red tape, the Chinese sent a cargo ship to Los Angeles, and the station wagon was put on board to be shipped to Tianjin, the northern seaport, and then driven to Beijing. The car arrived close to schedule and Mr. Yu was supposed to pick the station wagon up from customs and have it driven to Beijing. As always in China, nothing is ever as it seems to be or simple.

Mr. Yu called us from Beijing and told us the customs bureau would not release the wagon without customs duty, something Mr. Yu neglected to mention. He said the law stated that the duty would be one hundred percent of what the car cost when it was new. That amounted to almost $20,000. Sheldon told him that was ridiculous, and we had only charged the company $5000 for the wagon, and the most we should pay would be ten percent of that value or $500. Mr. Yu said this was a customs law and there was no negotiation, the same as US customs which doesn't negotiate. He added that they also wanted customs duty on the parts.

Sheldon told him this was not the US, it was China, and everything could be negotiated. Mr. Yu argued and said there was nothing he could do. Sheldon told him to just leave it at customs until they changed their mind. Mr. Yu defiantly said it would just stay there forever and hung up on Sheldon.

About a week later he phoned to say he had used all his influence to the highest level and that he had gotten them to accept $15,000, a twenty-five percent reduction. Sheldon told him that was unacceptable, and he should continue to negotiate.

We then received a call from Richard Chen, from Occidental Petroleum telling us he had received communication from his office in Beijing. It seems the government called the Oxy office, knowing of our relationship, and complained that this vehicle was sitting at customs, and we refused to pay the duty. The Chinese suggested that since Oxy was involved with World China Trade that they should pay the duty.

Mr. Chen politely refused and told us that it was our responsibility and that OXY should not be involved—they had enough difficulty with China business without this problem. Sheldon explained to Richard that we felt the duty was exorbitant and we could not afford to pay that much. Mr. Chen recited the mantra; it was Chinese law.

After five phone calls, and three weeks of negotiation, the Chinese agreed to $5000 in complete payment for the duties. We told Mr. Yu that was acceptable, however, we did not have the $5000 to make payment. Sheldon asked that he request terms, 30-60-90 days, after we took the car, to make payments.

Mr. Yu almost had a fit of apoplexy. He said that was absolutely impossible, it could not be done and there was no more discussion to be had about this issue. Customs did not give open accounts and it would be impolite for him to ask. Sheldon asked him to call the OXY office in Beijing and ask them to make the payment for us and we would pay them back, as per the payment plan, he had suggested. After much discussion, the Chinese took Mr. Yu's word, and we were able to make the payments as per the plan.

The next step was to register the station wagon with the Ministry of Public Security, as no vehicle could be driven without their permission. This was a long process and Mr. Yu somehow got permission for the station wagon to be driven to Beijing and parked at the Beijing hotel. It sat there for three weeks and finally we received permission for our office driver and personnel to drive the car. The purchase of gasoline was also monitored by the Ministry of Public Security. You could not just drive into a gas station. You had to have prior approval and gasoline certificates before being able to fill the gas tank. Fortunately, we received those approvals.

The wagon was a sensation. Everyone turned and looked at it. It was the first vehicle in Beijing with a sunroof and an alarm. When the alarm went off, which it did often, as our driver somehow could never figure out how to set it properly, the crowds would gather in wonder and delight. At one point, the Great Wall Sheraton hotel offered us $20,000 for the wagon, but after all the difficulty in getting it into China and the thought of what we would have to go through to replace it, we turned down the offer.

We loved having the station wagon there and available for our use. Mr. Yu, however, was always reserved about it, and he told us that it made too much of a spectacle and he was concerned.

One morning we went up to our office and were told that the station wagon had been borrowed and that it was uncertain when it would be returned. When questioned as to who had borrowed it and why, we received a look from Mr. Yu and no explanation. For the next three weeks we had a Japanese small sedan, and no one mentioned the station wagon. We asked several times, but our questions were never answered or responded to.

Three weeks went by and one day we met our driver downstairs at the hotel entrance, and wouldn't you know, he was driving the station wagon. It was very clean inside and out and I noticed that the lettering on the sides were a bit different color and font. It was obvious that it had been repainted. We asked Mr. Yu what was going on. He just looked at us and said that there were certain things that it was not necessary to explain.

We had the wagon for a year, and on one of our return trips to Beijing, Mr. Yu told us that the station wagon had broken down and he had to leave it. When he returned, it had disappeared. That was the last we ever saw of the wagon.

CHAPTER 16

Friendship Stores, Chinese Army, Pigeons

"Brainwashing is a Chinese Art Form."

Every trip back to China was a new adventure. We learned more about the Chinese each time, but we also came to realize it would always be a place of mystery and unanswered questions. Here are two stories that took place during the early development of the hotel project.

We always stayed at the Beijing Hotel, which had grown and expanded over the years as tourism and business increased in China. Our offices, located on the fourteenth floor with a corner view of the main avenue in Beijing, were one of the nicest in the hotel, and had been converted from hotel rooms. This part of the building was solidly constructed with thick cement walls. As the newer additions were built, the Chinese who were in a hurry to collect the foreign currency, changed their building standards and the construction was very different and hastily put up. At this point the hotel had over 1000 rooms.

We always requested rooms on the same side of the hotel as our offices, but on this trip, there were no rooms available on that side because there was a convention of Chinese Army high level officers from all over China. The hotel was fully booked so we were put in a room in the most recent addition to the hotel.

It was a very strange trip, and I should have realized that the karma was different from the first time when I walked into our office. The Chinese did not use screens on the windows and the air conditioning mostly did not work. If it did work, it just cooled the cockroaches and not much more. Therefore, the windows were left open in the summer.

When we arrived in the office that morning, we were surprised to see two pigeons flying around inside the office. Now in the US it would have been considered very strange, since it not only disrupted the day-to-day office business but there were pigeon droppings everywhere. I asked what was going on and Ms. Zhang replied that things were normal. I suggested that having pigeons flying around the office was not what I considered normal. She told us when a pigeon flies into your office it's a sign of good luck and they must not be disturbed.

I decided to take Ms Zhang out and buy her a gift, as she was working very hard, and it would be an opportunity to talk to her about the inappropriateness of having pigeons flying around the office, especially when we had many important people coming to visit us.

We went to a local friendship store. Friendship stores were department stores where foreigners could purchase Chinese goods, from clothing to food, appliances, jewelry, luggage, and more. The one we went to was not in the mainstream, but toward the northern outskirts of Beijing.

We found a leather coat that she liked, and I paid the clerk in FEC (Foreign Exchange Certificates) which is what foreigners converted their currency into when they came into China. The Chinese used RMB, the Chinese currency. The Chinese supposedly were not allowed to use the FEC 's but there was always a black market. We then returned to our office with the coat, but I had been unsuccessful in convincing Ms. Zhang to get rid of the pigeons.

Later in the afternoon two security people showed up. They were never uniformed, but you could always tell by their demeanor. There was a rapid conversation between Mr. Yu and the security people and then Mr. Yu told me that these people wanted to speak to me and that he would interpret. He told me not to be concerned and to tell them whatever they wanted to know, and if he felt the questions were inappropriate, he would intervene.

It seems that when I gave the clerk in the store payment in FEC's he put them in his pocket and put RMB's in the cash register to cover the payment for the coat. He was seen doing this by another employee, who immediately called the Local Ministry of Public Security. When you live in a country that's a police state, there's always a fear you will be turned in. I explained that I had given payment in FEC's, they thanked me and left.

Later I found out that within a two-week period this person was convicted and sent off to a farm (if you could call it that) in outer Mongolia. He would shovel night soil (human feces used for cultivation) for a few years to be rehabilitated.

The pigeons were really irritating us as we tried to work, especially Sheldon. One afternoon he decided to go to our room, in the new wing, and take a nap. The rooms were much smaller, and the location was not as convenient. The walls were paper thin and in the next room some of the Army contingent must have been having a party. It sounded like a whole army, with boisterous shouting, laughing and bouncing around. Since it was late afternoon, he just put some cotton in his ears and tried to get some rest.

It was very difficult with all that noise and about 7:00 pm, a somewhat cranky Sheldon joined me in the Western dining room. We talked about the pigeons and that made us laugh as there was not much we could do about it. About 10:00 pm we went back to our room and the noise was deafening. The party next door was raging on, and it did not stop until about 4:00 am. By that time, we were fit to be tied, exhausted, and then figured we would sleep until the early afternoon. Then at about 7:00 am it started again. We could not believe it.

We gave up, got dressed, and went off to our office. There we were greeted by two flying pigeons and pigeon shit everywhere. As the day progressed, we began to wonder what we were doing in China in the midst of this apparent insanity. People came and went, telexes were sent, and we had two important meetings with our Chinese sponsor, Mr. Wang. No one seemed to care about the pigeons. In fact, in one of the meetings, someone brought a flat box filled with live little ducklings, and Ms. Zhang ended up with three of them to take home. At one point we thought the ducks were also going to live in the office.

Through all this we conducted serious business, drank a lot of tea and ate very well. All meals were a treat and lunch was always very exciting. No business was spoken at lunch, and Mr. Yu always ordered. The minimum number of dishes were at least five or six with different varieties, which were always shared. Menus were for foreigners, and ordering was always a negotiation between the waiters and Mr. Yu, but the food was always great and the lunch was filled with laughter and carrying on.

After lunch, Mr. Yu and Mr. Wang would take a forty-five-minute nap and then we would resume our meeting. We told them that the office was becoming a mess and that we just had to get rid of the pigeons. They all looked at us and said it could not be done. They must stay.

We ate an early dinner in the Hot Pot restaurant in the hotel and returned to our room about 9:00 pm. The clamoring and noise were still going on. Between the noise and the pigeons, our nerves were frayed. Sheldon moaned and groaned and stuffed cotton in his ears. Finally, he had it. He got up and took his shoe and banged it several times on the wall. All of a sudden, the noise stopped, and we finally thought we would get peace and quiet. Then we heard pounding on the other side of the wall, obviously a shoe, and the noise started again louder than before. There was only one choice.

I put on my bath robe and went out into the hallway and knocked on the door. An older Chinese man opened it and looked at me. I told him I had a sick husband in the next room and would appreciate it if they could quiet down a bit. He looked at me and in broken English, told me he was alone in his room, was asleep when I knocked, and he had no idea what I was talking about. Of course, I could see into his room where there were several people drinking and shouting. He then politely said good night and closed the door.

Their party went on all night as usual, and we were very haggard when we got to our office the next morning. The pigeons were still there, the mess was worse, and Sheldon was not in a good mood. He asked Ms. Zhang to please call and find out who the person in the next room was. It turned out he was a very well-known and respected army general from the south, and the people coming in and out of his room were paying respects to him.

I implored Ms. Zhang to please call him and ask him to let us have some peace and quiet. She called and they were on the phone for quite a while, and she was laughing. She got off the phone, smiled at us and said he was very concerned, since we were respected foreigners, and he was a very important general in the PRC. He said that last night he was fast asleep, when there was a knock on his door and he opened it to find a foreign lady in a bathrobe, asking him to stop his party and be quiet. Since he was alone in his room and fast asleep, the only conclusion he could come to was that the foreign lady and her husband must be a bit insane, and he suggested that Ms. Zhang seek help for us.

He also told her to tell us that he would be leaving the following morning. That night they again partied all night long. In the morning he knocked at our door, shook hands with Sheldon and said he hoped we would be successful doing business in China. Brainwashing is a Chinese Art.

Later that day Sheldon told Ms. Zhang that if the pigeons were not gone by the following morning, he would personally grab each one, take them down to the kitchen and have them cooked for dinner. The next day they were gone, the place was clean, and when we asked her what she did with them, she looked at us as if to say, "What Pigeons?"

* * * * *

As the construction of the hotel project was progressing, Mr. Yu, and Sheldon and I were constantly looking for new business opportunities. Entrepreneurs from a multitude of Chinese Ministries would come to our office, after contacting Mr. Yu to review joint venture opportunities with us, to see if we had any interest.

One of the groups we met with were Chinese officials who were involved with the overall management of the largest friendship store in in Beijing, on the main street, where the Beijing Hotel and the Forbidden City were located. This store was four stories and was busy all the time.

I suggested that a new friendship store be constructed on the site of the existing one. I envisioned a twenty story building that would encompass the department store, the market, and an entertainment complex, which would include bowling, roller skating, ice skating, and movies. The Chinese side also wanted to have office suites that would be available for rental to Chinese provinces throughout the PRC that wanted to have a presence in Beijing, to sell their services and products.

Everyone thought it was a great idea and after we did some diligence work Mr. Yu arranged meetings with the officials we had previously met with, and we negotiated a Letter of Intent to be the joint venture partner in the project. The estimated cost was just under $100 million dollars.

We returned to the United States and began to contact a variety of potential funding sources including investment bankers, merchant banks, and real estate developers. We assembled a team of professionals to travel back to Beijing with us to attend the Letter of Intent signing ceremony, the banquet of course, and to view the sites and work with us to come up with a proper business plan.

It was an impressive group who included: Sheldon, the managing partner of the Los Angeles office of Arthur Anderson, Ivan, the national partner in charge of a large real estate development, Marvin, a partner in one of Los Angeles most prestigious architectural firms, Pei, a Chinese architect from Marvin's office, and Bernie, who was Vice President of MCA Entertainment.

We of course organized this trip with Mr. Yu, and he arranged our itinerary in Beijing. This was the first time we had traveled to Beijing with so many people and it was our responsibility to arrange the Chinese visas and take care of the group.

Our first stop was Hong Kong and we stayed there for a few days. Charles Wrangham from Standard Charter hosted a lunch for us, and we also met with and had dinner with Arthur Kwok, the architect of the hotel project.

The Chinese are great actors, and when they wanted to impress a foreign group, they would put on a show that could turn anyone's head and bring out human traits (such as greed) that would surface and change someone's total personality. We knew Mr. Yu would organize something very special for our group, but he really outdid himself on this trip.

We were met at the airport with Red Flag limousines. The drivers in these cars ruled the road, as all the top leaders would be driven around in these vehicles. It was a sign of great importance to the average Chinese citizen.

We were whisked to the Beijing Hotel and after everyone was settled, Mr. Yu had arranged for us to visit Tiananmen square, and the Beijing Zoo prior to the banquet that was being held that night.

We all got into the limousines and drove to Tiananmen Square. It's important to note that there is absolutely no public parking anywhere near Tiananmen Square and we usually walked over there from the Beijing Hotel, which was only three or four blocks from the Square.

Much to our surprise, we drove right onto Tiananmen Square. Sheldon and I had been to China many times and had spent hours and hours walking though Tiananmen Square, and had never, ever seen an automobile driven on the Square. Tiananmen Square is very large and can hold over a million people. We drove right up to Chairman Mao's tomb, stopped the limousine, and got out. There were two or three hundred people in line and one of the officials moved to the front and of course, we went in first. Chairman Mao is laid in state in a glass covered cubicle, (he was over six feet tall) and we filed by and looked at the remains of one of the great leaders of the modern world.

When we returned to the limousines there was a heated discussion going on between our driver and a uniformed Chinese. It seems that it was a gross violation to drive on Tiananmen Square. Then Mr. Yu got into the discussion, and it went on for several minutes. Finally, we saw Mr. Yu give the uniformed man some Chinese money.

We asked Mr. Yu what had transpired, and said it certainly was not proper to drive on Tiananmen Square, but because of his guanxi it was acceptable. We asked why then did he give the uniformed guard money? He explained that the man was one of the people in charge of keeping order on the Square and if Mr. Yu did not pay a minuscule fine, the uniformed Chinese would lose face. By charging a fine and having it paid, his face was saved.

We then headed to the Beijing Zoo, which is very large, but certainly not as modern as the Los Angeles Zoo. We arrived at the front entrance and again, Mr. Yu had the gate opened and we drove right in. We were not on any roads, but walking paths, that were almost too small for the limousines. All the professionals we were with were very impressed, but the best was yet to come.

We drove back to the hotel to rest and then we were off to dinner. Mr. Yu had not told us where the banquet would be held, and we were surprised when it turned out to be the newest and most plush Chinese hotel in Beijing. We arrived and were ushered into the grand ball room, and sitting there were various top Chinese leaders, including Mayor Yi Long Ki, who was the former Mayor of Beijing and had been Chairman Mao's secretary on the historic long march.

There were television cameras everywhere, reporters, and red carpets. Mayor Yi Long Ki walked up to Sheldon and me and gave us big bear hugs as did several other Chinese leaders. It was very exciting, and we felt like royalty. The banquet progressed and there were speeches about how respected our company, World China Trade, was in China, how Sheldon and I were old friends of China, and how we were liked and respected by the Chinese governmental officials.

The banquet was the most elegant we had yet attended. There was a lot of toasting and drinking to the success of our new project. The signing ceremony was filmed by several video and still cameras, and we were treated like celebrities. Our guests from the United States thought that our company was the most influential foreign trade company doing business in China and that's when the trouble started.

For the next few days, we toured the potential site for the new friendship store, and the architects discussed design and construction. The Arthur Anderson people talked about potential profits and Bernie from MCA discussed what the entertainment complex would contain and how his company would participate.

Sheldon, from Arthur Anderson, took us aside one evening and said he wanted to have a long talk with us. He said we had struck gold and that we didn't have a real concept as to how rich the vein was. He said he could bring whatever investment we would require, and he wanted to be a part of it. We listened and told him we would consider his proposition. Then Ivan, from Arthur Anderson took us aside and said that he could better whatever Sheldon offered and that he wanted to be part of it.

Then they got into a fierce argument about who should be our partner and how it should be handled. They were working for the same company, but that didn't seem to matter. It was like both of them were different people, their eyes were glazed with greed and power, and they ended up getting into a fist fight in the hallway of the Beijing hotel over this issue.

What no one realized at the time, was the game the Chinese were playing, pitting each one of us against the other. The dream of power was fleeting, and the Chinese gave it and took it away at will.

Everyone was very enthusiastic about the friendship store project and when we all left Beijing and traveled back to Hong Kong, we thought we owned the world.

Then the protests in Tiananmen square happened in April 1989 and everything changed.

CHAPTER 17

Interludes: The Great Wall of China and U.S. Customs

China is a land of contradictions. During our years there, despite becoming ensnared in a tangled web that included the most ruthless of China's security agencies, the FBI, the CIA, and a cast of characters who seem straight out of a Hollywood spy thriller, we were also fortunate to have many special experiences and cherished adventures.

Mr. Yu knew a great many Chinese Governmental officials and did many favors (guanxi) for them. Before he became president of our company, he was put in as manager of Occidental Petroleum when it first opened its office in Beijing, to watch and report back to the Government on its activities in China. He and Ms. Zhang were responsible for all the preparations, dinners, and events when Dr. Hammer came to Beijing. He was welcomed into China, as his reputation was far and wide, about his dealings with the Russians.

One of Mr. Yu's very good friends was Madam Deng Ling, the daughter of Deng Xiao Peng, a Premier of China. Madam Deng Ling had a twelve-year-old son named Maza, and he was friends with Mr. Yu's oldest son, Yishin.

On Sunday, all offices were closed, and Sheldon and I would spend time with Mr. Yu's family, going to dinner at their house and traveling and seeing some of the sights of Beijing. One Sunday he had Madam Deng Ling and Maza over and we all went out for dinner at a local hotel that had an English style restaurant

Madam Deng Ling was a very simply dressed person and you could not tell her from other Chinese of any class. This, you must remember was the Peoples Republic of China. Madam Deng Ling spoke a little English and Mr. Yu was not fluent but certainly could keep up a conversation in English.

When we were seated, Sheldon was having a great time with the kids, who included Mr. Yu's youngest son, YiYu. None of the kids spoke English, but we had flown kites together and we always brought them presents when we came to China. In fact, Sheldon taught them how to use the computer we smuggled in on Dr. Hammer's private jet.

This time Sheldon was showing them his spoon and fork trick. You take a glass and you put the fork with the top end laying down and touching the glass and the fork end up toward you. Then you take the spoon and lay the spoon top under the fork and the spoon surface toward you. Next, you tap the spoon and if you do it properly, it will flip the fork in the air and it will land inside the glass. Unfortunately, it may also land anywhere on the table and sometimes if you hit the spoon hard enough it will land on someone else's table.

The kids loved it and the forks were flying everywhere. Mr. Yu and Madam Deng Ling were giving Sheldon very dirty looks and the kids kept flipping the forks. It was really fun.

Afterwards, Mr. Yu told Sheldon that it was not a proper thing to do in a public restaurant and that he should remember that he was with the daughter and grandson of the most powerful leader in China.

Despite his admonishment, we all had such a good time together we decided that the following Sunday we would take a trip to a section of the Great Wall that was not open to the Chinese. The Great wall is

Interludes: The Great Wall of China and U.S. Customs

about two hours from Beijing, and we traveled in a van with Madam Deng Ling, Mr. and Mrs. Yu and the kids, plus the former head of the Beijing Ministry of Public Security, his wife and older children who were in their late teens.

We first stopped at a small village that was one of the new industrial areas where we were hosted at a lunch by the mayor, and his retinue. Since we were with such honored guests, we were wined and dined and the mayor and several of his colleagues decided to come with us. By the time we arrived at this portion of the Great Wall we had two vans and about sixteen people.

The Great Wall of China is about three to four stories high and wide enough to have a team of eight horses running side by side on the top. It stretches over 3500 miles and runs on the top of the mountains. It's hard to imagine how it was built, how the materials were taken up to the tops of the mountains, where the labor came from and how many Chinese must be buried up on top of those mountains who labored to build it. It was originally constructed to keep out the Mongol hordes.

There are no elevators, so you have to climb to the top. They had just constructed steps in this portion, so we all climbed to the top, which took a while. The kids, of course, were way ahead of us. Since Yishin and Maza were the same age and poor Yi Yu was younger, they left him out of their play and went along without him.

It was quite spectacular when we arrived at the top. There were many places where workmen were restoring parts of the wall. Once on the top, the wall did not necessarily continue on a level ground. It went up and down and followed the contours of the mountains. We walked at least two miles and were awed by this wonder of our world.

Refreshments were brought up by the mayor's people and he invited us to come back to his village and have a dinner, accompanied by entertainment, by a local group of the Peking Opera. After walking the wall for about three hours, Mr. Yu decided we should go down and head back to the village. We rounded everyone up, but somehow nine-year-old Yi Yu was nowhere to be found. Mr. Yu asked the two twelve-year-olds where the younger boy was, and they both looked at him, with an innocent look that tells you they are hiding something. They said they had no idea where he was.

We all fanned out and started to call to him. Mr. Yu was getting very angry. Madam Deng Ling was at the bottom of the wall with Mr. Yu's wife waiting for us and we were going to be late for the dinner that was being prepared in our honor. We were somewhere on top of the Great wall in a very remote spot and we just could not find him. Finally, Mr. Yu said let's all go down. He had a very knowing look on his face, as he glared at the two twelve-year-old boys. We tried to talk Mr. Yu out of going down because we were afraid that something must have happened to him. He could have fallen off, there are no guard rails and this portion of the wall needed repair. There were holes and broken pieces of stone and sheer drops.

Mr. Yu said, "Let's Go down," in a very authoritative voice. It was a long way down, through paths and stairs that were not finished. It took at least 45 minutes, and it was growing dark. When we finally got down to the bottom, there was little Yi Yu standing with his mother and he shouted out that the two boys were mean to him and chased him down. The two twelve-year-old boys ran to their mothers and Mr. Yu had blood in his eye. He was really angry.

He started to go toward the boys, and his fists were clenched. Mr. Yu had been through the cultural revolution and had seen and done things, that we as foreigners, living in the United States could never conceive. He was a very tough individual, and one that as one of the Americans we brought to China once remarked, "I would never want him as an enemy".

As he started toward the boys, Madam Deng Ling stepped in front of him and said in a very quiet voice, "Please leave the children alone, they are just boys. "He stopped immediately, unclenched his fists, and just stood there. Madam Deng Ling had a short conversation with all three boys, and they came forward with their heads bowed and formerly apologized to Mr. Yu and then to all of us for their behavior. They said they were ashamed of themselves and promised we would have no further trouble from them.

We all got into the vans and went off the village for our dinner. It was wonderful with local vegetables and a delicious fish we could not identify. We drank wine, Moutai, tea, and beer. The kids were really enjoying themselves and every once in a while, Mr. Yu would give them very stern looks. Once, just after he looked away, they made a funny face at him. Kids will be kids, which is one of the wondrous parts of our world.

The local Chinese opera we saw, was with children between the ages of eight and twelve. The music part of it was hard for us, as it has a screeching type of sound, but if you can understand the story line, it's very interesting. The costumes are elaborate and unique, and the makeup is just incredible. They portray not only people but dragons and snakes and an endless variety of other creatures. The stories are like soap operas and there is a great deal of emotion. We really enjoyed ourselves.

We arrived back in Beijing about 10:00 pm and Mr. Yu told us that he was going to the house of the former Minister of Public Security of Beijing, the very nice gentlemen that accompanied us to the Great Wall. We asked him why and he said they were going to play Mahjong. I told them I played Mahjong and asked if I could join them. They said of course and we went over to his house. It was behind closed gates, and you could tell nothing from the outside. It was a very special house with three floors, and several bedrooms, and it was obvious that he was a very important person.

Chinese Mahjong is a bit different then US Mahjong, but I fit right in, and we played for two hours. It was very unusual, because we were later told we were the first foreigners ever invited into the house.

We had several outings with Madam Deng Ling and also Li Pung, who at that time was the Coal Minister and then became President of China. Mr. Yu's associates were not from the liberal side.

* * * * *

Our custom incidents in China always involved Mr. Yu and were somehow resolved by his guanxi. Interestingly though, in the fifty-seven times over nine years that we came back to the U.S. from the Peoples Republic of China, we were only hassled by U.S. customs agents twice. And it was the second time when we were stopped, that we discovered we had our own form of guanxi.

On our return from our first trip to China, we were on United Airlines and our flight stopped in Hawaii. Since it was the first US stop, we were required to go through US customs, prior to our departure to Los Angeles.

Not knowing if this would be our only trip to China, we had brought several suitcases, much more then we needed, to bring souvenirs and gifts home for everyone. We were loaded with stuff, and it was difficult to fill out the duty certificate that must be presented to customs, outlining what you have purchased and the amounts.

Usually, customs officials randomly pick out people to examine as there is never enough time to deal with everyone, and we were selected. They examined everything, took apart everything, asked questions regarding everything and kept us for more than one and a half hours. It was very exacting and irritating, especially since coming back from Asia you lose twelve hours or so.

Finally, they let us gather our stuff and we passed through and got the plane back to the Los Angeles. After that experience we were always very leery and nervous going through customs.

Fortunately, until the incident in Vancouver many trips later, we were never hassled again. We would come through customs, they would look at our passports, check our names with some papers they always seemed to have, and just moved us on through, regardless of what we were carrying or how much luggage we had.

We started flying Cathay Pacific Airlines to China. It was a great airline, and the service was always incredible. We would purchase business class tickets to Beijing. United would fly us on business class to Vancouver and Cathay Pacific would upgrade us at no charge to first class from Vancouver to Hong Kong and then business Class to Beijing.

In those days, clothes and many other items were much cheaper in Hong Kong then in the United States. Hong Kong is one big shopping center, and we took advantage of that fact.

On this particular trip, I decided I wanted a fur coat. There was a Chinese fur shop very close to the Beijing Hotel. I picked out what looked like Chinese ocelot. When we told the shop keeper we heard it might be on the endangered species list, she said she was not aware of it and we would have no problem bringing it into the United States. I loved the coat, and the price was less than a wool coat in the United States.

Interludes: The Great Wall of China and U.S. Customs

We brought it to Hong Kong and settled into our hotel room for the night. About 2:00 am we woke up to a very strange odor. We searched and found that the odor was coming from the coat. We actually had to hang the coat outside the window, because the odor was so pungent. The next day it really stunk, so we took it to a local Hong Kong furrier, he remarked "Pretty smelly." He offered to trade the coat for what he said was a Siberian wolf coat, and we accepted the offer. Actually, we always joked that it was probably a German Shepherd. I also purchased a very pretty pearl ring for my mother and Sheldon bought an Omega watch.

We stayed in Hong Kong for about a week. The new coat didn't smell, and the owner of the shop told us that this type of coat was duty free.

On our flight back, our last stop before home was Vancouver. US customs has a unit in Vancouver that checks US citizens on the way through to the United States. We had been back and forth so many times, that customs was easy for us and this was a very small customs station. In our rush to fill out the customs form, we did not declare anything. I was wearing the wolf coat and the pearl ring was in the pocket of the coat. Sheldon was wearing his new watch. Most of the people went through and somehow, they stopped us.

They asked us if we had anything to declare and we said we did not. They then asked where the coat was purchased. I told them Hong Kong, and we were told there was no duty on the coat. They asked to see the coat and discovered the ring in the pocket. Yes, I fibbed and told them it was an old piece and that we had brought it to Hong Kong for repair. They flatly told us that they did not believe our story and we were in a great deal of trouble. Then they noticed Sheldon's watch and as the saying goes, the shit hit the fan.

All of a sudden there were five or six customs officers. They even had us take off our clothes and told us that they were going to confiscate everything and charge us triple duty. By that time, they were even inspecting the seams of our luggage. Everything was scattered around, and we were being questioned intensely.

Meanwhile our flight to Los Angeles was close to boarding. When we complained, they said that missing the plane would only be a small inconvenience compared to what we were up against.

I was very upset and arguing with the Customs agents, and at one point they told me if I did not calm down, they would put me in a room and restrain me. We felt certain that we were in lots of difficulty, and we were very concerned about the outcome.

They finally took Sheldon's wallet and pulled everything out of it to examine the contents. While searching through his business cards, they noticed that we had an office in Beijing and started to ask questions regarding our business ventures.

One of the customs officials took the business card and went into an inner office. He came back followed by the senior agent in charge. He asked us several questions and then said he would be back after he made some phone calls.

Meanwhile the search through our belongings continued, with questions on almost every article we had, and more threats about what was going to happen to us.

At last, the senior agent came back and called all the other agents into a corner and spoke to them for about ten minutes. He then came over to us and with a very strange look on his face, told us that we must hurry to catch our flight to Los Angeles. All the customs agents then started to repack our luggage and belongings and were very gracious. In record time we had everything back together. When we asked how much we owed, the senior agent said nothing, and that we should hurry and not miss our flight.

When we got on the airplane, Sheldon and I wondered who he had called and what had transpired to give us complete clearance. We were never bothered again. Customs would just look us up in a book and pass us right through.

That was when we realized that we had attained our own form of "guanxi."

CHAPTER 18

Mr. Yu's Other Businesses

"He that once deceives is ever suspected."
~Chinese Proverb

After the Tiananmen Square Incident, things changed dramatically in Beijing China. The Chinese maintained that what had transpired in Tiananmen Square was an insurrection and that they tried for days to find peaceful means to end the demonstration, but to no avail. For the safety of the city and the Government, the Chinese maintained that they used as little force as possible to curb the insurrection.

Not long after the incident in the square, we returned to Beijing. Mr. Yu had wired us before we left, saying that he had decided to move our offices out of the Beijing Hotel. Naturally, he had not consulted us. The People's Republic Army (PRA) had recently built a new hotel, The

Capital Hotel, according to the telex, and he had managed to rent us a modest suite of offices in the new development.

Sheldon and I were disappointed because we had come to feel comfortable and at home at the Beijing Hotel, even though we'd had only three small rooms there. The place had a unique ambiance and an interesting history, and we would miss it. Mr. Yu claimed that the Beijing Hotel had raised its rates, and the new offices were much cheaper than the old. We were just starting construction of our development and strapped for cash, so we were thankful for the savings and expected our new headquarters to be very modest. But we had mixed feelings about it.

By now, we didn't trust Mr. Yu at all and we never knew exactly what he was up to. He made decisions unilaterally and seldom explained the reasons. We knew he had considerable guanxi, which he usually wielded for his personal benefit rather than our own. We never knew if the joint venture or some other phantom business was the focus of his attention.

The language barrier was a constant problem. Mr. Yu would conduct transactions right under our noses, speaking Chinese, and we never knew what he was saying or to whom. We had suspected for quite a while that he was using joint venture funds for his own purposes, but we could not prove it. We were paying his wages, but he really was an employee in name only. We sent his salary to the state ministry, and in the end, he worked for himself.

Our new offices turned out to be quite different than we expected. They were located on the top floor of the hotel in a corner suite and were far from spartan. They were at least four times bigger than our old offices and much more luxurious. Mr. Yu had ensconced himself in a large private office behind a huge mahogany desk and a new leather executive chair that was obviously not made in China.

The scale of his furnishings made him look like a dwarf. There was a large oil painting of himself hanging on the wall behind the desk. The room read like a Freudian satire. Every object was an oversized icon of power. How could a culture so sophisticated, so adept at reading every nuance, produce a man with taste this crass? Mr. Yu's office only reinforced our suspicions. Something was going on.

Mr. Yu's Other Businesses

Ms. Zhang, who had served as Mr. Yu's assistant and as office translator, was in the United States. We had arranged for her to enter a special MBA program at the University of Southern California. We had become close to her, knew her parents and treated her like family. She spoke and wrote English expertly, but with a distinct accent. Mr. Yu had hired her replacement while we were gone. Her name was Jingua, but she preferred to go by the English name, Jennie.

Jennie spoke in perfect English, and in fact if she was not in China, you would think she was an overseas Chinese born and educated in the United States. I questioned her as to where she learned to speak English so well and she told me in school in Beijing. She then told me she had never been out of China. We later found out that Jennie attended a special Chinese spy school.

There were all new people in the office including a young man Mr. Xue. He was very pleasant, but still distant. When we questioned them about the comings and goings of the office activity, they would always give us vague answers and said we should talk to Mr. Yu.

There was a door to a small room near the entry way of the office. We asked Jennie what was in the room and why it was locked. She said she did not know, and they did not have the key. Just then we heard a sound from the locked room that sounded like a fax coming in. Sheldon called out to Mr. Yu and asked, "What's in that room? I hear a fax." He put his ear to the door and said, "Sheldon I don't hear a thing."

Later that day, I witnessed Jennie going to a safe in the office and taking out a large amount of FEC (Foreign Exchange Certificates), putting them in a large paper envelope and leaving the office for at least two hours. We were there two or three weeks, and I witnessed the same type of thing several times. It was obvious Jennie and Mr. Yu were involved in some type of payoffs.

Sheldon had become friendly with Denny Barnes at the U.S. Embassy. He had the title of Commercial Attaché but as we subsequently discovered, he was in fact with the CIA. Sheldon decided to pay him a visit. He was not aware that Mr. Yu had moved offices. He introduced Sheldon to a State Department official, Ford Hart, Jr., who asked if he could come visit the new offices. Sheldon arranged a lunch date with and when he arrived at our office he introduced him to Mr. Yu, who was very gracious. We had noticed that Mr. Yu was now growing the nail on his right small finger over an inch long, which was the custom of the old Chinese mandarins. Ford Hart had noticed it also, and we thought it was very curious.

Ford was very curious about Mr. Yu and his associates in the Ministry of Public Security. He told us that this was the most unusual Sino/Chinese business arrangement of which he was aware. Then he pointblank asked if we were involved in the buying and selling of armaments. We told him that we had no knowledge of the armament business, expect for the fact that at one point in the beginning of our relationship, Mr. Yu asked if we knew anyone in Washington. He said he had strong relations with the Ministry involved in the manufacturer of weapons, and if we were interested. We told him straight out that we and our investors had absolutely no interest in that type of business.

We noticed that most of the activity in the office seemed to have nothing to do with World China Trade business, but since it was conducted in Chinese, we couldn't figure out what was going on. When we went to look at documents, we would find them turned over and all the drawers in all the desks were locked. Mr. Yu seemed to make sure that we were never in his office alone and he kept nothing on the top of his desk, all in drawers and bookcases that were locked up tight.

We realized before long that the married Mr. Yu had taken up a personal relationship with Jennie, similar to the one he had with Ms. Zhang. We began to get friendly with Mr. Xue, and every time we asked him something he would get a sheepish look on his face and not answer.

When we asked Jennie about the Tiananmen Square incident, she gave us the party line. It was not the fault of the Government, and the government was now being much more liberal with the students, and everything was roses. Mr. Xue told us a whole different story. He said the recriminations against the students who had participated were very tough and he himself had friends who were jailed and sent away. He said we should be very careful, as Sino/China relations were very tense, and he intimated that Jennie reported back to secret government intelligence sources.

Mr. Yu's Other Businesses

Sheldon directly asked Mr. Yu if he was conducting any other business. He said he was not, and he was living up to our agreement. It was very frustrating for us because it was so obvious what was going on. Jennie was always watching us and when we would pick up a letter, or document from a desk, she would run over and grab it, before we could see it, and make some excuse.

Late one day, we were in the lobby of the hotel, and we met Mr. Xue who was leaving for the day. He was looking for us and said he had left a paper on his desk, in the edge of the ink blotter with the address of a wonderful restaurant, and on our way back up to the office we should retrieve it and enjoy ourselves.

We immediately went back up to the office. I went over to his desk and started looking for the address of the restaurant. I found no piece of paper but hidden under the edge of the ink blotter was a single key. We looked at the key and wondered. Then Sheldon took the key and put it in the keyhole of the top drawer of the desk. In the drawer were a variety of things, including a Sino/American flag pin in a small box, with the lid opened. Sheldon took it and underneath was another key, with a small piece of paper on the bottom of the box, with one word—FAX.

The puzzle was getting very interesting, and we took the key and tried it in Mr. Yu's door, Jennie's desk, and finally the door to the locked room. Bingo! We opened the door and sure enough there was a new fax machine and a large, locked cabinet filled with folders and papers.

The fax machine had several faxes and when we read them, we were shocked. We had suspected that Mr. Yu was carrying on private business, but never to the extent that we discovered. Sheldon looked at the fax machine (electronic equipment always interested him) and thought about the one-word message—FAX. Curiosity got the better of him and he started to look at all sides and then picked it up and looked underneath. There was a plate that was screwed into the bottom and it looked like someone had opened it, because there were scratch marks. For some reason he decided to unscrew the plate. Sheldon always carried a small tool kit with him in China, since he was always fixing things. And that's where he found three keys taped underneath the plate. One was for the locked cabinet in the room, one was for the door to Mr. Yu's office, and one was for the locked cabinet in Mr. Yu's office.

Even though we were in the office after hours, we realized that the monitors on the floor would call Mr. Yu and he might show up at any time. We discovered documents that proved not only did Mr. Yu create a new company that was doing business, but his partner was also one of our investors, who was a director of our company. We also found business cards, indicating that Mr. Yu was now an agent for the Chinese elevator company that we had purchased the elevators from for our hotel project and he was getting a commission on that sale.

The most damning documentation was that Dr. Hammer's OXY employees, directors of our company, were conducting an oil and gas business without the knowledge of OXY and Dr. Hammer. We also found two documents written in Chinese, that we later found out had to do with weapons.

I rushed to the copy machine, and started copying all the documents we found, which numbered more than fifty. While I was copying, Sheldon decided that he would give Mr. Yu a hard time with the fax machine. He set the fax machine on a setting that would disable it, realizing that if it didn't work, Mr. Yu might ask him to fix it, since he knew Sheldon was a technical guy. Then of course he would have to fess up about the fax.

True to our suspicions, we had just finished copying all the documents, when Mr. Yu showed up at the office. It was after 10:00 pm and we asked him why he had come back so late. He countered by asking what we were doing in the office at such a late hour. Sheldon told him he needed to use the computer to write a letter and I came along to keep him company. Mr. Yu's excuse was that he had forgotten a small piece of work, that he had to accomplish before tomorrow. He walked into his office and closed the door.

We went back to our room paranoid as to what to do with the documents. We knew without a doubt that our room was bugged, and we did not know if we had left any traces of our copying the documents. We were really upset. It was our office, we were paying the expenses, and we had to sneak around and copy documents in the middle of the night. We taped the large manila envelope under one of the drawers in the dresser and went to sleep.

The next day we returned to our office and throughout the day we could see that Mr. Yu and Jennie were in a state of anxiety. I even saw him go into the locked room, when he thought I had left the office. Nothing was said. Then someone we did not know, came into the office, and we later found out that he had tried to repair the fax machine, but could not.

The next day Mr. Yu called Sheldon into his office and in a very friendly way, told said he had taken his advice and purchased a fax machine. Sheldon replied that he had never suggested that he get a fax machine, he thought heard one in the locked room. Mr. Yu explained that he had gotten the key to the small room and had the fax machine installed, but unfortunately there was a problem, and the fax was not operating properly.

He asked Sheldon if he could try and fix the problem. It was hard for Sheldon not to laugh, but with a solemn face, he said he would do what he could. I watched Sheldon walk into the small room and sort of glance at the fax machine, while I tried to keep a straight face. Then he went back to Mr. Yu and told him he thought it was a serious problem and he should consider replacing it. Mr. Yu looked at him with a sickly sort of smile and told him that this was China and replacements were not available. Sheldon said he realized that, but at the moment it was his only suggestion. He asked Sheldon. to try again. After a day of delay and letting Mr. Yu sweat it out, Sheldon decided to reset the fax machine much to Mr. Yu's relief.

We were nervous about our safety this entire trip, concerned that the documents we had copied from Mr. Yu's office would be discovered, and the consequences could be dire indeed. We breathed a sigh of relief when we landed back in LA with the documents in hand.

CHAPTER 19

The Plot Thickens

"Fidelity, Bravery, and Integrity"
~FBI Motto

We had just returned home from Beijing and one of the first things Sheldon did was to check his messages. He was surprised to see one from a Mr. Robert Messemer, Special Agent from the FBI. Sheldon called his office and was told that he was not available and would return his call as soon as possible. We wondered why he was calling, but we were not overly concerned. We had much more pressing matters to deal with, namely what the documents we had brought back to LA uncovered about Mr. Yu's businesses.

Mr. Messemer returned Sheldon's call the same day and said that he must see Sheldon alone, immediately, to discuss an extremely critical matter of national security to our country. We were now very concerned. We assumed that our joint venture partner, The Ministry of Public Security, was deeply involved in Chinese politics, but we had always made it very clear that we were only interested in our business relationship and that politics was something we never discussed or got involved with.

I dropped Sheldon off at a local Westwood restaurant to meet Agent Messemer and when I picked him up a short while later, he looked ashen.

When Sheldon arrived at the restaurant, Agent Messemer was already there. At six foot six he was a very imposing presence. They sat down and the agent immediately informed him that the FBI had Mr. Yu and Ms. Zhang under surveillance for several years. They had determined that Mr. Yu was a Chinese spy working for the Ministry of Public Security and that our hotel joint venture was being used as a front for military espionage in the United States. He also informed Sheldon that we were "up to our eyeballs" in this intrigue. It was the FBI's contention that funds were being diverted from the joint venture to pay for this clandestine operation. He told Sheldon he should be very careful because the Chinese would not hesitate a moment, as he bluntly put it, "to spill your blood" on the streets of Los Angeles.

FBI Agent Messemer then informed Sheldon that he was going to speak individually to me and our attorney, who was a principal in World China Trade, to determine just what our involvement was and how, if at all, we were connected to the alleged espionage conspiracy. By then Sheldon had lost his appetite completely, and he left the restaurant with FBI agent Messemer telling him that he would be contacted again shortly and to keep this conversation in strictest confidence.

After Sheldon finished the story, I was flabbergasted. How in the world could we have gotten ourselves into this situation? After talking about it further, we decided that we would take an aggressive approach and not be interviewed individually. Sheldon called FBI Agent Messemer and asked to arrange a meeting to include all of us – Sheldon and me, our attorney partner Joe Brightman, and Marty an independent legal counsel representing us. Sheldon made it clear that we would not separately meet to discuss any aspects of the joint venture, or its participants.

We all met for lunch, and FBI Agent Messemer brought an additional agent along with him from the Federal offices in West Los Angeles. He reiterated what he had told Sheldon. We explained to him that although we were partners in the joint venture with the Ministry of Public Security, we had absolutely no knowledge of any doings other than the business of the joint venture. We then provided him with the documents we had discovered in Mr. Yu's office. After examining them, he told us that these were indeed valuable to his investigation and cautioned us not to disclose this meeting to anyone.

It reminded us of a conversation we had a few years back with Mr. Yu in our office in Beijing, where we voiced our concern about being involved with the Ministry of Public Security as American citizens. Mr. Yu said we didn't have anything to worry about and we could always live in China if any political problems arose. We realized at that moment that our relationship would always be on a strictly business and no political basis. Now, here we were years later, and the meaning of Mr. Yu's comments were coming to light.

We assured Agent Messemer that we would cooperate with him, but we were concerned about the joint venture and our investment in China. Mr. Messemer assured us that it was not the FBI's intention to create any havoc with the joint venture, however their intention was to prosecute, if possible, the individuals involved in the alleged espionage.

From that moment on and until our interest in the joint venture was sold back to the Chinese Government, we cooperated and worked with U.S. government intelligence agencies in several different respects.

CHAPTER 20

The Chinese and Israeli Ambassadors

"A well begun is half done."
~Chinese Proverb

It was very tense returning to Beijing and continuing to work with Mr. Yu. At one point during the construction of the hotel, Sheldon became friends with the Chinese Ambassador to the United States, Ma Yu Zen, and on this trip, he introduced us to the Minister of Culture, who arranged a visit to Tianjin that was a welcomed relief. Ambassador Ma was later to play an important role, with our assistance, in forging a relationship between China and Israel.

This trip was not too long after the Tiananmen Square incident that was televised to a shocked world, and the Chinese were looking for ways to improve their image. Ambassador Ma suggested that we meet with Ying Ru Chen, who at that time was the Minister of Culture for the Peoples Republic of China. Mr. Chen was an actor, who played

Willie Loman in *the Death of a Salesman* in China and played the Warden in *The Last Emperor*.

The meeting took place in The Forbidden City which reminded us of *The Last Emperor*, and we felt like we had traveled back into the past. Ying Ru Chen was very gracious and spoke excellent English. After we were served tea, he explained that Ambassador Ma told him we were friends of China and could assist in a creating a better image, by dealing with the children of China and the local people.

He wanted us to visit Tianjin, the largest seaport in Northern China, to meet with their Minister of Culture. From Beijing, it is about a three-hour trip by train, and he had arranged for one of his assistants to take us to the train and provide us with tickets. We thanked him and he thanked us.

The next morning, we were picked up by his assistant, who unfortunately spoke little English, and we were taken to the Beijing Train Station. During a normal day there can be as many as 300,000 people in the station at one time, and foreigners need to have a guide in the station. The assistant escorted us to a local train, and we of course were the only foreigners aboard. When we stopped at a small-town crossing, several people were purchasing rice and vegetables wrapped in lotus leaves, from a vendor that was cooking it right beside the train. We bought some too and it was delicious.

When we arrived in Tianjin we were met by the Minister of Culture, his secretary, and his driver. It's interesting to note that the people of Tianjin are very tall and it's not unusual to see many people over six feet. Our first stop was of course a restaurant. In China the normal greeting that people give each other is not "how are you" but "have you eaten lately." We were told the restaurant was very famous for its dumplings, called Chaozhou. Joining us were three additional people, who were either friends or part of the Ministry of Culture of Tianjin.

The Chaozhou started coming to the table and we thought it would never stop. It's a dumpling similar to Kreplach which are Jewish dumplings. Each one is filled with something different, from meat, to poultry, vegetables, fish, and other things that would probably make your stomach queasy. There must have been thirty different types and of dumplings and it would be insulting not to try each one.

And of course, along with the food they served Moutai and wine. Everyone would down a shot glass of Moutai while shouting ganbei which is the Chinese equivalent of the Jewish toast, La Chaim. It was by far the most memorable meal we had in China. We also noticed there were security people attending the meal, who were quiet, and observing.

After the lunch our retinue had grown to over ten people and two vehicles. We traveled through the very crowded streets of Tianjin, which reportedly has ten million bicycles, and arrived at a local family adult center. In China, all communities have centers for adults, teenagers, and small children. These centers are not free, but the costs are minimal. We were introduced to the director of the center, who gave us a tour. It was old and in U.S. terms dilapidated, but it had a movie theater with a small projector and some seats, snooker tables, and several project rooms, where adults could sit and do creative things. We spent about forty-five minutes there and then we were off again. By this time, there were three vehicles and about fifteen people in our retinue.

Our next stop was the teenage center, where there was a roller-skating rink, basketball, baseball and other activities. The teenagers were interesting as several were wearing sunglasses, which was their way of being a bit different. There was a lot of excitement as we were honored guests, and the teenagers had a brief performance for us tumbling and skating.

We then were off to the small children's center and our caravan was growing by leaps and bounds. On the way there, we made a stop. It seems there was a musical recital of six- to eight-year-olds and we were invited. The recital was held in a building that had a dirt floor and I am sure most of the children and their parents had never seen a quailo before (the Chinese word for foreigners which means round eyed white barbarians). I took one of the children in the audience and sat her on my lap. She was very nervous, but many pictures were taken. As a side note, we were told that there were more teenagers in China then people in the United States.

By this time, we were really overwhelmed, and as had happened so often, we were not quite sure what the Chinese agenda really was for us in Tianjin. The Chinese are very clever, and their purposes have long range results, that most of the time are not evident in the present. The next stop at the children's center was a treat. There were about fifty to sixty little children, and in one instance we were sitting on the floor with the kids all around us jumping around and touching us with wonder.

When we left, there were now five vehicles and many people and as the caravan passed though the city thousands of people were looking at us. The next stop was very strange, and to this day I cannot understand the purpose, except maybe to expose us to a high official in an unofficial surrounding.

We stopped at a large apartment complex. These apartment complexes are several stories, with elevators, but the elevators only stop at every third floor. This saves construction costs, and it is expected that people can walk up and down two flights of stairs. The apartments are very small, and the walls are all concrete. Most have no refrigeration, and no hot water. There is a drain, where they heat the water in the kitchen and then use it to wash over the drain. The kitchen is a small area that has just two gas burners, no oven. The apartments are about 600 square feet at the most, but they are considered luxury.

The people who live in these apartment units come from living in houses that are more like huts, that are hundreds of years old. The only heat is peat that they buy in the streets, and the only water is a cold-water spigot that is in the central courtyard outside. Toilet facilities are not worth mentioning here.

Our entourage had expanded to over twenty people and we all entered the apartment of what we were told was a retired army general who had cancer. He was most gracious, and the apartment was filled with fish tanks, in every room. It was the largest variety of fish I had ever seen outside of a public aquarium. It was very interesting, but Sheldon and I could not figure out what we were doing there. Most of the people we were with did not speak English.

We finally left and the next and last stop was also in an apartment complex. It was much smaller and with so many people we were all crowded in, much like China is everywhere. This was the home of

Mud Family Zhang. This family had for centuries created mud sculptures. The technique was handed down from father to son and their sculptures were incredible. They were not sold but were exhibited in museums and had been in the hands of the emperors and such royalty throughout the past.

We always talked about our family, and at that time, our niece was undergoing surgery for her back deformity and Sheldon told all the people present, the story. The ten-year-old son of the father, who was just learning the craft, showed us Snow White's seven dwarfs, which he had made over a period of time. Then, much to our surprise, they gave us a gift of one of the dwarfs and the father presented us with a statue of an old Chinese judge. We told them that these priceless gifts were too much, and we were not able to take them. But they insisted. While we were there, we had our niece call and thank them for the gift of the dwarf, and since there was only one phone for the entire complex it was quite an experience.

Somehow, we got to the last train in time to return to Beijing but ended up in a train station that was not the one we had left from. We were concerned because it was an area that we were not familiar with, at the southern outskirts of Beijing, and of course no one spoke English, another Chinese test. We wandered around for a bit and of course before long, someone tapped Sheldon on the shoulder and there was an English-speaking person who was sent to pick us up.

It was a wonderful day, and we told many people of our adventure, but we are not at all sure what the visit was about, and if it had any impact on changing the image of China after Tiananmen Square.

* * * * *

Sheldon's friendship with Ambassador Ma Yu Zen ultimately led to a very gratifying relationship with China and Israel, that we did have an impact on.

From the very beginning of traveling to China, Sheldon never hesitated to tell everyone that we are Jewish, and that our heritage and history was as long or longer than the Chinese. In Beijing, we met several Jewish people who had lived in China for many years. The most interesting was Israel Epstein, a Polish-born Chinese journalist and author. He was one of the few foreign-born Chinese citizens of non-Chinese origin to become a member of the Communist Party of China. He had lived in China for sixty-five years and had been a personal friend of Chairman Mao.

During one of our trips home, Sheldon received a call from Ambassador Ma Yu Zhen who was Los Angeles. He invited Sheldon to lunch at the Chinese Consul located near downtown Los Angeles. He was a very important man in the Chinese political circles and Sheldon was honored to be invited to lunch.

When he arrived at the Chinese Consul, he was ushered into a private dining room, where he was greeted by the Ambassador and the Vice Consul. They were served an elegant lunch and the Ambassador asked how our joint venture was proceeding, and he said the Chinese Government was very interested in a positive outcome. He told Sheldon that we were very respected in China and had attained a foreign status called lau pengyou (old friends). This status was a high honor for a foreigner.

After lunch we moved into a small conference room, with soft couches and Chinese antiques and were served tea. Ambassador Ma then told Sheldon that the conversation they were about to have would be confidential and that it was very important. He explained that he was speaking in an unofficial capacity. China and Israel did not have diplomatic relations however, the Chinese Government was very interested in forging a relationship that would have mutual benefit. He asked Sheldon for his help in starting the relationship.

Sheldon told him he was very interested in helping because he thought there was a great similarity between the Chinese and the Jews, and that he would speak to me, and we would come up with a plan. He also suggested that a good start in opening up lines of communications would be for him to arrange with the Israeli Ambassador for a Chinese representative to come to Tel Aviv and an Israeli representative to come to Beijing.

Sheldon and I decided that an unofficial dinner at our house between Ambassador Ma and his wife and some prominent Jewish leaders would be a good beginning. We called our friend Harvey

Schacter who was the head of the local office of the Anti-Defamation League (ADL), and he suggested that we bring the head of the ADL and some other prominent Jewish leaders to the dinner.

I arranged a typical Jewish dinner, with chicken matzo ball soup, roast chicken, egg bread, and kishke. The people from the ADL questioned Ambassador Ma repeatedly about the human rights issues in China and Ambassador Ma, being somewhat of a smooth politician, answered the question in a soft manner. The dinner went very well, and it was the beginning of several dinners, unofficial of course, between Ambassador Ma and the Jewish community.

Then one day Sheldon received a call from the Ambassador inviting him to lunch at the Chinese Consul again. He told Sheldon he had arranged with the Israeli Ambassador to have the Chinese open a tourist office in Tel Aviv and the Israelis would open a science office in Beijing. He thanked Sheldon for his suggestion and help, and said it was still unofficial but the first step toward relations. He suggested that on our return to Beijing we should meet with the Minister of Foreign affairs for North Africa, whose area encompassed Israel. The Minister was a friend of his and he would arrange the meeting.

Sheldon went to visit the Israeli consul in Los Angeles and met with the Vice consul and asked him for the address in Beijing where the Israeli office was being opened and the name of the representative. He told the Vice Consul he would visit the office, meet the representative and try to open some doors for him in Beijing. The Vice Consul replied that he was not aware of any relations between Israel and China and had no knowledge of any Israel office opening in Beijing. Sheldon suggested that he meet the Vice Consul from the Chinese Embassy in an informal way, and he arranged a lunch in Chinatown with the three of them.

The lunch went very well, and when the Israeli Vice Consul asked the Chinese Vice consul if he was aware of the Chinese opening an office in Tel Aviv, he said he was not, but that it certainly sounded like a good idea. Sheldon was certain both Vice consuls knew of the arrangement, but it was not politically correct to admit it at this time.

Sheldon asked the Israeli Vice Consul if he would communicate with the proper officials in Israel and tell him where the office was in Beijing. He sent several communications, and they all came back, saying that they had no knowledge of any office. He then called Ambassador Ma and asked him where the Israeli office was in Beijing, and he said that unofficially it was already opened, but he did not know the location.

When we returned to Beijing the next month, Sheldon told Mr. Yu that he wanted to meet with the Minister of Foreign affairs for North Africa. He wanted to know why, and if it pertained to our business, and not politics. Sheldon explained to him that our being in China was more than just doing business, and that the more relationships you make the more opportunity will come.

The next day Mr. Yu arranged the meeting with the Minister. The Ministry of Foreign affairs was a huge complex with gates in the front and a guard. His driver waited for him. He was escorted into a typical Chinese conference room with couches, and antiques. They sat side by side and the Minister told Sheldon that China would like to have diplomatic relations with Israel, but that they also had friends in several of the Arab countries, who had embassies in Beijing and diplomatic relations with China.

He said China wanted to have relations with all countries and not get involved in the internal politics of each country. A relationship with Israel was very important for China, because the Chinese could learn many things from the Israelis and the Israelis could learn many things from the Chinese. China and the Jews have had thousands of years of history between them, and there were Jews in the court of Kubla Kahn. In his opinion, the thinking processes between the two peoples were very similar.

Sheldon asked if he was aware of the Israeli office in Beijing. He replied that had heard something about it and was pleased as it was a good step forward. When Sheldon asked for the address, he said he had no idea where it was located. Sheldon thanked him for his time, and gave him a personal letter Ambassador Ma had given to him for the Minister.

He was very frustrated and told Ms. Zhang that everyone was telling him there was an Israeli office in Beijing, but somehow no one knew where it was, and he wanted her to find it. Her response was if the Minister of Foreign Affairs didn't know where, how was she to find out. Sheldon patiently explained that he knew she could find the office, because of her Guanxi and her ability. She laughed and in fifteen minutes Sheldon had the address of the Israeli office in Beijing. It was located in the Jing Gua hotel, which was where the JAL office and other foreign offices were located.

Sheldon walked up to the front desk and asked where the Israeli office was, and the Chinese Clerk said they had no Israeli office in the hotel. He wandered back to the ground floor where the offices were located and found a closed door with no markings. He opened the door and saw an Israeli calendar on the wall. There was a Chinese sitting at a small reception desk, and he asked him if this was the Israeli science office. He said he was assigned here by the Government. When Sheldon asked who was in charge and he said an Israeli gentlemen named Yoel Guillat. Sheldon asked to meet him, and within moments Mr. Guillat came out of the office and greeted him warmly. The office had been open for a month and Sheldon was the first visitor.

The Chinese had opened a tourist office in Tel Aviv and staffed it with five Chinese, but he was the only person sent from Israel. He brought a gift for the Chinese, a software program, that converted Pin Yin (Chinese into English and vice versa.) His goal was to meet with as many Chinese as he could, but he was having a problem, because all his attempts were rebuffed with a polite no. He asked Sheldon for some assistance. That night Sheldon and I had dinner with our new friend Yoel and we really enjoyed ourselves.

The next day, Sheldon asked Mr. Yu for some assistance in inviting some of his friends in the different Ministries to meet with Mr. Guillat. Mr. Yu said he could ask, but that none of the Ministers or other officials would meet with the Israeli, because the office was just an experiment and if it went badly for whatever reason, they would not want the visit on their record.

Sheldon then asked Ms. Zhang to come with him to try and convince some of them to visit the office or at least invite Mr. Guillat to visit them. Everyone was very polite and said they understood, but they all refused. Mr. Guillat was very disappointed but continued doing what he could. Sheldon finally convinced his friend who was one of the officials at the Ministry that had to do with high tech and computers. He had been trained at a school in London and was interested in the software that had been brought by the Israelis.

Sheldon arranged to have lunch together in one of the dining rooms at the Jing Gua hotel. His friend was very nervous that he could be criticized for going to this lunch, but his interest exceeded his fear. Mr. Guillat gifted his Chinese friend with a software product that had been designed in Israel and that could automatically fix hard disk errors in a DOS based system. This was a valuable tool for any person that dealt with PCs. Then they decided to visit the Beijing Computer economic zone.

The computer zone consists of five street blocks, lined on both sides of the street with nothing but computer stores. When they arrived, trucks were pulling in and out filled with American and Japanese computers and products. They discussed the future of computer products and computers and spent most of the day together. Sheldon's Chinese friend was very impressed, and Sheldon asked him for his assistance in getting other Chinese officials to visit Mr. Guillat, so that the process of the relationship between Israel and China could move forward. He said it would be difficult, but he would do his best.

A few years later when we finished our final negotiation and sold back our interest in the hotel project to the Chinese, we were invited to the Israeli Consul in Beijing. By then, China and Israel had diplomatic relations and we attended a party with a multitude of Israelis, including several members of the Israeli Parliament. We were happy to have played a role in establishing those relationships.

The ox moves slow, but the Earth is patient. We were beginning to understand that.

CHAPTER 21

Interlude: The Silk Road to Couture

"The silkworms die when the spring silkworms die, and the wax torch turns into ashes and tears begin to dry."

~Li Shangyin, poet Tang Dynasty

While the hotel was being constructed, I had the time to focus on other opportunities in China that were far less stressful and much more enjoyable. Since our early days there, I had been interested in China's silk industry, and had visited several silk factories, including the episode with the "ugly Americans," the two brothers from Los Angeles who were in the garment industry. China's woven silk goes back thousands of centuries and was the fabric of choice for Chinese and Roman emperors. Silk was also what linked the Western world to China. The Silk Road was the ancient trade route starting with the Roman Empire and China. For centuries, China dominated the silk industry, until the early twentieth century when Japan became the world's top silk producer. However, by the mid-1990s China once again resumed dominance as the world's largest producer of silk.

What I discovered after visiting many silk factories in China, was that their technology was still behind the Japanese, and because they were not able to weave silk in a 52- or 60-inch width, couture designers were not able to use Chinese silk, even though it was beautifully woven. I approached the Silk Ministry and told them I could help to get equipment that would retrofit the factories to produce silk fabrics in a wider width, which would open up China's silk manufacturing to more markets. They were very open to this idea, and by the time the hotel was built, several factories were able to produce the wider widths of silk. Now we had to get the word out to couture designers.

That's when I had the idea to approach *Vogue* magazine, the top women's fashion magazine, to support us. Through a friend of a friend, I was introduced to Alexandra Shulman who was the editor-in-chief of *British Vogue* at that time. I told her about my idea to showcase new silk designs and the fashion that was going to come out of China. Alexandra, who was from England and Hong Kong loved the idea. The Ministry of Silk was very excited too.

Vogue had seven magazines around the globe that published in different languages. We asked the editor or of each magazine to select two designers to come to China. We would take them to the silk factories that we had now remodeled, so they could come up with designs created from the woven silk. Once the designs were completed, I knew we needed a memorable way to present them and introduce China silk to the world's fashion elite.

It was now 1990 and the hotel was open. Holding the event there would showcase the hotel and the China silk fashions. I happened to remember when Queen Elizabeth II visited China and Hong in the fall of 1986 to acknowledge the Sino-British pack to return Hong Kong to China in 1997, that she had given a speech in Hong Kong to talk about all the years they had been a part of England. She gave the speech on the waterfront on a beautiful pavilion float that had been built for her.

I talked to the head of the silk ministry, and he contacted Hong Kong, and lo and behold, they agreed to send the pavilion to our hotel. We set it up in the front of the hotel, where the circular driveway entry was, and that's where we did our fashion show. It was a spectacular event, and was covered by all of Vogue's magazines, as well as by fashion reporters from every corner of the world.

Today of course, almost everything you put on your body is made in China. Whenever I see something made of China silk, I smile with great pleasure.

CHAPTER 22

Mr. Wang's Nefarious Businesses

*"Tension is who you think you should be.
Relaxation is who you are."*

~Chinese Proverb

It was the spring of 1990 and the hotel project, now the Asia Hotel, had been opened for about ten months but the construction, which was not fully complete, was nearing forty million dollars. The intrigue and tensions with our partners were rising, and now we trusted no one in China. We were constantly getting telexes and phone calls from Mr. Yu telling us that the Chinese side Mr. Wang (BLIPU) was concerned because the hotel was not making any money and there were payments due to Standard Chartered Asia for the construction financing, among many other debts.

Mr. Wang had called an emergency board meeting. With trepidation, Sheldon, Joe and I traveled to Beijing. We were told this was going to be a show down and since we had only sketchy information about the finances of the project, we felt ill prepared. But we knew it was necessary for us to attend, because of our fiduciary responsibilities to our investors.

The short-term loans from Chongqing (CHITIC) were long overdue and so were the payments to the Bank of China for the three-million-dollar loan to our joint venture. Mr. Yu informed us that the Bank of China and CHITIC would no longer loan the joint venture any funds. That's what Mr. Yu told us, but he also said that the books and records were being kept by five different entities, World China Trade, BLIPU, the City of Chongqing, the Beijing Branch of the Bank of China and Ramada who was running the hotel. Each set of financial records for the project were different. We could never get a true number on the escalating costs of the project.

Mr. Yu had now moved our offices from the Capital Hotel to the Asia Hotel. Our company, World China Trade, occupied two small offices on the floor that contained snooker tables, a bar and lounge area. Jennie and two other employees were located in one of the offices and Mr. Yu had the other office, which was always locked when he wasn't there. When we asked Jennie for the key, she said only Mr. Yu had it, but from time to time we would catch her unlocking the door to his office and going in. When Jennie left for the day, she would also lock her office, and when we asked for the key, she said there was only one.

The board meeting was held in a closed room on the second floor off the lobby, which had three ballrooms and a restaurant. The room was designed as a board room and had a large conference table that sat twenty people and then chairs and couches around the walls that sat an additional twenty people or so.

At this point, our joint venture was composed of our company, World China Trade which owned 50% of the joint venture for 30 years, the Beijing Ministry of Public Security (the Chinese counterpart of the KGB) which owned 25%, and CHITIC (Chongqing International Trust and Investment Corporation) which was the financial arm of the City of Chongqing, owned the other 25%. Our original joint venture contract was with the Ministry of Light Industry of Beijing, but unbeknown to us the Chinese changed partners in the middle of the joint venture and never informed us of the change.

Sitting at table was the Chairman of the joint venture, Mr. Wang, who the CIA referred to as a Mafia boss, four other directors who were members of the Ministry of Public Security, five directors who were with CHITIC, and Mr. Li who was the chief spokesperson for the group. He was about 70 years old and had traveled with Mao on his 2000-mile march through China.

Our group consisted of Sheldon (Vice Chairman of the joint venture, me as a director, and Mr. Yu, President of World China Trade and the first Chinese citizen given the right to participate in a foreign company, and our and partner Joe. Also present were Mr. Lu, the senior interrupter for the Chinese government (now Manager of American affairs for World China Trade), and Richard Chen, Vice President China operations Occidental Petroleum Corporation. There were also several other people in the room taking copious notes.

The Board meeting lasted four days and it was a circus. All the accountants from all the groups were present, including representatives from the Bank of China. Mr. Wang started the meeting and informed everyone that the hotel project was in dire financial straits and that if we were unable to get additional funding, then the hotel would have to be closed. This of course caused a great deal of agitation among all the board directors, the assorted accountants, and other members attending the board meeting.

The next two days were filled with recriminations, each side blaming the other side, and then the accountants started to argue with each other. Each side had a different set of financial records, and each side argued that their records were correct. There was a large disparity between the different sets of records, and they all blamed Mr. Wang. He of course blamed the City of Chongqing and Mr. Yu, and the Bank of China blamed everyone.

Then Mr. Wang, in his very charismatic way, asked the representatives from the Bank of China to fund the project an additional five million dollars. Mr. Li from the City of Chongqing thought that was a very good idea, and we thought the representative from the Bank of China, who was manager of the Beijing branch, would have a fit of apoplexy. His face got very red and flushed and he started to holler at Mr. Wang, who calmly sat and looked at him, and said since the City of Chongqing had refused any more short-term loans, the Bank of China was the only source left for funding. The representative from the Bank of China then looked at Mr. Li from Chongqing and asked why they would not loan any more money to the joint venture.

The answer went on for a while. Mr. Li never lost his composure. He was with Chairman Mao on the long march and was a very patient man. He explained that they had originally put up the guarantee, and had yet to receive the guarantee fee. They had made a short-term loan of over twenty million dollars to the joint venture and had not received any payment at all. The loans were seriously overdue, and the costs of the project were continuing to escalate, with no end in sight. He stopped short of calling Mr. Wang a thief.

Then the accountants started to really argue and scream and holler at each other. We didn't get much of the translation as things were really getting out of hand when one Chinese accountant got up, jumped over the table and pushed another accountant against the wall and started screaming at him nose to nose. Mr. Wang stopped the board meeting, and we all went out to lunch. Everyone calmed down and lunch as usual was a treat. We were in a private dining room, the food came directly from the kitchen, and it was really excellent.

After lunch we resumed and the fighting and arguing continued. Mr. Wang produced a bank statement showing that we had almost no funds in our joint venture account and that all this arguing and bickering would not solve the problem. We needed cash immediately.

The Board meeting ended for the day with no resolution and Sheldon, Joe and I went back up to our office with Mr. Yu for discussion. Mr. Yu who had his own set of accountants for the joint venture had no explanations, except that he also suspected Mr. Wang of misdoing, but we suspected that explanation was only for our benefit.

Mr. Yu left the hotel for an unknown appointment. Shortly after we received a call from Mr. Xue, who was now an ex-employee whom we met when we had our office at the Capital Hotel, and who helped us find secret documents. He said he understood there was difficulty with the joint venture. He also said that you never know what people would throw away, and that's when we realized he was trying to tell us something. So, Sheldon and I contrived a plan to get Jennie out of the office, so that I could search it.

There was an American movie playing on the TV in the lounge and we knew that Jennie was always very interested in the United States, so Sheldon grabbed her and asked she wanted to go and watch the movie with him. That was my chance. I went into the office and started to look through the desk while Sheldon kept talking to Jennie and telling her about life in the United States. I knew I had to work quickly, and that she might suspect something.

Within twenty minutes I found something very disturbing and went to the lounge and gestured to Sheldon that we had to talk. Jennie went back to the office, and I quietly told Sheldon we had to find Joe because I had something to tell them, but not here in the hotel. We found Joe in his room and through hand gestures motioned him to follow us. Our rooms were always bugged with microphones, and we were concerned about our conversations in the public areas because the Chinese always had spotters who would casually listen. We decided to leave the hotel and go out in the street to talk.

Once we got in the street, I showed them copies of two money transfers amounting to over two million dollars, from our joint venture account into a bank in Toronto, Canada. Most of the documentation was in Chinese, but we were able to make out the number of our joint venture account and the dollar amount, and the words Toronto, Canada.

Our first thought was to fax a copy of the money transfers back to Los Angeles, but on second thought we realized that the fax machine in our office was also bugged. We were very concerned, and apprehensive. We did not know what Mr. Wang would do to us if he found out that we knew about the money transfers, after he had told everyone at the board meeting that the joint venture account was depleted, with no funds, and the same day he transferred over two million dollars out of the country.

I had found the copies of these fund transfers in the wastepaper basket in Jennie's office. That, in itself, was very unusual as money transfers or financial dealings were always taken care of in the accounting office. Why Jennie would be privy to that was a mystery, and why anyone would make copies of the illegal fund transfers and then leave them next to the top of the wastepaper basket was indeed strange.

The Chinese had more than one agenda, and we later found out that there was another strong Chinese faction that was trying to bring Mr. Wang down and using us as the bait and lever to do it.

We had made some friends with a large international public relations firm, Hill and Knowlton, who had offices in Beijing, and we decided to ask their advice and see if they were willing to expose what was going on. We met with them and told them who our joint venture partners were and about the money transfers. The manager of the office got a very panicky look on his face and told us that if he was in our position, he would leave Beijing immediately. He advised and pleaded with us to take his car and driver and go immediately to the airport and do whatever we could to leave China. He said our lives were in danger, we were involved with very dangerous people and that he would have nothing to do with this at all.

We all got very scared but decided that we had to go back to the board meeting, as we could not leave the country even if we wanted to, without permission. We left his office, and went back to the hotel, just as the board meeting had started again. Mr. Wang had copies made of the bank statement, which of course we knew was a phony since it showed no money transfers, and the arguments continued. We thought of asking Mr. Yu about the transfers, but decided against it, as we realized that he was definitely in league with Mr. Wang.

After much thought we agreed that Joe who was leaving the next day, would put a copy of the money transfers in his shoe and when he got back to the United States, he would have the documents translated and then call the bank in Canada for an explanation. Sheldon and I also had copies that we carried with us in our shoes.

The board meeting continued, and the arguing went on for another day. Periodically one group or another would get very upset and walk out of the meeting, returning at a later time. Then Sheldon suggested that we call in the Ramada manager and question him as to the finances of the hotel, since Ramada was managing the property.

There was a lot of discussion, and it was obvious Mr. Wang did not want the Ramada manager reporting to the board.

Sheldon told Mr. Yu that it was very necessary and begrudgingly he agreed, and after more discussion Mr. Wang agreed. We had told the Ramada manager to be prepared with a report just in case he was allowed to join the meeting. His report was much different than Mr. Wang's. His sales figures were much higher, and he did not understand why we had no funds in the joint venture account, since according to him, there should have been a large fund of money available.

Mr. Wang said that it was obvious that the Ramada analysis was incorrect. Interestingly there was not much comment from any of the Chinese. The Ramada manager left the meeting and the arguing started again, almost as if the Ramada manager had never made a report.

Then Mr. Li informed the board that Mr. Shi (his second in command and also a director of the board) had been diagnosed with liver cancer and the doctors believed it was terminal. We had spent much time with Mr. Shi since the beginning of the joint venture and everyone in the room was very sad and concerned. Finally, the Bank of China agreed to lend the joint venture additional funding and the meeting was adjourned. Mr. Shi died about a year later and we were all very sorrowful. He was a good soul.

The accountants all agreed that they would get together and try to compare notes and create a set of books and records that everyone would agree upon. That of course, was never done.

When Joe returned to the United States, he investigated the money transfers and found out that the funds were transferred into an account in Toronto, Canada. The account listed a business owned by Mr. Wang. The business was a real estate company that was purchasing for cash, office buildings and condominiums, and other activities of funds being funneled into other areas, that we had no knowledge of.

Joe turned everything over to FBI Agent Messemer who concluded that these funds were being used for illegal criminal activities including possibly buying nuclear secrets.

CHAPTER 23

Interlude: The Briefcase

At the same tension filled emergency board meeting where Mr. Wang informed the board that the joint venture had no money and more funding was required to complete the hotel construction, Sheldon's briefcase, containing highly confidential and secretive information, disappeared.

There was a great deal of intrigue going on as each joint venture partner had its own agenda. Mr. Yu, being a Chinese Citizen, was walking a tightrope, as he was president of an American corporation and a high-level Chinese citizen. Sheldon was also walking a tightrope as Chairman of an American company doing business in China and also secretly reporting (in a fashion) to US Governmental intelligence agencies.

Sheldon had a slim leather briefcase, which contained several documents, that were supposedly secret from the other partners. It also had correspondence from the American intelligence service, and it was highly confidential. He carried this briefcase with him everywhere, and we were so paranoid, he even put it under the mattress at night.

At one point, he excused himself from the board meeting and went out into the lobby to clear his head, as most of the discussion was in Chinese and we had to deal with our interpreter, which was very difficult to say the least. On each floor of the hotel, there was a desk, manned by hotel employees who not only reported to management, but also to the Ministry of Public Security. Sheldon sat on one of the couches for about ten minutes, and Mr. Yu came out of the board room. They had a heated discussion and then returned to the board room.

A few seconds after they returned, Sheldon realized he had left the briefcase on the couch in the lobby. He rushed out to the lobby and to the couch, and lo and behold, the briefcase was gone. It could not have been more than one or two minutes at the most. He immediately went to the Chinese at the desk and asked where the briefcase was. They motioned that they did not understand English, but of course they did in some fashion. Sheldon gestured with his hands and by now was frantic because he was concerned about the consequences if the Chinese side got hold of that briefcase.

The desk boys just kept denying any knowledge and he finally went back in the board room and told Mr. Yu about the disappearance. Mr. Yu now became very agitated. At the time, China was controlled to some extent by the Ministry of Public Security. Mr. Yu had a family and there was no telling what might have happened to him or his family if the contents of that briefcase were exposed.

Mr. Yu immediately went out with Sheldon to started questioning the desk boys who kept repeating that they had no knowledge of the briefcase and that they saw no one take it. Mr. Yu got very angry and there was a great deal of shouting and threatening. He finally made a call from the desk and in less than ten minutes two very serious looking Chinese showed up and started interrogating the desk boys.

In just a short period of time, all three of the desk boys looked very frightened. One started to cry and then just burst out in a torrent of Chinese. He then pulled up a chair, stood on it and pulled a ceiling tile out, stuck his hand in and as you can well imagine, he pulled out Sheldon's briefcase, wrapped in plastic. Sheldon was relieved but also angry to be treated like that in a hotel that our company owned.

Somehow the story circulated all through Beijing and Sheldon received calls from several news agencies asking for a story. He declined because we did not want to cause any difficulty with our joint venture relationships. The next day a story was circulated by the Chinese officials as follows:

"When Mr. Krechman came and sat down at the couch, the desk boys observed him and were concerned, as he was an honored guest, and a partner in the hotel project. When Mr. Yu came out to join him and they got into a heated discussion, the desk boys were concerned and took a special interest. When Mr. Krechman and Mr. Yu went back to the board meeting, the desk boys noticed immediately that Mr. Krechman left his briefcase on the couch. They instinctively realized that the briefcase must be important, therefore they decided to protect it in a plastic case and put it in a safe place, and the safest place they could think of was in the ceiling. They didn't understand Mr. Krechman when he asked them because they did not speak English. They were trying to protect Mr. Krechman and his briefcase and therefore were entitled to commendation."

The US Embassy and the news agencies just laughed at that version, but in China, one always expects the unexpected. And we were just relieved that the contents of the briefcase had not been exposed.

CHAPTER 24

Mr. Yu, LA, and the FBI

*"It's the oldest question of all George.
Who can spy on the spies?"*

~John le Carré

After our initial meeting with Agent Messemer when he told us of the suspected espionage by Mr. Yu, he and Sheldon had several meetings. We wanted to make sure that we were giving our government all the assistance we could, not to mention that were also very concerned about our own involvement, as we had never dealt with an investigative agency.

Sheldon called his friend Ford Hart Jr., who was now at the White House. We had met him at the U.S. consul in Beijing and were never quite sure what his job was, but we knew that he was involved in the intelligence business. We later discovered that he was part of the White House intelligence agency that reported directly to the President. Sheldon told him of our meetings with Agent Messemer and what had transpired. He said he was unaware of the FBI investigation, but we should cooperate with the FBI, and continue to report to him at the White house on all events concerning Mr. Yu and the FBI.

The very next day, Agent Messemer called Sheldon and asked to meet with him. When Sheldon arrived, he asked if he had spoken to the White House Intelligence agency. When Sheldon confirmed he had, he asked why. Sheldon replied that our group had no secrets, and that for our protection we wanted everyone to know what was happening.

Messemer had a very funny look on his face and his manner was much more subdued than it had been in previous conversations. He told Sheldon that the FBI Director in Washington had called him and asked for all the details after he had received a call directly from the White House regarding this issue.

This put Sheldon on an even footing with Agent Messemer. He said we must have serious friends at a very high level in the White House, and now that the FBI Director in Washington was directly involved, he would be under scrutiny from not only the FBI office in Los Angeles, but the National FBI office in Washington as well. The case had high priority in the FBI agenda, and he considered it to be the most serious case of espionage ever uncovered in the United States. Agent Messemer spoke fairly fluent Chinese and had uncovered another Chinese espionage plot, located in Chicago a few years earlier.

At this time, Mr. Yu was trying to get a visa to come to the United States. There was a quota by the U.S. Government as to how many Chinese Citizens would be allowed into the country. They had to apply at the U.S. consul in Beijing, wait in long lines, have a good reason for their trip, and be prepared to be rejected most of the time.

Every time Mr. Yu wanted to come to the United States, we would write a letter to the U.S. visa bureau in Beijing requesting that Mr. Yu be allowed to enter for a pre-determined length of time for purposes of the business of World China Trade. Mr. Yu also requested on several occasions that we write a letter to the visa bureau for different groups of Chinese who he said were important for our business. Agent Messemer told Sheldon that the visa letters we had written were for many Chinese who were involved in the alleged espionage business.

When Sheldon told Agent Messemer that Mr. Yu wanted us to write another visa letter for him because he was anxious to come to the U.S. to pursue his Green Card application, he said we should just continue along with our business as if nothing had happened.

Sheldon went to the International Terminal at Los Angeles' LAX Airport to wait for Mr. Yu's arrival. You were only allowed to go to a certain point and look down at the ramp where the travelers would come up after going through customs. That's when he caught sight of Mr. Yu and to his disbelief, he was walking up the ramp with Agent Messemer. As they came toward him he was very uncomfortable, but Agent Messemer, without acknowledging Sheldon, said goodbye to Mr. Yu and went on his way. When Sheldon asked Mr. Yu who that was, he said just a fellow traveler he met at customs, that he had never seen before and changed the conversation.

After Sheldon dropped off Mr. Yu at his hotel, he received a call from Agent Messemer, and Sheldon said he was surprised to see him walking with Mr. Yu. He explained that when Mr. Yu was last in the United States, he had interviewed him and he had denied everything. He told Agent Messemer he was just a businessman and had nothing to do with politics.

Agent Messemer then informed Sheldon that there was a 24-hour surveillance on Mr. Yu and that he was being followed wherever went. He gave Sheldon his cell phone number and said to call him as to our whereabouts. He said our safety was of paramount importance and that the FBI would be watching. He was under the impression that we might be in some kind of physical danger. We never thought so. The Chinese were always cordial especially when we had meals together. I have to admit though that Sheldon and I were excited about this kind of double life. Our relationship with Mr. Yu had cooled somewhat and we were not aware of all his meetings when he was here in the United States.

Ms. Zhang by that time was in graduate school at the University of Southern California, a special program called IBEAR, which was an MBA program for non-residents that I had helped her get into.

About a week after Mr. Yu arrived, we had arranged to have dinner at a local Chinese restaurant with Mr. Yu and Ms. Zhang. It's important to note that our relationship with Mr. Yu and Ms. Zhang was very family like. We had spent years together, had hundreds of meals and our whole family knew them and treated them like part of the family.

Mr. Yu, at this point, was very frustrated with Sheldon who had promised to help him obtain his green card, and he accused him of hindering the process. (Sheldon later found out that meant falsifying the application document, which he refused to do.) In fact, on our last trip to Beijing, Mr. Yu had been told that his Green Card was approved and to go to Guangzhou to receive the final documents. When he arrived at the U.S. visa office in Guangzhou, they interrogated him for three hours and then refused to grant him Green Card status.

He flew back to Beijing and accused Sheldon of stopping the process. Sheldon of course denied that he had anything to do with that, but the reality was that he was correct. Sheldon had discussed the issue with Paul Kelly, supposedly a retired secret service agent, and they decided to slow down the process.

Mr. Yu had a weakness which was always causing him problems. He had affairs with his senior office assistant, Ms. Zhang and then Jennie. He of course had a wife, Lily, whom we knew, and she always suspected. He told us not to make any waves. Since Ms. Zhang was now in the United States going to school, Mr. Yu took up with Jennie in the office in Beijing. Ms. Zhang knew what was going on and she was not happy at all.

Mr. Yu had asked us not to mention Jennie's name in front of Ms. Zhang when we met for dinner. But being a pot stirrer, Sheldon causally asked him how Jennie was doing at Ms. Zhang's old job. There was a very strong relationship between Mr. Yu and Ms. Zhang, that went far beyond an affair or a business relationship. We in the United States cannot understand what a person had to do to survive the Cultural Revolution, and these two had met during those times, and through their suffering, a very strong bond was formed.

Ms. Zhang looked at Mr. Yu and casually said that she had heard that Jennie was a spy. He looked at her and went totally crazy. He jumped up in this crowded restaurant and started screaming (very unlike a Chinese), "Spy, spy, spy, it isn't true," and ran out of the restaurant still screaming. Ms. Zhang just sat there calmly, eating her dinner, and smiling. People all around us were staring and at a table next to us, two men in suits and ties, smiled at us and nodded their heads.

Concerned about Mr. Yu, I went out and found him pacing and muttering outside the restaurant. I convinced him to come back in and he did. He gave Ms. Zhang a dark look and she very sweetly looked at him and said, "How is Jennie the spy doing?" He totally flipped out, and we thought he would punch her out, but he just ran out of the restaurant and somehow got a bus back to his hotel.

When we returned home later that night, Sheldon got a call from Agent Messemer, who laughed and said, "It must have been quite a scene in the restaurant." The two men at the other table were FBI.

CHAPTER 25

OXY becomes a Shareholder in World China Trade

"Tough times pass. Tough people last."
~Plaque on Dr. Hammer's desk

After the Tiananmen Square incident, all the bank lines from outside China closed to the Chinese Government and our hotel project, for lack of funding, was moving very slowly. The original budget of twenty-five million dollars was now over sixty million dollars and the Chinese were requesting funds from World China Trade to cover half the deficit.

We kept rejecting those requests. Not only had we invested what all parties had agreed upon into the joint venture, we did not have any additional funds. Our position was that if the Chinese wanted to make the project larger or grander, it was their responsibility to provide the funding. This of course did not sit well with Mr. Wang.

He repeatedly requested more funding and we kept refusing. Then he started to threaten to close down the project. Our response was, "Go ahead." We were in the midst of construction and closing it down was an unlikely scenario, at least we hoped so.

Union Bank in Los Angeles, our equity lender for the project, was getting very nervous. The project was far behind schedule, and the interest on the loan was growing day by day. We had several meetings with the bank, and they threatened to call the loan and take the collateral which we had put up to guarantee the loan. The collateral was a combination of Letters of Credit, CD deposits, and personal guarantees from friends and investors.

Standard Chartered Bank in Hong Kong was also pressuring us because they had already lent the joint venture over twenty-five million dollars, and they got very concerned when Mr. Wang threatened to stop the project.

We met with the bankers in Hong Kong, and they told us that it was our responsibility as joint venture partners to share fifty/fifty in whatever the overruns were at the hotel. Furthermore, they would not lend one more penny to the joint venture and if the payments were not made in a timely basis, they would foreclose. That was an idle threat, because Standard Chartered Asia Bank would never foreclose on a China project, realizing that if they did, there would be no future for them in China. Bankers always threaten, but we took it seriously.

We went back to Beijing and met with Mr. Wang and told him that the banks were frozen, and he could expect no more funds from outside China, including any funds from World China Trade. After much negotiation, sitting in a room for ten hours where there were twelve people, nine of whom were chain smoking Chinese cigarettes (the smoke was so thick, you could hardly see across the table), Mr. Wang told us that it was possible to arrange a series of short-term loans, inside China. But he warned that these short-term loans would have to be paid back on the date that they were due or there would be dire consequences.

OXY BECOMES A SHAREHOLDER IN WORLD CHINA TRADE

Of course, Mr. Wang said as long as the Chinese side would be financing the balance of the construction, then World China Trade would have to give up some future rights in exchange for the Chinese shouldering the financing load. We argued about this point for a long while and finally agreed to give the Chinese side some small advantage when, and if, profits came from the project.

We called a board meeting and Mr. Li and his group came down from Chongqing to attend. The purpose of the meeting was to determine where the joint venture would get the funds to complete the project. As far as Mr. Wang was concerned, the purpose of the meeting was to get the City of Chongqing to agree to loan these short-term funds. Mr. Li was very upset and started the meeting off by asking Mr. Wang why the guaranteed fee of one hundred thousand dollars was still not paid to CHITIC. The hotel was in the middle of construction, the fee should have been paid prior to the start of construction, and he demanded payment.

Mr. Wang in his inimitable way, started a dialog that lasted hours. He went through the whole history of the joint venture, and somehow never got to the point. Of course, we only heard what was interpreted for us, so the true meaning might not be what we were told. This went on for about three days, and then Mr. Wang told the officials from Chongqing that the joint venture needed more funds to complete the project. The Hong Kong Bank had refused any additional funding and World China Trade had refused to put in any more funds. If the City of Chongqing didn't lend the joint venture more money, the hotel project would be stopped.

Mr. Li got very red in the face and started shouting at Mr. Wang. He said that Mr. Wang had suckered him into putting up the whole Chinese side of the investment, even though Chongqing only had a twenty-five percent share in the project. They had also put up a twenty-five-million-dollar guarantee and had not even received their guaranteed fee. And to make matters worse, the project was fifty percent over budget. And now Mr. Wang wanted the City of Chongqing to loan more money to the joint venture?

Mr. Wang, in his very political way, just kept on talking and as a last resort the city of Chongqing started funding more money to the project. The loans were to be paid back in 60 days, 90 days, and 120 days. As far as we know, they were never paid back.

Meanwhile Union Bank in Los Angeles, started pressing us to either sell the joint venture back to the Chinese or come up with the money that was owed them. The Chinese, seeing an advantage, offered to purchase our share, but since the joint venture was not complete, the amount was minuscule and all the investors would have lost most, if not all of their money.

The stock in World China Trade, was held in the following manner. Sheldon and I owned thirty-three percent. Mr. Yu, Richard Chen, and Dean Lee, each had twelve percent. Dean worked for Richard and Mr. Yu worked for Dean when he was manager of the Oxy office in Beijing. The rest of the stock was in the hands of our investors, which totaled about twenty different people.

At that time, Occidental Petroleum Corporation had no legal interest in the joint venture. The only connection as far as the public was concerned, was that their two top China employees, Richard Chen and Dean Lee, were stockholders. The Chinese on the other hand, came to the conclusion that Occidental Petroleum was a partner, and that was the way that Richard Chen and Dean Lee acted toward the Chinese officials when they came to Beijing.

Union Bank finally got their lawyers involved and made a formal demand for payment. We owed them 3.75 million dollars plus accrued interest of several hundred thousand dollars. The demands started to come on a frequent basis. We had our own legal counsel involved and things looked very bleak. It was like being on a Ping Pong table, both sides at us all the time. We were constantly writing telexes, arguing with Mr. Wang, and fielding telephone calls from our investors who were upset, to say the least.

The hotel project was more than a year overdue, the original budget was a joke, and we were already past forty-five million dollars and climbing. Our investors were very upset after Tiananmen Square, and the banks were ready to grab all the collateral and put us out of business.

On a Monday morning we received a call from Richard Chen, who said he wanted to meet with us immediately. He came over to our house and after we had some tea, he told us that Dr. Hammer had made him an offer he could not refuse, for his stock in World China Trade. The Oxy lawyers were drawing up the papers and they wanted the transaction to be completed within a few days.

The next day we were contacted by Ray Gill, the in-house lawyer for Occidental Petroleum, requesting a meeting. Ray told us that OXY was willing to purchase our shares also. The price he quoted was much too low and we realized that it was just a legal gesture.

Within four days, Occidental Petroleum Corporation was a twenty-four percent owner of the stock in World China Trade. Ray Gill and Jack Dorgan (Chief Financial Officer for Occidental Petroleum) were now on our Board of Directors, replacing Richard Chen and Dean Lee.

The next day, we received a written offer from Occidental Petroleum Corporation, to purchase all the shares in World China Trade at a price that would pay off Union Bank and return to the investors their original investment with no profit. It was an open offer to be taken at any time, with no time limit.

The OXY lawyers sent a copy of this offer to Union Bank, informing them that they now owned a significant share of World China Trade. Union Bank stopped their demands immediately and left us alone to deal with the Chinese.

Once OXY became a shareholder, everything became much more formal. We had several meetings with Jack Dorgan and Ray Gill, and of course our secret meetings with Dr. Hammer.

The construction continued and the Chinese side stopped their demands for funding from us. The intrigue continued, but that of course is part of the story.

* * * * *

Except for Richard Chen, the OXY people were much more formal with the Chinese. The rapport that we had thought we had established with our Chinese partners changed considerably at the joint venture board meetings, now that two OXY executives were present.

OXY was having severe difficulties in their coal joint venture in Shanxi Province and Dr. Hammer realized that dealing with the Chinese was very different then dealing with the Russians.

Our first board meeting in Beijing with the OXY executives present, was very tense and Jack Dorgan and Ray Gill asked many pointed questions as to Mr. Wang's activities regarding the joint venture. It was obvious that Mr. Wang was irritated but did his best not to show it. He realized that with Occidental Petroleum involved, he was dealing with a multi-national corporation, with influence that reached to the highest levels of both the Chinese and U.S. governments.

The hotel construction was nearing completion, the overruns were horrendous, and the graft was obvious. Sheldon and I, Richard Chen, Mr. Yu, Jack Dorgan, and Ray Gil, decided prior to the first board meeting we were all attending in Beijing, to tour the construction site. Mr. Dorgan asked about the three-story energy center that was constructed by the joint venture on the backside of the hotel property. We were told originally that the energy center was necessary because the hotel would have to have its own source of power, and not depend on the city of Beijing to provide it. The electrical power produced by the Beijing City Authority was very erratic, and there were always dark hours in some part of the city.

I had always questioned the size of the energy plant and the cost of constructing it. The Chinese engineers consistently said it was necessary. After we toured the project, I decided to visit the relevant city authority that dealt with plans and specifications of all the new construction in Beijing.

Through an interpreter, I made friends with a woman who was one of the Beijing City Clerks, and with my knowledge of architecture, design, and construction, I went through all the plans and specifications. One of the things I discovered was that the energy plant was not only supplying electrical energy to our hotel project, but to twenty other new apartment buildings and Mr. Wang's personal office building that was under construction. The joint venture had paid for the construction of the energy center and was also paying for the maintenance, upkeep, and all expenses, including payroll.

Our directors from Occidental Petroleum were not at all pleased when they heard this information along with a multitude of other actions and misdoings that came to light about Mr. Wang's and Mr. Yu's activities with the joint venture. Finally, the OXY people requested

OXY becomes a Shareholder in World China Trade

that the next board of directors meeting be held in Los Angeles, not in Beijing. Because of their concerns, they wanted to bring to light several issues with the Chinese.

At first, Mr. Wang refused to have the board meeting in the United States. He said this was a China project, and all business that had to do with the project should be held in Beijing, China. We argued that point and told Mr. Yu and Mr. Wang that we had traveled to Beijing for eight board meetings. We always had to pay for our own airfare and hotel accommodations, and it was time that Mr. Wang and the Chinese came to America.

Mr. Wang finally agreed and of course the joint venture had to pay for all the expenses. Mr. Li and the Chinese directors from Chongqing also came. We arranged for them to stay at a hotel in Westwood close to the OXY offices and Dr. Hammer graciously offered to have the board meeting in the OXY board room, which was on the sixteenth floor of the OXY building and the same floor that Dr. Hammer's office was located.

We took the whole Chinese contingency to Las Vegas for a visit, and then returned to Los Angeles for the board meeting. It was a pleasant time in Las Vegas, and we of course had to play tour guide, which was always our role with the Chinese outside of the PRC.

When we returned from Las Vegas, the Chinese contingency, which consisted of fifteen people, asked me to take them shopping. They complained to me that when they had traveled to New York and had asked to go shopping they were taken to Fifth Avenue and all the upscale trendy shops. When the large U.S. corporations invited mainland Chinese to the United States, they would always treat them to the finest restaurants and the best shops.

The Chinese would always be polite, but what they wanted was a local Chinese restaurant and a department store where they could purchase items for their families at reasonable prices. I started taking the Chinese to a local Montgomery Ward Department store in a mixed ethnic neighborhood and they all enjoyed it. Every time I would host a group of Chinese, they would always ask to go that store. First, we would all have an ice cream cone in the Thrifty Drug Store and then we would go to Montgomery Ward. The Chinese would purchase a variety of clothes and small appliances and would always be very grateful to me.

Just prior to the board meeting at the OXY offices, Sheldon and I had a meeting with Dr. Hammer at his house. We had related to him all the facts about what was going on with the joint venture and he was clearly not pleased. He told us that whatever transpired at the board meeting, to be very calm.

The meeting lasted three days. The board room was spectacular. On the hallway walls just outside the room were some of Dr. Hammer's priceless art collection. The boardroom itself was very large, with high tech electronics and a vast conference table that could comfortably sit thirty to forty people. We decided that we would give the Chairman's seat that was reserved for Dr. Hammer to Mr. Wang, as he was the Chairman of the joint venture.

The American side sat on one side of the table and the Chinese contingency sat on the other side, so we were facing each other. Sheldon and I sat on Mr. Wang's immediate right, and Mr. Yu sat on Mr. Wang's immediate left.

Aside from the normal board of directors, there were two attorneys from the OXY office who also joined the board meeting. Dr. Hammer made a brief visit and said that he hoped the meeting would go smoothly and the project would be a success.

The OXY building was designated as a no smoking hi-rise office building and it was up to me to tell the Chinese contingency, since almost every one of them were chain smokers. I went to Mr. Wang and explained to him the smoking situation and told him that because OXY wanted everyone to feel comfortable, they had designated a room on the same floor as the boardroom, where the Chinese could go and smoke if they wanted.

Mr. Wang said that this was very inconvenient and that he and the others would not be comfortable sitting in a board meeting and not smoking. I explained to him that not only was "no smoking in public places" a law in the state of California, but that Dr. Hammer had graciously allowed us to use his personal board of directors' room and that no one ever smoked in there. If he did smoke, it would be very insulting and discourteous and would reflect badly on the Chinese Government. Mr. Wang just looked at me and walked away.

Mr. Wang started the board meeting and within a few minutes, after the prior board minutes were read, the meeting became very argumentative. There was a lot of blaming each side for the overruns, the obvious corruption (which of course was never admitted to), the amount of money we owed on the short-term loans we borrowed, and the ongoing manipulation of the joint venture for the Chinese benefit by Mr. Wang, and several other issues that needed explanation and closure.

Two times Mr. Wang stormed out of the room in anger, and I expect frustration. At first the Chinese would leave the room and go to the designated smoking room and then return. They kept this up for the first day. By the second day of the board meeting there was obviously enmity between the Chinese side and OXY. It appeared that we had been somewhat naïve in our dealings with Mr. Wang and the OXY lawyers were dealing with those issues in a very stern corporate way. Since Sheldon was the Chairman of our company, World China Trade, it was his responsibility to bring those issues up at this meeting and then the OXY lawyers would jump in.

Every morning at the start of the board meeting, waiters would bring in carts of fresh fruit, rolls, sweet rolls, and a large variety of breakfast items. These would be replaced during the day with other foods. All this was served on a special bone China that Dr. Hammer had ordered from China. It was very elegant, unlike the rest of the meeting. If looks were daggers, by the end of the second day we all would have been dead. It was by far the most difficult board of directors meeting we every had up to that point.

Dr. Hammer came to the meeting at the end of the second day and spoke to everyone about Sino American relations. He said that the future of China depends on the foreign companies that want to do business with China and share the modern technology, so that China could grow and become a major player in the world community. He also told the Chinese that he appreciated their not smoking in the board room, as he realized from his many trips to the PRC that the Chinese love to smoke, and that it's difficult for them not to have that freedom.

Things had not improved by the third day and were rapidly deteriorating. Mr. Wang accused the OXY people of being obstructionists, and not understanding the Chinese, and causing trouble. The OXY people based their conversation on facts that Sheldon and I had uncovered and proceeded to push for explanations, in a very stern, direct, and rigorous way.

At one point in the meeting Mr. Wang looked at everyone, took out a cigarette, lit it up and started to smoke away. I was a bit stunned, and the OXY people got very red in the face. One of them said in a very polite way that if Mr. Wang wanted to smoke, they would agree to pause the meeting while he went out to the smoking room. Mr. Wang just looked at them and continued to smoke, while dropping the ashes on one of the bone China plates in front of him.

Mr. Dorgan got up and said he would leave the meeting if Mr. Wang continued to smoke. Mr. Wang smiled at him and crushed out his cigarette on the bone China plate. He then casually lit up another cigarette and continued to smoke. I thought there would be a physical showdown, but Mr. Dorgan sat back down, and the meeting ended shortly after that.

As we filed out of the board room, Mr. Wang came over to Mr. Dorgan and the OXY attorneys, and with a smirk on his face asked Mr. Dorgan and the OXY employees, if they would join him for dinner at a local Chinese restaurant. One of the OXY attorneys looked at Mr. Wang, and with a very straight face, said they could not accept Mr. Wang's offer as they had a much more pleasant evening planned—they were going to have their fingernails pulled out with pliers. With that statement, they all turned around and walked out. Mr. Yu asked Sheldon and me to join Mr. Wang and the group for dinner, but we refused.

It was a bad ending to our board meeting.

CHAPTER 26

The Beijing Asia Hotel is Open

"Elegant and Graceful."
~Beijing Asia Hotel brochure

B y the time the Beijing Asia Hotel was finally completed in 1990, after years of intrigue, nefarious activities, and the stress of doing business in China, it seemed almost anti-climactic. But our adventure was far from over.

The Asia Hotel, which is still thriving in Beijing, is a golden palace that soars several stories high. At the time it was built, it boasted many amenities like a spa and health club which were not common at the time. It had 300 tastefully furnished rooms, each with a comfortable work area, and luxury suites as well. The executive floors included a reception center, business center, small meeting rooms, a reading room and a lounge area. Office space was also available. There were several restaurants and a state-of-the-art conference center that could accommodate a thousand people.

Before the hotel opened, we started looking for a hotel management group that could run the hotel. Our board had interviewed the Sheraton hotel chain, Holiday Inn, the Furama Hong Kong Chain, the Nikko Hotel chain, and several other hotel companies. We decided that an American hotel chain was the best for the joint venture, and Ramada was selected.

Ramada had a worldwide network reservation service, the expertise to manage a modern hotel, and they understood how to deal with foreign tourists. They were a protection for World China Trade as they would report to the joint venture on all aspects of the hotel operation and there would be no secrets. They would handle all the money and we would get an honest count. At that time, the Chinese had little or no knowledge of the operation of a modern tourist hotel.

The terms of the Ramada contract with our joint venture were much more liberal than any of the other hotel chains we interviewed. The Ramada management in their offices in Hong Kong were all Chinese including the General manager of the whole Asian territory. They came to Beijing several times to make presentations and finally agreed on a fee structure that was thirty to forty percent less than any of the other competing hotel management companies that we interviewed. It was Ramada's second hotel management contract in China, the first being in Southern China, near Guangzhou. We signed a five-year contract with them.

Ramada had brought in two or three managers for our approval prior the opening of the hotel and we had all decided on an Austrian who had years of experience in several hotel chains and was married to a woman from Thailand. He had a lot of experience in Asia and his manner was acceptable to the board. The joint venture had also financed a large group of young Chinese and sent them to the first hotel school opened in Beijing for training.

Ramada was very concerned that they would be allowed only ten expatriate personnel, as the hotel would employ over two hundred people that Ramada would be responsible for the day-to-day management of the hotel. The Chinese were adamant about that fact and would not bend. Several of the other hotel companies we interviewed, requested at least thirty to forty expatriate personnel, and said they would not even consider managing the hotel without proper management in place. Ramada was very anxious to have this management contract and they reluctantly agreed. And since the General Manager of the Asian area was Chinese, Mr. Wang was comfortable.

Unfortunately, the Chinese General Manager of the Asian area was not so comfortable. Hong Kong Chinese were always concerned when they traveled into mainland China, because they knew that if the PRC wanted, they could detain them and there would be little or no recourse.

There was a case of a Hong Kong Chinese who traveled back and forth from Hong Kong to Mainland China. His relatives lived in Guangzhou, and he found out that the Guangzhou authorities had a long dossier on him and because he was a Hong Kong Chinese, it was not very positive. On one trip as he was leaving Guangzhou, he was stopped at the airport and detained for about two weeks. His airline ticket from CAAC airlines had his name spelled incorrectly, misplacing only one character. When they detained him, their reason was that he had a forged ticket, with the wrong name. He later found out that they had purposely misspelled his name, so that they could detain him in the future.

Our hotel had three sets of offices. One was the Ramada management office, the second was Mr. Wang's office, that was set up to monitor the activities of the Ramada management, and the third was the Chinese office. That office was set up to deal with all the local Chinese, since in fact they worked and were paid for by the Chinese Government, and the hotel joint venture paid the Government bureau for the services of the employees.

Ramada was hemmed in, and their activities were watched and questioned all the time. The Austrian manager could hardly purchase a fountain pen, without the permission of Mr. Wang. He would constantly complain to us because he was apprehensive about dealing directly with Mr. Wang. There were always Ministry of Public Security agents around the hotel, and the Ramada offices were bugged with microphones.

The Ramada manager did the best job he could under the circumstances but got little help from his boss in Hong Kong. He was also fearful of Mr. Wang and almost never traveled into China, with the exception of when we had the grand opening of the hotel.

Ramada management did as good a job as they could with all the restrictions placed upon them by Mr. Wang. But as time passed, Mr. Wang began talking about how ineffective the Ramada management was and that we could save money by having the Chinese manage the hotel themselves. This was their plan from the start, but it was easier said than done, because we wanted Ramada to continue the management for several reasons.

We had only recently discovered that the rooms on the top floor of the hotel, were not being rented out. Every time we questioned as to why, we received a variety of answers, like, the air conditioning was not working on that floor, or the heat was inoperative. When we walked the floor, all the rooms were locked and when we asked for the keys, we were told they could not be found, but they would look for them. We were able to view into the room through the key holes and found them filled with air conditioners, refrigerators, mattresses, television sets, and other items. The Chinese side had purchased the items with joint venture funds and were selling and keeping all the profits for themselves.

When we questioned Mr. Yu, he denied any knowledge and said he would investigate and if this was true, he would talk to Mr. Wang and straighten out the problem. Of course, this was nonsense as Mr. Yu was part of the whole process and was receiving part of the profit from all these nefarious activities.

Ramada managed the hotel for about a year and a half, and we constantly argued with Mr. Wang about eliminating them. At each board of directors meeting the issue would come up and Mr. Wang would have a long list of complaints. We would try and counter those complaints expressing the positive aspects of the Ramada management.

We also explained many times that part of the Standard Chartered loan construction agreement expressly said that the joint venture must have a foreign experienced hotel management company, and if we made the change that Mr. Wang kept requesting it would be a violation of our loan agreement and the bank could theoretically call the loan.

Mr. Wang said that Standard Chartered Bank would never call the loan. We countered that Mr. Wang was not giving Ramada fair chance and that he could not just break their contract. Mr. Wang's position was that this was Beijing, China and that he was part of the most powerful agency in the country, and he could do anything he wanted. It was said in a much more subtle way, but that was the gist of what he meant.

Our manager was in a constant turmoil, not knowing from day to day what embarrassment or difficulty he might encounter. He repeatedly spoke to the Ramada Hong Kong office about his problems and was told that he in essence would have to solve them himself.

Ramada management in Hong Kong invited Mr. Wang and our group to come to Hong Kong and stay at the Ramada Renaissance for a visit. This was a new plush four-star hotel, and we were given suites and wined and dined for three days. Mr. Wang was honored and received several gifts from Ramada and graciously accepted them all. He even told the Ramada Hong Kong management that he was satisfied with the Ramada management and as he was in the middle of developing a new hotel in Hainan Island, he would give them the opportunity to manage that also.

When we returned to Beijing, he reverted back to his insistence that we eliminate Ramada from the management. The Ramada manager of our hotel invited his mother-in-law to come visit he and his wife and two children in Beijing. She was with the family for about three weeks and then decided to go back to Thailand.

When you enter China, you are required to fill out an identity card. This card gathers information regarding who you are, your passport and county and other pertinent information. These cards are either collected at the airport or the hotel you stay in. The cards are then sent to a division of the Ministry of Public Security and filed.

The manager's mother-in-law and his wife had both filled out these cards when they entered China and assumed they were filed with the Ministry of Public Security. His mother-in-law had been scheduled to leave the following morning and they were having tea in one of the restaurants in the hotel.

Two Public Security people walked up to them and politely asked them if they had filled out identity cards when they arrived in China. It was a ludicrous statement, because the Chinese would not allow anyone in the country without filling out the identity cards.

Both ladies said that they had indeed filled out the identity cards. They were told by the security people that their cards must have been misplaced, because they could not be located. They requested that the two women fill out new cards, so they could have them on file. The women agreed. They filled them out at the table and gave them to the Public Security people. They looked at the cards and then told the two women they were under arrest and to come with them immediately.

They took them away in a van and brought them to the Ministry of Public Security and put them in a locked room. The room had couches and they were served tea to make them as comfortable as they could under the circumstances. Meanwhile, the manager went looking for his wife and mother-in-law and was told by the manager of the restaurant that they had been taken away by the Public Security officials.

The poor man got frantic and ran to see Mr. Wang to ask what happened. Mr. Wang told him that he did not know what was going on, but he would try and find out. Two or three hours went by. The manager was beside himself and called his boss in the Ramada office in Hong Kong and told him that he wanted him to come to Beijing immediately to help him with his wife and mother-in-law. He refused, and said under these circumstances he would not enter the PRC, because he was fearful they would not let him out of China.

When we heard what happened, we went to Mr. Yu and told his that this was an intolerable situation, and he had to immediately find out what was going on. He went to see Mr. Wang and came back about half an hour later and said that since the wife and the mother-in-law filled out new identify cards, it was an emission that they never filled out identity cards when they entered the country, and therefore had violated Chinese Law and were being held for prosecution.

We were furious and told Mr. Yu that was ludicrous, and that anyone with any sense would see right through this obvious attempt to extort the Ramada manager. He told me there was nothing he could do about it, as they had violated Chinese law.

The Ramada manager got in touch with an international law firm with offices in Beijing and we all met for a conference. The Ramada manager's wife and mother-in-law had been held in the Ministry of Public Security overnight. They were treated very well and respectful but were not allowed to leave. After a lengthy conversation with the lawyer and the manager, the lawyer finally said the Chinese could do whatever they wanted, and there was very little anyone could do about it.

We then met with Mr. Wang and several other directors of the joint venture. We told them we knew that Mr. Wang was part of the Ministry of Public security and that we were convinced he set this whole thing up to intimidate the manager. We told them that this was a foreign joint venture, the hotel was for foreign guests and if this is the way foreigners would be treated, the hotel would be a failure. Sheldon actually said, "This is not Nazi Germany, and you can't treat people like this."

Mr. Wang said he had once been part of Ministry of Public security, but no longer was, but that it was obvious that the two women had violated Chinese law and there was nothing he could do about it. We told him we did not believe that, and we knew he was pulling those strings and that he should immediately have those women released. He asked if he could do something, would we be more amenable to discuss a change in management. We told him we would not make any decisions based on extortion.

The manager, meanwhile, told Mr. Wang that if he could help, he would resign his position as manager, and leave the country. Mr. Wang said he would do what he could. Two hours later the women were released. The next day the manager, his wife, mother-in-law and the children left China.

CHAPTER 27

Mr. Wang Comes to LA

"Be careful who you call your friends."

~Al Capone

Mr. Yu's phantom business, as we would eventually confirm, included arms trading, petroleum deals, kickbacks from suppliers to the joint venture and most likely other illegal activities. Mr. Yu became the subject of much interest on the part of U.S. authorities, both in China and the United States. After we had first met with Special FBI Agent Messemer, we continued to have a relationship with him, as he and the FBI were investigating Mr. Yu and Ms. Zhang and the investigation was on going. However, it was Mr. Wang, who really captured the attention of U.S. law enforcement.

Mr. Wang's long-standing relationship with the Chinese espionage community was of considerable concern to the FBI, who believed he was using World China Trade as a front for illegal activities in North America, including buying nuclear secrets. The LA office was responsible for monitoring U.S. security interests for the Pacific Rim, including China. Messemer spoke fluent Mandarin and had an in-depth understanding of Chinese espionage and criminal activities in the U.S. He referred to Mr. Wang as a "Mafia boss" and was very interested in getting him to visit the U.S. He repeatedly asked if we could arrange for Mr. Wang to come to Los Angeles. Mr. Wang was no doubt aware of the FBI's interest in him, and he steadfastly refused every invitation.

One day Mr. Yu called us at home from Beijing and said that Mr. Wang and some of his associates were in Toronto, Canada. We suggested that since he had come so far, he ought to fly down to LA and visit. It would provide an opportunity for us to discuss some of the current problems with our joint venture and also give us an opportunity to reciprocate Mr. Wang's hospitality.

Mr. Yu said that Mr. Wang had his daughter with him (actually his mistress) and he might come if we could visit Las Vegas, too. We told him all things were possible and Mr. Wang should definitely come. Mr. Yu made the arrangements and called back to say Mr. Wang would arrive in two weeks. and he was coming as well. Sheldon called Agent Messemer with the news. He was pleased and said Mr. Wang would be thoroughly watched every minute he was in the United States.

Mr. Wang arrived in Los Angeles with great fanfare and the first night we all met for dinner at a local Chinese restaurant in the Los Angeles China Town area. Agent Messemer told us that there would be FBI Agents following closely and gave Sheldon a cell phone with a private number and asked him to convey our whereabouts as we changed from location to location. He also told us that part of this very intense surveillance was to ensure our safety, which he thought could be in question if Mr. Wang found out about our cooperation with the FBI.

The FBI agents took the hotel rooms above and below Mr. Wang's room and had microphones and video cameras hidden in his room. We had invited Mr. Wang to our house for some tea and a meeting the next morning. Our son Robert, who was living with us at that time, remarked that there was a green van parked across street of our house, with very dark tinted windows and several antennas. Sheldon immediately called Agent Messemer and told him about the van. He denied any knowledge, and Sheldon remarked that whatever or whoever that was, it was much too obvious, and that Mr. Wang could be suspicious.

A short time later, Mr. Wang called and said something had come up and he couldn't make it over to our house, but he invited us to dinner that night at a Chinese restaurant in Monterey Park, a community southeast of Los Angeles that had become almost entirely Chinese. The dinner was at a small out of the way restaurant called Dumpling Master, and the owners were from Beijing.

Sheldon called Agent Messemer and told him where we were having dinner, and wouldn't you know it the green van disappeared, at least for the moment. We were never quite sure whether Mr. Wang came to our house, saw the van, and drove off because it was so obvious. Before Mr. Wang became Chairman of our joint venture, he was a policeman on a very high level with the Ministry of Public Security.

The restaurant was not crowded and Mr. Yu, after negotiation with the waiter, ordered dinner which was delicious. Dumpling Master is well known for the large variety of dumplings they have to offer, and a very special Chinese baked garlic. Sheldon and I noticed two Chinese at a table not far from us and later we found out they were FBI.

Mr. Wang asked us to go to Las Vegas with he and his daughter, plus the three other people in his party along with Mr. Yu and Ms. Zhang. We of course agreed and rented a large van to drive to there, so we would be comfortable. Agent Messemer told us that the FBI would have surveillance vehicles both in front and in back of the van and that just in case we lost their surveillance they had placed a tracking device on the van.

He kept telling us that we needed to be concerned for our safety and to be very careful. With the special cell phone he gave Sheldon, all he had to do was press one button, and It would automatically connect to the surveillance team. Agent Messemer was convinced that there would be a drop contact for Mr. Wang in Las Vegas and highly sensitive documents pertaining to military intelligence would be passed on. When we loaded the luggage in the van, Mr. Wang kept his briefcase separate and carried it in his lap. Maybe Messemer was right. We left for Vegas in the late morning and headed east on Interstate 15, into the Mojave Desert.

Mr. Wang Comes to LA

It was quite a ride to Las Vegas, and a lot of Chinese was spoken. When we reached Barstow, Mr. Yu said that he wanted to stop at a friend's Chinese restaurant. We drove into the city to a small Chinese restaurant in a shopping center. Mr. Wang and Mr. Yu got out of the van and told the rest of us to wait and said they would only be a few minutes. Mr. Wang was carrying his briefcase. They returned in about 15 minutes, and Mr. Wang put his briefcase in the back of the van, with the luggage. They said nothing and we continued our trip to Las Vegas.

We arrived about 6:00 PM and went directly to the Desert Inn where we had reservations. We all went to the buffet which the Chinese love. They pile everything they can on their plates and then they share everything. Sheldon went to the bathroom and as he was washing his hands, a man came up next to him and told him not be concerned, the bureau was on the case and asked Sheldon to take Mr. Wang to a local casino that was in downtown Las Vegas.

When Sheldon returned to the table, he glanced at me, and then suggested to Mr. Wang that we try the casinos in downtown Las Vegas, where the betting limits would be much lower, and we would have more fun. He agreed and we all piled into the van and went to the place the FBI agent suggested.

We arrived at the casino which was much smaller than the casinos on the strip, and it was very crowded. We stayed and gambled for about an hour. As we were leaving, a very boisterous group of people, who looked like they had a bit too much to drink, pushed their way through us and jostled us, especially Mr. Wang, as they made their exit. He was upset at being pushed and commented on the bad manners of some Americans.

We got back to our hotel and Sheldon and I went directly to our room. It has been a long day and as we were preparing for bed, the phone rang. It was Ms. Zhang, and she was very agitated. She said Mr. Wang had lost his purse at the casino. He was frantic because all of his travel documents were inside. She asked Sheldon to drive her back to the casino and see if someone had found it. He told her it would be an exercise in futility. This was Las Vegas, and pickpockets were common. But Ms. Zhang persisted, and Sheldon agreed to drive her back. When they asked the manager if anyone had turned in a lost purse, he of course, said "no."

When they returned to the hotel Sheldon asked Mr. Wang's "daughter" what was in the purse. She said it contained more than $20,000 in cash. Sheldon told Ms. Zhang that Mr. Wang should not carry such large sums of money. She replied that it was a misunderstanding. There had been only $2,000.

Wearily, Sheldon returned to our room. A moment later the phone rang, again. It was Agent Messemer. He said it was a shame Mr. Wang had lost his purse—which, of course, no one had told him. Sheldon said that it reputedly contained $20,000. He replied that it was substantially more. When Sheldon asked him if he intended to return it, his reply was that he knew nothing about a purse or who might have taken it.

The ride back to Los Angeles was peaceful without much conversation, other than Mr. Wang and Mr. Yu who were sitting in the back having a private conversation.

Mr. Wang stayed in Los Angeles for a few more days and we had a meeting at our offices in West Los Angeles. We of course had allowed Agent Messemer to place microphones and a video camera in the office and everything was recorded. We wanted to have a conversation with Mr. Wang regarding the money transfer documents we had uncovered that showed transfers from the joint venture account to a bank in Toronto. Although Agent Messemer asked us not to mention it to Mr. Wang, we had decided we wanted an explanation.

We showed Mr. Wang copies of the transfers and asked for an explanation. He asked where we had gotten copies of those documents and we him told him we could not disclose that to him. He turned and gave Mr. Yu a very dark look. We again asked him for an explanation. He then told us a long story.

It seems that another entity that he was involved with had several million dollars of excess cash and wanted to use it to finance the purchase of some business and condominiums in Canada. The relevant Chinese law at that time prohibited the transfer of those funds outside of China. Since he was a partner in the joint venture, he asked Mr. Yu if he could deposit the funds in our joint venture account, and then wire those funds to Canada. He said that Mr. Yu told him that since he was a joint venture partner and that it was not costing the joint venture anything, it was okay. We then asked Mr. Yu why he never told us, and Mr. Yu said that it was such a small matter, he didn't feel it was necessary to bring it to our attention.

We then told Mr. Wang that what he had done, with Mr. Yu's approval, was a crime in the United States. It was called money laundering. We also told him that if it was against Chinese law to send those funds outside of China then he had committed an illegal act in China as well, and he had put our joint venture is jeopardy. He replied that we should not be at all concerned with any violation of Chinese law, and he would take care of any problems that might emerge.

We then asked him for proof that the funds were not part of the joint venture account and were indeed separate funds. He gave us some wrinkled-up pieces of paper with Chinese writing and said that was the proof. It was ludicrous. It was obvious that Mr. Wang, with the help of Mr. Yu, had taken funds belonging to the joint venture.

Then Sheldon paused for effect and with great seriousness told Mr. Wang that the FBI was aware of the transfers and had already contacted us to discuss them. Mr. Wang sat up straight in his chair and asked for the name of the agent. He told Mr. Wang, who was now paying rapt attention to his every word, that Special Agent Robert Messemer had contacted us. Sheldon added that we were very uncomfortable with the situation, and we didn't want to make excuses for Mr. Wang or have the joint venture investigated because of his actions.

Sheldon reminded him that the FBI was a very serious intelligence organization, something he well knew. Then he leaned across the table and asked him quietly what, exactly, was his relationship to the Ministry of State Security. He made no reply, but gathered up his things, said the meeting was over and left. Mr. Yu and Ms. Zhang, who had been translating, followed him out. Two days later Mr. Wang and Mr. Yu were back in Beijing.

Agent Messemer called Sheldon after the meeting and said he was upset that he had disclosed to Mr. Wang our knowledge of the money transfers. Sheldon told Agent Messemer that he and I, and our investors had a lot at stake, and we wanted Mr. Wang to realize that we had knowledge of his illegal actions, and that we were cooperating with our government, not his.

CHAPTER 28

A Visit to the Ministry of Security

"Only two U.S. citizens had ever been in the building, and both were taken to the Ministry unwillingly and under guard. They're thugs."

~Denny Barnes, Commercial Attaché, U.S. Consul, Beijing

When we returned to Beijing a month later, we were determined to do something about Mr. Wang. He was taking advantage of the joint venture in ways that were becoming increasingly shameless. He was now wearing a gold Rolex with a diamond bezel and was chauffeured around town in a late model, long-body BMW. In addition to the illegal funds transfer from the joint venture account, he had turned the top floor of the hotel into a personal warehouse. The whole floor was full of refrigerators, TV's, mattresses, and other equipment which we discovered had been purchased by the joint venture but sold by Mr. Wang on the black market. He was making a fortune at our expense.

We decided to drop by the U.S. Embassy and visit Denny Barnes. As he listened to our story, he told us that we were not the only American joint venture that was full of corruption. Ours was very blatant, however, and the U.S. government was interested in making it an issue with the Chinese government. Most foreign corporations in China were large, multinational companies who knew they were being exploited, but didn't care enough to do anything about it. They were betting on the future and were willing to put up with the present.

Mr. Yu had been cheating us too. We weren't sure what the relationship between Mr. Yu and Mr. Wang was, but it seemed they were both collaborators and competitors at the same time. When we confronted Mr. Yu, he denied having any knowledge of the corruption, but agreed that Mr. Wang was probably doing some things that were not legal. Mr. Yu told us that the Minister of Public Security was a friend of his and would certainly want to know of any misdeeds by Chinese members of the joint venture team. If Mr. Wang had committed crimes, he would be punished, he added. We didn't know whether to believe him or not, but since he was President of our company, and conducted all our business in the PRC, we had no one else to rely on.

We decided to meet with one of our other joint venture partners and decided to fly to Chongqing. The city was a 25% partner, and we were to meet with the mayor, Mr. Li and all the other officials involved in the joint venture. The city is one of the largest, if not the largest city in China, and at that time had over 18 million people. It sits on the banks of the Yangtze River in central China and is known as the furnace of China because it's so hot. No one could ever understand why the city of Chongqing would be a partner in a hotel project in Beijing which was 1500 miles away.

We had never been to Chongqing and thought the trip would be interesting and we wanted our partners to know about Mr. Wang's usage of our joint venture funds. We were fortunate because instead of the old Russian jets CAAC flew around China, we were put on a new 737, which the Chinese were introducing into their flight system. When we were seated the Chinese stewardess came out and told everyone that we should stay in our seats through takeoff and landing. The aircraft took off and immediately everybody got out of their seats and started looking out the windows. It was crazy that they all just ignored the stewardess, and she didn't seem to mind either. There were also a few live chickens on the plane in the seat across the aisle from us.

We arrived and were met by members of the mayor's office and taken in a Red Flag limousine to the Holiday Inn on the banks of the river. It was very spectacular. We checked into the hotel along with Mr. Yu and Jennie who had accompanied us. They had taken separate rooms, even though one of them was never used.

Mr. Yu suggested we go to a special restaurant that he had been to before and thought we might enjoy. The mayor had provided us with a car and driver and off we went. Somewhere deep in the heart of the city, we were dropped off and we walked up the stairs of this very crowded place and into the restaurant. Each table had a large steel pot that was heated by live coals. The pot was divided into two compartments, and each compartment was filled with bubbling liquid. One side was a brownish red and the other was almost a bright red. All the tables were filled with people who were sweating profusely.

It was hot outside and of course there was no air-conditioning. We sat down and the waiter brought us platefuls of raw food, meat, fish, poultry, vegetables, and some food items that were not recognizable. We were instructed to take whatever pieces of food we wanted and to dip them into either side of the pot and when they cooked, which was very fast, then we would eat it. Chongqing is known for the hottest spiciest food anywhere. The first piece of food Sheldon tasted almost took his head off it was so spicy. He coughed and sputtered and could hardly catch his breath. That's when I put my food in the brownish red side, which was milder then the bright red and Sheldon did the same with his next pieces of food. Mr. Yu put his food in the bright red side and ate with relish. He must have had a cast iron stomach.

We then went off to a meeting at the mayor's office, and were ushered into a very large room, with couches and chairs facing the front doors and maybe thirty chairs on each side. As per Chinese custom with foreigners, we sat on one side of the mayor and Mr. Yu sat on the other side. We were served tea, and then Sheldon made a

A Visit to the Ministry of Security

speech about how we admired China and how appreciative we were to the Chinese for giving us the opportunity to join in the hotel project, and how thankful we were that CHITIC had so graciously put up the guarantee for the construction financing. That of course brought up the issue of the guarantee fee.

The mayor told us he was very upset, that they had not received their fee. He told us that their guarantee was the first for a hotel project and asked why the fee was still not paid after five years. We then got into a discussion about Mr. Wang and the Ministry of Public Security in Beijing. Sheldon told the mayor that we suspected some very serious misdoings and that since he was a partner, he should be aware of what was going on.

Just about that time, one of the mayor's assistants started to shake his head and, in a few seconds, it looked like he was having an epileptic fit. He fell to the floor with froth coming from his mouth and was thrashing around for a few seconds. Everyone stopped talking and just looked at him. Then two other men from the group jumped up and one took his head and inserted something in his mouth and the other started to massage him with pressure points in a variety of places.

Everyone just stared and didn't make a sound. After a few minutes, the shaking stopped, they wiped his head, he sat back up, looked at everyone, and smiled. The mayor continued talking, just where he left off, without missing a beat. The meeting continued and no one said a word or offered us an explanation about what had just transpired, but we realized we had once again witnessed the miracle of Chinese medicine.

The meeting finally ended with the mayor's assurances that he would support us in any way that he could. He also said Sheldon should personally meet with the Minister of Public Security in Beijing and tell him of the corruption in the hotel project and ask for an immediate investigation by Chinese authorities. We realized we were being used, and once again we didn't know why, but now Sheldon was even more determined to meet with the Minister.

When we returned from Chongqing, Sheldon dropped by for another visit with Denny Barnes. He told him of our meeting with the mayor and that he intended to meet with the Minister of Public

Security as soon as possible. He didn't think much of the idea. He explained that U.S. citizens were not allowed in the Ministry building and were prohibited by Chinese law from having any direct contact with Public Security personnel.

Barnes said that to his knowledge only two U.S. citizens had ever been in the building, and both of them were taken to the Ministry unwillingly and under guard. "They're thugs," he said. Sheldon told him that unfortunately the Ministry of State Security thugs were our partners in the joint venture, and he intended to have his meeting, anyway. He wished Sheldon luck and said that if he were detained the embassy would lodge a formal complaint. That was supposed to be comforting.

When Sheldon returned to our office, he asked Mr. Yu to set up the appointment. Mr. Yu told said it was very difficult to do, as only a few foreigners were ever in that Ministry, and since Sheldon was an American citizen, it was a very sticky issue. This discussion went on for several days, and it seemed we were no closer to the meeting. Everyone in our office was very nervous, and one day, Jennie received a phone call and all of a sudden, she started to shake and cry. She finally put the phone down. Mr. Yu came out and they had a long conversation in Chinese. It was obvious she was very upset.

We repeatedly asked Mr. Yu what was going on before he finally told us. Jennie had received a threatening call from someone in the Ministry of Public Security. They warned her that she was too close to the Americans, and she should remember that she was a Chinese citizen living in China, she had a family, and if she was not careful, she and her family could disappear or worse.

Sheldon finally told Mr. Yu that if he did not arrange this meeting, we would call a press conference, and tell the world what was going on. One hour later a meeting was set for the next day. Mr. Yu always played both sides. This time he said Sheldon should tell the Minister what was on his mind. When Sheldon asked if he would go with him to the meeting, he had an excuse and said that Mr. Ming, a translator and one of our office staff, would go instead.

Mr. Ming was not happy about going to this meeting. He told Sheldon that he should be very careful about what he would say, and that he really had no idea about the reality of the power that the Ministry of Public Security had and what they could do. Sheldon told him not to worry, but Mr. Ming was thoroughly frightened. And to be honest, Sheldon and I were both anxious the next day when he kissed me goodbye, and he and Mr. Ming went off to the meeting.

The Ministry of Public Security is located next to Tiananmen Square in a location that communicated to everyone its importance. It is headquartered in a large, drab, cement-colored building, more reminiscent of post-revolutionary Russia than anything Chinese. If architecture is language, then this building bespoke machine-like, anonymous power – all efficiency and no ornamentation. It's the only building that has armed guards in the front with large iron gates with barbed wire. As they drove in, Sheldon was sure he saw Mr. Wang's BMW ahead of them.

They were greeted at the door of the car and escorted into the building by armed guards. Sheldon admitted to having a very queasy feeling in the pit of his stomach and tried to be as calm as possible. They were taken to a meeting room where four people awaited them, each one dressed differently. The Minister was dressed in a blue Mao outfit and was a small man, about 65 years old. There was another larger heavyset man, dressed in a gray Mao outfit, also about 65 years old. The other two were younger. One had thick glasses, an ill-fitting western style suit and the other looked like a thug. He had on casual clothes, and it was obvious he was armed.

Sheldon was introduced to the Minister and his secretary/interpreter, the young man with the glasses. The thug just glanced and nodded, and the older man in the gray outfit didn't say a word. Sheldon asked Mr. Ming the identity of the older man in the gray suit. Mr. Ming looked at him and whispered that he should not ask that question. They were getting off to a bad start. They hadn't even begun to discuss Mr. Wang and were already arguing.

When Sheldon persisted, he started to shake and said he was afraid. Sheldon insisted and finally in a very shaken voice, he asked the question. The answer was, "It is not necessary for Mr. Krechman to know the identity of this gentlemen." Sheldon told Ming to tell them that if they did not identify this man, he would leave the meeting, because he would not stay in a meeting with someone he was not introduced to.

Mr. Ming panicked. He was very frightened and pleaded with Sheldon to just forget it and continue with the meeting. Sheldon insisted. Choking out the words, Mr. Ming complied. From the background the thug glared and then took a step forward. There was silence for a few seconds and after a nod from the Minister, the translator introduced the other man.

He was in charge of all the Ministry of Public Security's business affairs—and was Mr. Wang's father-in-law.

With the tension somewhat relieved, they sat down and had some tea. Sheldon sat next to the Minister, and the thug sat across from him. There were no business cards exchanged, which was very unusual in Chinese meetings.

Sheldon told the minister what our suspicions were, and he took notes on the back of an envelope Sheldon had given to him with a copy of a very strong letter we were going to send the Chinese central government. Sheldon explained that we had put all our assets on the line for this project. We had taken investment dollars from many of our friends and neighbors, and we had worked diligently to make this project a success, with little or no financial rewards. We had been told that the Chinese were honorable people, and that before we would allow ourselves and our friends to have such a financial set back, we would expose this story to the world.

Sheldon told him that, if necessary, we would go before the U.S. Congress and report this story and that it could hurt, if not eliminate, China's most favorite nations status, which was just coming up for renewal. (Denny Barnes had told him to say that.) He added that we were Jews and that if they pushed our backs to the wall, we would never stop talking about this miscarriage of justice.

Mr. Ming was absolutely white that Sheldon had actually threatened the Minister of Public Security, in the Ministry of Public Security. Sheldon had said those words in a very respectful way, but he wanted the minister to know that we would not stop. The minister looked at him, and in a very gracious way, said there was nothing we could do to harm Sino U.S. relations. He also said that he would look into the allegations and pursue an investigation. He assured Sheldon that if Mr. Wang or any parties were guilty, they would be ferreted out and prosecuted. Sheldon thanked him.

As they drove out of the building, Mr. Ming started to cry and told Sheldon he had made a serious mistake and he feared that his life was now in danger. The next day he disappeared, and we later learned that he escaped from China. We also found out that the Minister Sheldon had met with, had a condominium in Vancouver, purchased with funds from our joint venture project.

CHAPTER 29

Threatened in Beijing

"Get out of China or great harm will come to you."
~Ministry of Security Thug

After the hotel project was completed, our Chinese partners mounted a campaign to eliminate World China Trade from the joint venture. It was a process at times subtle and at others crass. We were being cheated by Mr. Yu and Mr. Wang, and perhaps others, of that, we were sure. But it was difficult to pin anything down and since the Chinese authorities were fully complicit, there was no one to whom we could appeal and expect anything to be done.

We had several meetings at the U.S. Embassy with Denny Barnes to complain about the situation. It seems every American business in China was being similarly cheated but no one else seemed particularly interested in putting a stop to it. The embassy wanted to cooperate with us in bringing the situation to light, but the political pressures from Washington put a finite limit on their zeal.

The State Department was engaged in a tense dialog with the Chinese following the Tiananmen Square democracy protests, and powerful American corporate interests considered corruption a price of doing business in China. There was little political support for a crackdown. The only people who were worried were those within the embassy who monitored Chinese organized crime and espionage. They knew that Americans were being used as fronts for the illicit businesses of Chinese officials and for the benefit of the Chinese espionage agencies.

The Chinese security agencies acted just like organized crime in the United States. Double dealing, embezzlement and intimidation were the norm. Our joint venture partners kept four sets of books, each different, and most of the written records were kept in Chinese. It was impossible to figure out where money went and to whom. The Chinese were masters of ambiguity. Direct questions were answered by exquisitely vague replies. By the time our project was completed three different banks held notes on the project and none of them was ever paid on time or given a straight answer to the simple question: Where is the money being spent?

Standard Chartered Bank, our original lender, threatened to throw us into default several times but never did. The bank knew that it had little recourse within the Chinese judicial system, particularly against partners who were themselves instruments of the Chinese government. Mr. Wang always insisted we needed more money and the banks, especially the Bank of China, would grumble for a while and then come up with the funds.

We suspected that officials at the Bank of China were being paid off. If so, it was a slick deal. They would lend the money, our partners would kickback a portion of the proceeds and then siphon off the rest for themselves. We soon found ourselves in a situation where the Chinese side stole every new loan dollar that came in, by whatever means, while expecting World China Trade to pay the debt. Our joint venture agreement, loan agreements, corporate bylaws and subsidiary contracts of every kind were honored only when convenient or necessary to save face.

Now when we traveled to Beijing, there was a complete lack of trust between Mr. Yu and us. We would rarely have dinner at his house, and he kept his office door locked when he wasn't there. Jennie was standoffish and distant. We were treated as if we were dissident strangers and not part of the company. Of course, we took as much control as we could and we questioned many things, and mostly got evasive answers.

Mr. Wang was more antagonistic than ever since Sheldon's meeting with the Minister of Public Security and consequently more dangerous. Denny Barnes made it clear to us that Mr. Wang was no better than a common criminal and we better watch our backs.

On this particular trip, as the situation worsened, one of our American investors, Joe Massie, a director of our corporation, came to Beijing to attend a board meeting. We were expecting a showdown and felt we might need outside assistance. Sheldon asked Denny Barnes, who spoke Chinese, to attend the board meeting. He had never attended before and with the strained relations between China and the United States, he had to get permission from Ambassador Lily. Denny got the okay, and we decided that we would not tell the Chinese or Mr. Yu prior to the meeting. We wanted to make the point to Mr. Wang and his cohorts that our government was standing up for us.

Denny met us at the hotel entrance just prior to the meeting, and we all walked in together. Mr. Wang looked at us and Sheldon introduced Denny. He then explained that we had invited him to the board meeting because we were concerned that the American side of the joint venture was being swindled and we wanted a representative from the U.S. government at the meeting so that our government would have firsthand knowledge of the actions of Mr. Wang and the Chinese.

Mr. Wang was very reserved, and he asked for Denny's credentials. Denny produced them and surprised Mr. Wang by having a conversation with him in Mandarin. Mr. Wang finally said that it was his understanding that the Chinese side should have been given notice that we were bringing a representative from the United States government to the board meeting and that if they had been notified, they could have also brought a representative from the Chinese Government.

After about ten minutes of arguing and discussion, we all agreed that Denny Barnes would have to leave the meeting, but our point was made. Denny asked us for an immediate briefing after the meeting was concluded.

Mr. Yu told us we had made an egregious mistake, and that the Chinese side would now realize that the American side did not trust them. That would have been laughable had he not said it in all seriousness. We explained to Mr. Yu, that was indeed the case, and we did not trust the Chinese side. We also voiced our concerns about Mr. Yu's business loyalty. While we realized he was a Chinese citizen, he was also president of our company and had a fiduciary responsibility to all the shareholders.

The Board meeting ended after three very frustrating and contentious days with several issues unresolved, including the Ramada management situation. It left everyone with a bitter aftertaste.

That night Sheldon, Joe, and I had dinner with Denny Barnes and discussed what had occurred at the meeting. Denny told us that the Chinese were taking advantage of all the American companies that were trying to do business in China and ours was one of the most blatant. He said he also suspected that the Chinese had other purposes for this joint venture, because of the way it was being conducted and that our partners included Mr. Wang, who Denny referred to as a mafia chief (which is also how the FBI referred to him), and the Ministry of Public Security.

Denny was pushing us to hold a press conference. Exposure to the foreign media was one of the few things feared by the Chinese. It was possible, he thought, that the government could be forced into arresting Mr. Wang in order to save face. Ostensibly, the punishment in China for graft was execution by firing squad. Public executions were held right down the street from our hotel in the Worker's Stadium. It was a public spectacle in which the family of the executed person was charged for the bullet. It was the ultimate loss of face.

If we exposed Mr. Wang and forced a trial, the press conference would be interpreted as nothing less than a death threat. It would be a high stakes gamble. We decided not to do it. On the one hand we didn't want Mr. Wang to die for his sins, and on the other we weren't convinced he'd ever be charged. If every Chinese official involved in graft were arrested, the government would fall overnight. Corruption was endemic

As we were leaving the restaurant, which was in our hotel, two men (obviously security people), bumped into Denny and knocked him forcefully against the wall. They grunted sort of what was supposed to be an apology, but you could feel the hostility emanating from them. Denny left and went back to the U.S. Consul, and we retired to our rooms, which were next to each other on the fifteenth floor of the hotel.

We were sound asleep when the phone rang at 11:30 pm. Sheldon answered, and a man asked in broken English if he was Mr. Krechman. When Sheldon asked what he wanted, he started threatening him in a very antagonistic angry voice, saying the Chinese wanted Ramada out and that we were no longer welcome in China. We better leave the country immediately or we would be in physical danger, and they would get us. Sheldon asked him who he was and offered to meet him immediately to discuss just what he wanted. He refused and said we better take heed of his warnings and hung up.

About five minutes later, Joe started pounding on our door. When Sheldon opened it up, he told us he had just received a threatening phone call too. There was nothing we could do but go back to sleep. We put a chair under the doorknob of our room, but realized it was just an exercise in futility. We were in Beijing China, in a hotel that was owned by the Ministry of Public Security, and in reality, they could do anything they wanted. Still, it gave us a psychological measure of comfort and we went to sleep.

We were awoken again at about 3:00 am by a pounding on the door. Sheldon got out of bed, put on a bathrobe and slippers and opened it. Standing there were two public security men demanding that he turn over his passport. He refused and told them to go away. They said they were sent to get his passport and they would not leave until they had it. Sheldon told them that if they continued to pressure him for the passport, he would immediately go to the phone, call the American Embassy, and report that he was being harassed by the Ministry of Public Security.

They told him to try the phone which he did—it was dead. Sheldon told them the only way they would get his passport would be to physically take it from me and that he would put up a fight before he would let them have it. He then slammed the door shut, put on the skimpy little chain. We were shaken but tried to go back to sleep. They pounded on the door for another half an hour and then finally stopped.

Obviously, we got little if any sleep that night. In the morning we met Joe and went down to the Western restaurant in our hotel for breakfast, which was our normal routine. They served a buffet every morning that included eggs, bacon, fruit, ham, Chinese bread, and cheeses. Joe ordered his usual coffee to start, and Sheldon and I had some tea.

When Joe took his first sip of coffee, he spit it out all over the floor and started to cough heavily. I immediately started pounding him on the back and when he finally stopped gasping, he said the coffee was laced with some evil smelling liquid that was almost unbearable. We looked around and saw what looked like some of the kitchen help staring at us with malevolent dark looks.

We decided that we should immediately go the U.S. Consul and ask for advice. We got one of the hotel cars, with a driver to take us. When we arrived, we met with Denny Barnes and the chief intelligence officer of the Consul. They took us into the courtyard, because they suspected that all the rooms in the embassy were bugged. We related the events of the prior night.

The chief intelligence officer looked at us in a very serious manner and said that we were dealing with thugs. He said that it's been known that if these people wanted to get to someone, it would not be out of the question for them to take away that person's children if necessary. He also told us that based on our circumstances, and the people we were dealing with that we should take the threats very seriously and immediately take refuge in the U.S. embassy. He said that the United States Government could not protect us, unless we were in the embassy, and that if we left, we would in his opinion, be taking our lives in our hands.

Joe and Sheldon and I talked about what our next course of action should be. Joe thought we should take the advice of the intelligence agent take refuge in the embassy. Sheldon and I rejected that thought, maybe because we were naïve, but we did not want to be prisoners in the U.S. embassy. At that point, we had spent over 1200 days in China dealing with the Chinese and their children and had developed the hotel complex that was obviously successful. We had personal guarantees at stake and all our investors' capital. We talked the situation over for a few minutes and made a decision that Joe, who still had his passport, would leave the country right away and we would stay and try to hold things together.

Joe went back to the hotel with us to get his things but cautioned Sheldon to be very polite with Mr. Wang. He told Joe okay because he didn't want to worry him, but I knew Sheldon was really angry and that was not the course of action he would take.

Mr. Wang had been made aware of our presence the moment we entered the hotel. We found Mr. Wang in his office, and Sheldon requested an immediate meeting. He told us that he and other directors would meet with us in the board room in one hour. When we entered the board room, Mr. Wang was there with the two-security people that had pounded on our hotel room door and three of the other board directors.

He asked Sheldon the purpose of the meeting. That's when Sheldon, from the perspective of the Chinese, went berserk. He started pounding his fists on the table and shouting at the top of his lungs that Mr. Wang and the Ministry of Public Security were no better, and in fact far worse, than Hitler's Nazi Gestapo. His face was blood red, the veins were popping out on his forehead, and he was shaking with anger.

He screamed out, "How dare you threaten us? Carole and I have put our hearts and souls into dealing with China and the development of the hotel project. If this is the payback that we are receiving, being threatened and intimidated, then the Ministry of Public Security is filled with nothing but thugs and hoodlums, who have no respect for their joint venture partners, human dignity, and humanity, and were obviously the dregs of society." He added that Mr. Wang was the worst of the lot, since he was in charge.

Mr. Wang jumped back from his chair and the two Public Security men that had pounded on the door of our room jumped up and started toward Sheldon with menacing looks on their faces. Mr. Wang waved them back to their chairs, and in a very calm voice, (through an interpreter), he asked Sheldon why he was so upset, and could he explain to him just what a Nazi was and what was the Gestapo.

Sheldon calmed down and did the best he could to explain what Nazi Germany was like and told him of the telephone threat the night before and the two Chinese that pounded on our door and demanded his passport. Mr. Wang insisted it was all a mistake and that it would never happen again and that he would personally guarantee our safety.

Then he invited us to dinner that night in a small room off the kitchen of the hotel, where the food was always the best. As usual, we didn't talk business at meals. We shared food, talked amiably, and toasted each other. Our problems were far from over, but something had happened. The threats had suddenly stopped. Mr. Wang, an agent of The Ministry of State Security, had never had anyone stand up to him before. We had not solved our business problems, but we had gained respect. It was a quintessential moment. In China, they steal you blind, threaten you and then take you to dinner.

CHAPTER 30

The Final Negotiation

"Armand Hammer, the financial entrepreneur whose extraordinary career spanned seven decades and half a dozen different businesses and whose avocation as a collector of art added to an already controversial life, died Monday at his home in Westwood."

~LA Times, December 11, 1990

After a brief illness, Dr. Hammer died on December 10, 1990, at the age of 92. He was still at the helm of OXY, although in February of that year, he finally named Ray Irani, OXY's president and COO, as his successor.

He died the day before he had planned to celebrate his own belated bar mitzvah. He was raised in a non-observant family, and two rabbis in Beverly Hills were to perform the ceremony for a fund-raising dinner at the Beverly Hilton Hotel to benefit two organizations, the Pacific Jewish Center and the Jerusalem College of Technology. The ceremony was changed to a private memorial service attended by 200 people including celebrities and titans of industry who celebrated his accomplishments in business, art, diplomacy, and philanthropy.

We were saddened by the loss of our mentor who had guided us into China, the adventure of a lifetime, and we were soon to find out the nearly devastating impact his death would have on our company.

Within days of his passing everything dramatically changed for World China Trade. The two OXY employees on our board of directors resigned immediately, and that same day OXY revoked their standing offer to purchase World China Trade's shares.

Union Bank went into attack mode and employed outside legal counsel. Occidental Petroleum employed outside legal counsel. Standard Chartered Asia employed outside legal counsel. World China Trade investors then employed their legal counsel. And there we were in the middle of it all, with lawsuits flying. It was a constant legal barrage on a daily basis from all sides.

With so many large corporations and banks involved, no one knew quite what to do. The judge who was trying the case in superior court, was a well-known woman who was the wife of the District Attorney of the City of Los Angeles. She remarked that this was the most complicated case she had ever been involved with.

The Chinese, knowing all too well what was transpiring, realized our weakened position and tried to use it to their advantage to negotiate with us to purchase our shares. At this point, Mr. Yu was in the United States and had been here for several months. He was having his own troubles with the FBI and his green card status and did not want to leave the country in fear that he would never be able to obtain a visa to return.

The negotiating was going on via phone and fax between Mr. Wang in Beijing, and Sheldon, Joe and me in Los Angeles, and the pressure was mounting. We had refused any offer that would not pay back the banks and our investors. The bank of course had no regard for our investors, and they were only concerned about repayment of their loan.

Finally, we agreed on a value with Mr. Wang, and we negotiated an agreement which was faxed and signed by Sheldon and me, and the Chinese side. Mr. Wang requested that the three us (Sheldon, Joe, and me) travel to Beijing to sign the final papers. We said yes, but only after

Mr. Wang agreed that the joint venture would pay for all our expenses including business class air travel.

The night we arrived, we were given rooms on either side of the elevators on the fourteenth floor, no doubt to remind us of who was in control. We anticipated having the final meeting the day after we arrived, but of course we ended up waiting for three days, without any notice.

We met with Mr. Tian, the Chinese lawyer representing Mr. Wang and his company BLIPU. He told us that he had reviewed the agreement and was looking forward to consummating the transaction. We asked Mr. Tian when the meeting would be, and he told us shortly.

As we wandered through the hotel, we were proud of what we had created. We tried each of the seven restaurants, including a Korean barbecue. Our hotel also had the first fast food type diner, that was located on the street at the end of the office building.

We wanted to go to our company offices which Mr. Yu had moved to the hotel, and we could not get in. Jennie and Mr. Yu's wife locked themselves in and refused to open the door for us. We got Mr. Wang and asked him to open the door with a passkey, which he said he didn't have. We then asked him to forcibly open the door. He refused and we argued for a while and then we gave up the idea.

On the third day, as we were leaving the western restaurant after lunch, a young man came up to us and asked us to follow him, as the meeting was about to begin. We had received no advance notice whatsoever. We followed him to our board room and as we entered the room, we realized that sitting at the table were Chinese we had never met before. Mr. Wang was not even sitting at the table, but in a chair on the side of the room. He demeanor was very different than ever before. Instead of blustering and taking charge, he was quiet and very respectful.

We were positioned in the middle of the table and through an interpreter, we were introduced to Mr. Jin Li Zhou, seated directly across from us. He was the head of the Ministry of State Security, which is a much more powerful and influential body, then the Ministry of Public Security. The company that was purchasing our shares was a Hong Kong front company owned and controlled by the Ministry of State Security. The FBI later told us that they had known about Mr. Jin

The Final Negotiation

for years but had never had the opportunity to speak to an American who met with him. He had an infamous reputation.

Mr. Jin made the first statement. "Mr. Krechman, Mr. Wang and I have been friends for over 30 years." Sheldon tried to remain nonplused, since over the past several months, he had been sending letters to many top Chinese officials accusing Mr. Wang of theft, mismanagement of funds, and a variety of other charges, that if proven correct, would entitle Mr. Wang to be executed.

Sheldon thought for a while, having learned the valuable lesson to think before speaking in China, and then replied, "Mr. Wang has done a wonderful job in the development of the project, and we should thank him, for without him the project would never have happened." Mr. Wang looked at Sheldon, smiled and gave him a thumbs up.

Mr. Jin smiled and looked at Sheldon in a very pleasant way, and said, "Mr. Krechman, you don't really expect me to pay this amount of money for your shares. The hotel is a losing proposition and as a good businessman, I am sure that you will agree with me that the value of your shares is considerably less then what is stated in this agreement."

Sheldon told him that this was negotiated by Mr. Wang. Mr. Jin replied that Mr. Wang was not the buyer, he was. We all looked at him, and even though we were surprised, we understood after years of doing business in China that the unexpected was considered normal.

Sheldon told Mr. Jin that as far as we were concerned the meeting was over, and that we were going to go directly to the United States Embassy and file an international complaint. Mr. Jin replied that we were welcome to use a hotel car and driver. That was the beginning of a negotiation that lasted three weeks.

After the initial meeting, we went off to the U.S. Embassy and spoke to Denny Barnes even though we understood that there was really nothing that the Embassy could do, since it was a commercial transaction.

We returned to the hotel and met with Mr. Tian, Mr. Wang's lawyer and asked him for some help. He explained to us that Mr. Jin was a very important and powerful personage, and it was all his decision.

Over the next two weeks we had several meetings with the Chinese, and the time went by without any resolution. Mr. Jin seemed to have disappeared and all our negotiations were with Mr. Wang who was friendly but stubborn. He said that the real price for our shares would have to be half of what we had agreed upon. We told him that was unacceptable and the only thing we could accept is what we agreed upon.

Every night about 11:00 pm, the second elevator, which was next to the door to our room, would stop and open and then stop and open continually. Sheldon would go out and wedge one of the plastic slippers that came with our hotel room, into the elevator door track to hold it closed. (The maintenance department was never to be found). At about midnight, someone would pull out the slipper and the door would open and close all night long until about 8:00 am when it would start functioning properly again, somehow miraculously repaired. We eventually almost got used to the noise of the opening and closing of the elevator doors.

There were several impromptu meetings, where someone would come and find us, and we would meet in small groups with endless discussion. We were getting weary, and we knew the Chinese were trying to wear us down for their advantage.

But the food was great, and we had a chance to enjoy the hotel project that we had worked on tirelessly over the years. We ate in all the restaurants, examined every inch of the hotel, from the inside out. I even made several lists of things to be repaired, replaced, or changed. We met all the employees, and we were treated like owners. All our expenses were paid for by the joint venture. We had a car and driver, and the only expense we argued about was the overseas telephone charges. We actually argued about that until the day we left.

There were frequent telephone conversations with Marty our lawyer in Los Angeles. The three or four law firms involved, the judge, the banks, and of course OXY were all very interested in settling this issue and things changed daily.

Finally, we agreed on a value of $7.5 million dollars that was close to our original agreement. However, when we sat down with Mr. Jin after negotiating this new agreement, he informed us that the Chinese Government would deduct the relevant Chinese income tax from the payment. What that tax was and how it was to be calculated no one quite knew.

The Final Negotiation

We told him that the agreed upon payment was to be paid in full, with no deductions. Mr. Jin said that he was not responsible as this was a PRC Government tax issue. We informed Mr. Jin that he could do anything he wanted and that we would not agree with the settlement if there were any Chinese taxes deducted.

We negotiated for another week and then Mr. Jin said that if we worded the agreement in a specific way, we could avoid the taxes. The wording he wanted had no material change in the agreement. It was just a face-saving tactic.

After three weeks of stomach aches, headaches and confusion, everything was agreed upon—at least that's what we thought.

We then arranged a board of directors meeting to agree and ratify the sale agreement. Ms Zhang flew in from Los Angeles to attend the meeting, as she was a director, and she was also representing Mr. Yu's interest.

At the board meeting she introduced a letter from Mr. Yu complaining that we asked for a resolution that the funds be put into a joint account, whereby none could be released without the signatures of both Sheldon and Mr. Yu. The new quasi buyer, Mr. Jin, said that maybe the process should be stopped if there were difficulties among the World China Trade directors. Sheldon, Joe and I held an emergency board meeting in the next room.

Since collectively we had more than 50% of the stock in World China Trade, we removed Ms. Zhang and Mr. Yu from the board. Ms. Zhang refused to vacate and the Chinese for the first time did not know what to do. We argued in the board room for two more days and finally we convinced Ms. Zhang that we were not going to take advantage of anyone, and she would get her rightful share. She then voted our way and we re-instated her to the board.

Two hours before the signing ceremony, we met with Mr. Wang and told him that we had some unpaid expenses that were due, and we were also entitled to a director's fee for all the board meetings we had attended. He of course refused. We told him that we would not sign the agreement without getting paid our reimbursables and our fees.

Mr. Wang started screaming, "Now you want this, then you want that." I replied that it was in or contract, and we hadn't seen a dime of that money. Mr. Wang walked out in a huff and headed to his office upstairs. I took the contracts off the table, rolled them up, and went after him, yelling, "This isn't right. We've always been promised our board fees. We paid our own way here for years to have meeting after meeting to get this thing done, and we don't have a deal until we get paid." With that, Sheldon and I stormed up to our room.

About half an hour later, the doorbell rang and when I opened it, a man handed me a suitcase and left. I put the suitcase on the bed and opened it—it was filled with money, lots of money. Sheldon and I laughed, and a great time playing with the money, and throwing it around on the bed. I finally put it in a bag and then into the suitcase it came in. Then we went to sign the documents.

Minutes before the signing ceremony, I produced some additional invoices for more reimbursables. Mr. Wang ran out of the room saying it was finished, no more, it was finished, as I followed out after him waving the bills in my hand. They also paid those.

Prior to the signing ceremony the documents had to be translated and printed in both Chinese and English. We told Mr. Wang that we wanted an independent translator, having learned this lesson the hard way, so that we could be assured that the documents said the same thing in both Chinese and English.

We requested Mr. Fan Shi Long, a friend who was not connected to or joint venture partners. He was the editor of the magazine *China Reconstruct*, which was printed in six languages and distributed throughout the world. Mr. Fan did not have a private phone, so Mr. Wang sent a car and some public security officials to get him. Mr. Fan arrived, commanded respect and did a very good job on the documents.

Mr. Jin took Sheldon aside, with an interpreter and said, "Mr. Krechman I want you to know that I have seen all the letters you have written about Mr. Wang to our government, and when we had our first meeting, you said such nice positive things about him, and I wonder why."

Sheldon looked at Mr. Jin and after a few moments of thought, replied, "Mr. Jin, you are a master and I would like to become your pupil, as I could learn much from you." Mr. Jin smiled, put his arm around Sheldon's shoulders, gave him a small hug and walked away.

The Final Negotiation

We expected a formal banquet, which we were not looking forward to. Much to our surprise, Mr. Jin had the special private room prepared for us and only twelve people attended. It was very intimate. Mr. Wang was not invited.

Mr. Jin ordered the food and then ordered a very special rare (150 proof) Moutai wine. We started toasting. Mr. Jin would give a toast to me and then Joe would give a toast to Mr. Jin and then so forth around the table. By the time the first course of food was served we were all blasted and didn't eat a thing. We just kept toasting.

Mr. Jin told Sheldon that I was a very smart person and very forceful, and that he was henpecked. Sheldon agreed and told him that him they could share me. He laughed and we all continued toasting for over two hours. Poor Joe was really gone, and we had to take him up to his room. We left him sitting on his bed and when we returned three hours later, he was still sitting stiff on the bed. We laughed and a lot of the tension was released from all of us.

The final moment was with Sheldon and me and Mr. Jin in the lobby of our hotel, hugging goodbye, in front of a multitude of Chinese people.

We then went off to visit the Israel Embassy in Beijing. We were invited to a party with seven members of the Knesset, and a group of Israelis wanting to do business in China. At the party, we were asked by the group to help them in how to do business with the Chinese. We told them to treat the Chinese like they were Israelis, but remember, "The journey of a thousand miles begins with the first step, and the ox moves slow, but the earth is patient."

The next day our friends at the U.S. Embassy including Denny Barnes and Agent Messmer, who was now assigned to the Embassy, took us to the airport. We were flying to Hong Kong and from there, back home. I was carrying the suitcase full of cash. The only flight we could get that day to Hong Kong was on China Airlines, which we rarely flew. We got onto the plane which has a very strange configuration. We were in first class, and the galley was right behind us in the middle of the plane. Everyone from the embassy was standing on the boarding bridges waving goodbye to us, happy that we had safely made it on our flight.

Then they took the bridge down and we rolled out to the tarmac, where we just sat on the tarmac, not moving at all, for quite a long time. I was getting nervous, and then all of a sudden, right where I was sitting, the carpet on the floor of the plane rolled back to reveal a trapdoor. At the bottom of the trap door were two men in black overalls coming up the ladder. My heart was pounding so fast I could hear it beating. I was sure they were going to take us off the plane, take our money, and we would just disappear. That's what went through my mind in the five seconds it took them to get to the top of the ladder.

Well as it thankfully turned out, they were mechanics who were fixing something in the gallery behind us. When we got to Hong Kong, we were able to turn the money over to our banker at Standard Charter Asia and they wired it to our bank in America.

When we returned to the United States all the lawyers and the banks told us that we had failed – the Chinese would never send the funds as we agreed.

The day the agreement specified for the funds to be in our bank account in Los Angeles, Mr. Jin wired the total amount we had agreed upon.

CHAPTER 31

The Deportation of Mr. Yu Xue Wen

Fool me once, shame on you; fool me twice, shame on me.
~Chinese Proverb

In the summer of 1992, Agent Messemer called us from the Federal Prison in Terminal Island, Wilmington, California. He stated that Mr. Yu was on trial, and a deportation hearing was scheduled for 1:00 pm that day. He was concerned that without our testimony Mr. Yu might succeed, and if left on his own recognizance might disappear in the United States. Agent Messemer was frustrated. He had previously told us the political powers in Washington were against the FBI prosecuting Mr. Yu for his alleged espionage activities here in the United States. He needed our help.

At one point in the past when Mr. Yu was under heavy FBI surveillance, he told Agent Messemer that if he would travel to Hong Kong to meet him, he would report the details of the espionage activities in the United States. Agent Messemer received permission from his superiors in the Justice Department and headed to Hong Kong for the meeting.

When he arrived, he contacted Mr. Yu and asked to meet him in a local restaurant. Mr. Yu said he was prepared to tell all to Agent Messemer but asked him to travel with him in an automobile to an undisclosed location. Agent Messemer discussed this with the security personnel at the United States Embassy and was told he would be putting his life on the line. Mr. Yu might have devious plans and Agent Messemer's safety was at risk.

He took the advice of the security personnel and declined to go. Mr. Yu then refused to give Agent Messemer any information and he returned to the United States.

After Agent Messemer's call, we immediately contacted our attorney who worked with us in China. The three of us then got into our cars and drove down to the Terminal Island Federal Prison. The guard at the gate was very reluctant to allow us entry as we had no papers or credentials, and only the name of Agent Messemer. Finally, he made a call to the prison officials and Agent Messemer came down to the entry gate, and we were allowed into the prison compound.

Agent Messemer was wearing a special name tag, and the prison officials questioned him as to who we were and what was out status. He explained that we were critical witnesses to the upcoming deportation hearing.

We were ushered into a room with a conference table and several chairs. We sat down as the deputy closed the door to the room which had a small window, which was steel mesh. I remarked to Agent Messemer that there were no doorknobs, and we were effectively locked in the room, which was obviously for interrogation purposes. Agent Messemer was surprised and clearly uncomfortable being locked in a room, with no access out except for pounding on the door for a prison guard to unlock it.

Agent Messemer explained to us that he was very concerned that Mr. Yu would be released and that it was critical that we and our lawyer testify to Mr. Yu's activities and the history of our joint venture. Agent Messemer then went to the door and knocked very loudly. It took ten minutes before a prison staff member came to open the door and release us. The prison staff person questioned Agent Messemer as if we were in custody and could not leave the room. He told him that we were civilians and were here to testify in the upcoming deportation hearing.

We were then ushered into another room, this one with inside doorknobs, and left alone. On the desk was a brief that described what had transpired since the arrest of Mr. Yu, three days earlier. The brief stated that Mr. Yu was arrested and detained when he arrived at the Los Angeles office of immigration, where he went to supposedly receive his green card status.

Mr. Yu was being sponsored by a local California businessman, who had falsified his application for his green card status. When the California businessman learned that Mr. Yu was under heavy surveillance and investigation by the FBI, and that Mr. Yu had been less then truthful with him, he wrote to the Immigration Bureau and canceled the application and sponsorship. When the Immigration bureau received these documents, they concluded that Mr. Yu was in this country illegally, and after consultation with Agent Messemer, they decided that he should be detained, manacled, and held incommunicado, until the deportation hearing could be convened.

The Immigration Bureau and Agent Messemer decided that it was in the best interests of our country that Mr. Yu not be allowed to see anyone prior to the hearing, so they moved him in manacles from jail to jail, until they brought him to the Federal Prison in Terminal Island for the hearing, the morning we arrived. Agent Messemer brought in the Federal Immigration prosecutor to meet with us, and it was obvious that she was not fully prepared and did not have all the pertinent facts regarding this case. We briefly discussed some of the facts and then we entered the court room for the hearing.

The immigration judge was a women and Mr. Yu's attorney was also a woman. I could see the strain on Agent Messemer's face, as he had spent many years investigating Mr. Yu and was very concerned that the hearing went in favor of the United States Government and not Mr. Yu.

We all assembled in the courtroom. If looks could kill, we would have been eliminated by the dark dagger looks Mr. Yu sent our way.

The hearing began with the prosecuting attorney making an opening statement. She then called each of us to the stand to testify regarding Mr. Yu and his past activities. Our lawyer then took the stand and produced several documents that were most damaging to Mr. Yu.

Mr. Yu became very agitated, started stamping his feet on the floor and started shouting that he was innocent and was being persecuted by Agent Messemer and the United States Government. The Judge warned him to be quiet and after a short while Mr. Yu calmed down.

Mr. Yu then took the stand and denied all the allegations against him. He reiterated that he was being persecuted by Agent Messemer and the United States Government and that he was a Chinese citizen in good standing and not related to any political party. The prosecutor asked him why his passport bore the stamp that he was a member of the communist party. He replied that it was an error when his passport was issued to him.

The judge finally called a recess and told the court and Mr. Yu that she would not make any decision in this matter for at least six weeks. During that time Mr. Yu would be held incommunicado, in the same manner as he was being held now. His lawyer objected and requested that Mr. Yu be allowed to at least go to his apartment and collect his clothes and other possessions. The judge refused and said that after hearing the testimony she believed that Mr. Yu posed a potential threat to our government and its national security.

She then offered Mr. Yu and his attorney the choice of immediate deportation, with the stipulation that Mr. Yu and his immediate family would never again be allowed into the United States for any reason whatsoever, and that copies of these proceedings would be sent to immigration authorities in other countries having the same sympathies as the United States. Mr. Yu's attorney asked the judge for a recess so that she could discuss this choice with Mr. Yu.

The court reconvened an hour later. Mr. Yu's attorney stated to the judge that he would agree to be deported immediately if he could spend a few days saying goodbye to all his friends and collect his personal belongings. Mr. Yu also requested that he be allowed to take a regularly scheduled airline back to China.

The judge listened to the request and then stated that this was not acceptable at all. If Mr. Yu accepted what the judge suggested, then the court would notify the Chinese Government that Mr. Yu was being deported and he would be taken in handcuffs by a federal marshal to San Francisco and then handed over to CAAC the official Chinese Airline for transportation back to Beijing.

Mr. Yu, seeing that he had no choice, accepted the proposal. He was taken to the airport that day, and with a federal marshal traveled to San Francisco. CAAC, the Chinese airline, refused to take Mr. Yu on orders from their superiors. The federal marshal then arranged to fly Mr. Yu to Tokyo, where he was handed over to the Tokyo authorities, who then sent him back to China in disgrace.

EPILOGUE

"When China wakes, the world will shake."

~ Napoleon Bonaparte

After we sold the hotel back to the Chinese and Mr. Yu was deported, Sheldon and Bob Messemer continued to meet on a regular basis for many years. He always asked when we going to write a book about the experiences. He continually told Sheldon that if we really knew the whole story, it would totally surprise us, and that this investigation was the pinnacle of his career.

Finally in 1998, Sheldon started to put down on paper some of our experiences. When he told Bob we had decided to write the book, he was very encouraging and in the next several months, they emailed each other and met for lunch frequently.

He told Sheldon that there were going to be some very unhappy people in China when this book surfaced and that we might be the target of retaliation. He then suggested that we consider hiring a bodyguard, when the book is published, a suggestion he reiterated several times in subsequent conversations.

Every time they met, Sheldon kept asking him questions about the FBI files on World China Trade and us. He kept saying there were voluminous amounts of material, but it was classified, and it would be difficult if not impossible to get the files. At one lunch, he suggested going through FOIA (Freedom of Information Act) to see if we could obtain the files.

Sheldon secured the proper form and sent it to the FBI (FOIA) office in Washington D.C. Three weeks later they acknowledged receipt of our request but said it was necessary to send them a notarized statement that Sheldon was the person who was requesting the information. He sent it off and four weeks later he received a form reply that they had searched their data bases for the past twenty years and that there were no files that corresponded either to World China Trade or Sheldon Krechman or Carole Krechman. Sheldon then posted an appeal. Another four weeks passed, and he received a letter, that was obviously not a form letter, that stated they had again searched all the files and that they were closing this issue. They suggested that he contact the FBI office in LA.

By then we very frustrated and we traveled to Washington D.C. and met with Senator John Kerry's chief of staff and explained our situation and asked for some help. She in turn introduced us to John Kerry's intelligence aid, who met with us, asked a lot of questions, "Do you still have those papers that you found?" (referring to the two million dollars that was transferred from our joint venture account by Mr. Wang) and said that he would investigate the matter.

We also met with the State Department's liaison to the White House, and he promised to investigate. He also said he would keep our documents in a safe. Later on, he shared with us that intelligence told him "Not to touch this with a 10-foot pole."

Sheldon then wrote to the FBI office in Los Angeles and waited for several weeks. We finally received a letter stating that they had found the files, but Sheldon had to go through the process of notarization, again, which he did.

After several more weeks, he then called the FBI legal counsel who was the signatory to the letter we received and asked about the files. He complained that their office was understaffed and over worked and that he had no idea at all when we could expect the files. He explained that every word in every document would have to be gone over to see if any of the content was classified, and if so, it would be stricken from the file.

EPILOGUE

We waited several more weeks and received a letter from the Los Angles FBI office saying that the request had been sent back to the head office in Washington D.C. and we were assigned a file.

Finally, after several weeks, we received the thousands of pages of highly anticipated documents, but to our immense disappointment they provided absolutely no insights into what the FBI and the CIA had uncovered. Why? Because nearly every single page is redacted with huge blocks of blacked out information. Would we ever know if any the two million dollars Mr. Wang had transferred from our joint venture into various banks in Canada and the U.S. was used to buy nuclear secrets?

Coincidently in 1999, not long after we received the redacted documents, a federal court hearing in Albuquerque made national news when *The New York Times* reported that China, working with nuclear secrets stolen from the United States, had taken the lead in the development of miniature nuclear warheads. The investigation centered on a Los Alamos nuclear scientist Wen Ho Lee who was accused of 59 counts of mishandling classified information by downloading nuclear secrets—"weapons codes" used for computer simulations of nuclear weapons tests—to data tapes and removing them from the lab. He was suspected of having shared U.S. nuclear secrets with China.

The investigation was led by none other than FBI Agent Robert Messemer who testified at Lee's arraignment that he effectively had declassified the equivalent of more than 400,000 printed pages of highly classified computer data.

Investigators were never able to establish what Lee did with the downloaded data and there was a huge public outcry that he had been made a scapegoat. After ten months in jail, Lee pleaded guilty to a single count and the other 58 charges were dismissed with an apology from U.S. District Judge James Parker for his incarceration.

In 2021, as this book was underway, I once again reach out to the Los Angeles FBI department under the Freedom of Information Act, to see if I could get the FBI documents on World China Trade. Since nearly thirty years have passed, I thought perhaps some of the classified information might now be declassified and we might discover the long-awaited answers to our questions. After several phone calls, I was told there were no records of World China Trade, and the files did not go back that far.

* * * * *

Throughout the years on our trips home from China, we would occasionally visit Dr. Hammer, usually at his home. Richard Chen kept him up to date on our business activities and often we would talk about his art or other interests of his. He once gave me a beautiful poster signed by the artist Chin Yiffi Fey from his gallery. We were like family, and he was excited and proud of what we had accomplished.

Our experience in China, including all the drama, intrigue and frustrations, was the adventure of a lifetime, and it would not have happened if Dr. Hammer had not facilitated our entry into this land of mystery, ambiguity, incredible culture and history, and a chance to meet the real Chinese people in the People's Republic of China. I am often asked if Sheldon and I thought Dr. Hammer had an agenda for us and if we were just pawns in a bigger game. Looking back, I think he truly believed the roller rinks had potential in China, and he also came to realize that our presence there was good PR for him during his difficult negotiations with the Chinese for the coal mines. Over the years, he made many wonderful connections for us, and up until his death, he did his best to protect our financial interests there as well.

* * * * *

After we sold the hotel back to the Chinese, Sheldon returned to China once with our son. (That's a story for another book.) I have not been back, but I look forward to returning one day. The Asia Hotel is still thriving in Beijing. We created a world class hotel that was ahead of its time in many ways, and one that has stood the test of time. It's an accomplishment I will always be proud of.

Epilogue

* * * * *

We live in very uncertain and perilous times. China has made no secret of its desire to dominant the world. We can continue to ignore the very real threat that China presents to a free world and our global economy, or we can take charge of our destiny.

Let's not forgot Napoleon's prophecy.

www.ingramcontent.com/pod-product-compliance
Lightning Source LLC
LaVergne TN
LVHW091533070526
838199LV00001B/43